180 Days
behind the
Curtain

A Deeper Life Daily Devotional

180 Days behind the Curtain

A Deeper Life Daily Devotional

DAVID FRAZIER MABC, Th.D. (c)

Foreword by Glenn Meldrum,
MA in Theology and Church History

iUniverse LLC
Bloomington

180 DAYS BEHIND THE CURTAIN
A Deeper Life Daily Devotional

Copyright © 2014 David Frazier.

All rights reserved. No part of this book may be used or reproduced by any means, graphic, electronic, or mechanical, including photocopying, recording, taping or by any information storage retrieval system without the written permission of the publisher except in the case of brief quotations embodied in critical articles and reviews.

All scripture is in the New American Standard version, (NAS) unless otherwise noted.

iUniverse books may be ordered through booksellers or by contacting:

iUniverse LLC
1663 Liberty Drive
Bloomington, IN 47403
www.iuniverse.com
1-800-Authors (1-800-288-4677)

Because of the dynamic nature of the Internet, any web addresses or links contained in this book may have changed since publication and may no longer be valid. The views expressed in this work are solely those of the author and do not necessarily reflect the views of the publisher, and the publisher hereby disclaims any responsibility for them.

*Any people depicted in stock imagery provided by Thinkstock are models, and such images are being used for illustrative purposes only.
Certain stock imagery © Thinkstock.*

ISBN: 978-1-4917-2933-5 (sc)
ISBN: 978-1-4917-2935-9 (hc)
ISBN: 978-1-4917-2934-2 (e)

Library of Congress Control Number: 2014905853

Printed in the United States of America.

iUniverse rev. date: 04/02/2014

Contents

Day 1.   The Beginning and the End 1
Day 2.   The Curtain of Intercession; Not Separation 3
Day 3.   Repair the Altar First (Part 1) 5
Day 4.   Repair the Altar First (Part 2) 7
Day 5.   The Man behind the Curtain 9
Day 6.   Hired and Qualified 11
Day 7.   Have You Entered? 13
Day 8.   Teach Us to Pray Like That! 15
Day 9.   Cleansing the Temple 17
Day 10.   Heart Melting Mercy 19
Day 11.   A Life Hidden in Christ (Part 1) 21
Day 12.   A Life Hidden in Christ (Part 2) 23
Day 13.   Have You Been with Jesus? 25
Day 14.   Christ-like or Anti Christ-like? 27
Day 15.   Jesus Stopped! 29
Day 16.   Justice in Who's Hands? (Part 1) 32
Day 17.   Justice in Who's Hands? (Part 2) 34
Day 18.   Like His Unlikeness (Part 1) 36
Day 19.   Like His Unlikeness? (Part 2) 39
Day 20.   Loving Jesus Produces Hatred for Evil 42
Day 21.   Mocker or Beggar? 44
Day 22.   Caught off Guard 47
Day 23.   The Balanced Walk of the Saint 49
Day 24.   The Crest and the Trough 52
Day 25.   The *Winds* and *Fires* of God 54
Day 26.   The Discipline of Listening 57
Day 27.   The Joy of Suffering 59
Day 28.   Trading Worthy For Worthless 61
Day 29.   Show Me the Coin 63
Day 30.   What Makes You Unique? (Part 1) 65
Day 31.   What Makes You Unique? (Part 2) 67
Day 32.   What Makes You Unique? (Part 3) 70
Day 33.   Love without Hypocrisy 72
Day 34.   Clinging is Two-Handed 74
Day 35.   Godly Relief or Ungodly Release? 76
Day 36.   Merciful Contempt 78

Day 37.	Staying in Light or Playing with Wax?	80
Day 38.	Sacrificing Idols or Isaacs?	82
Day 39.	Make the Eternal Exchange	84
Day 40.	The White Squirrel	86
Day 41.	A Worship-full Heart is not Noisy to God	89
Day 42.	Victory is Losing (Part 1)	91
Day 43.	Victory is Losing (Part 2)	93
Day 44.	What is Your Recharging Base?	95
Day 45.	Whose are You?	97
Day 46.	The Day the Earth Swallowed the Son (Part 1)	99
Day 47.	The Day the Earth Swallowed the Son (Part 2)	101
Day 48.	The Day the Earth Swallowed the Son (Part 3)	103
Day 49.	The Day the Earth Swallowed the Son (Part 4)	104
Day 50.	The Only Eyewitness on Earth	106
Day 51.	Walking Forward Backwards	108
Day 52.	Be Careful What You Love	110
Day 53.	Righteous or Rebellious?	112
Day 54.	Beware what Makes a Lot of Sense!	114
Day 55.	"Abba, Father" Not Abracadabra (Part 1)	117
Day 56.	"Abba, Father" Not Abracadabra (Part 2)	119
Day 57.	Seeing is Not Necessarily Believing	121
Day 58.	Fire of Redeeming Love	123
Day 59.	"But" Does Not Follow God	125
Day 60.	Tear Down the Wall!	127
Day 61.	The Fullness of Forsaking Sin	129
Day 62.	When You See War	131
Day 63.	When God Stops Paying	133
Day 64.	Come to Jesus Like a Dead Person	135
Day 65.	The Evil of Motivational Manipulation	137
Day 66.	The Futility of Solomon's Futility	139
Day 67.	How Could a Good God Allow Evil?	141
Day 68.	Spirit-Filled Equals Sin-Restrained	144
Day 69.	The Smiling Scowl	146
Day 70.	Turn Cope into Hope	148
Day 71.	Seek and Find, Not Hide and Seek	150
Day 72.	Don't Settle for 'Only Human' (Part 1)	152
Day 73.	Don't Settle for 'Only Human' (Part 2)	154
Day 74.	Would You Be Blessed?	156
Day 75.	A Baptism of Prayer and Faith	158
Day 76.	A Large Heart Means a Little You	160

Day 77.	The Hand and the Glove (Part 1)	162
Day 78.	The Hand and the Glove (Part 2)	164
Day 79.	Self-Love Multiplies Sorrows	166
Day 80.	The Way Out	168
Day 81.	God's Dwelling Place	170
Day 82.	Prayer-paration	172
Day 83.	Fearful and Amazed	174
Day 84.	Disillusioned but Not Disappointed	176
Day 85.	Disillusioning Your Thoughts	178
Day 86.	The Source of Life, Not its Decoration	180
Day 87.	The Agoraphobic Hoarder	182
Day 88.	Timely Words are Tidy Words	184
Day 89.	Don't Remember what God Forgets	186
Day 90.	Give it All or Keep it All	188
Day 91.	God Counts it as "Done"	190
Day 92.	Others-Supplying is Self-Denying	192
Day 93.	I'm Still the Chief!	194
Day 94.	Falling is Rising	196
Day 95.	The Weight of Guilt (Part 1)	198
Day 96.	The Weight of Guilt (Part 2)	200
Day 97.	The Weight of Guilt (Part 3)	202
Day 98.	The Weight of Guilt (Part 4)	204
Day 99.	Compassion Versus Pity	206
Day 100.	Lifted by Love into Holiness	208
Day 101.	The Dirtiest Becomes the Cleanest	210
Day 102.	Two Steps Too Far!	212
Day 103.	Just Keep Walking!	214
Day 104.	Our "Dash in the Middle" (Part 1)	216
Day 105.	Our "Dash in the Middle" (Part 2)	218
Day 106.	Expense is Immaterial	220
Day 107.	The Goodness of Loneliness	222
Day 108.	When Our Answer is "No!"	224
Day 109.	Branches are Not Fruit	226
Day 110.	Nothing but the Present (Part 1)	228
Day 111.	Nothing but the Present (Part 2)	230
Day 112.	Who's Touching My Bride?	233
Day 113.	The Authority of a "Never" Promise	235
Day 114.	He Reigns! (Part 1)	237
Day 115.	He Reigns! (Part 2)	239
Day 116.	Do You Really Know Him?	241

Day 117.	The Spring in the Desert	243
Day 118.	Becoming the Message	245
Day 119.	Obeying the Message	247
Day 120.	Hating or Loving the Message	250
Day 121.	It's a Worship Problem	253
Day 122.	The Standard Transcendent	255
Day 123.	The Standard Despised	257
Day 124.	Not Boxing the Air	259
Day 125.	Minor Corrections	261
Day 126.	Humbled or Stumbled?	263
Day 127.	Thief or Sheep?	265
Day 128.	Don't Be a Right-Fighter!	267
Day 129.	Killed with Kindness	269
Day 130.	Who is My Neighbor? (Part 1)	271
Day 131.	Who is My Neighbor? (Part 2)	273
Day 132.	Who is My Neighbor? (Part 3)	275
Day 133.	Who is My Neighbor? (Part 4)	277
Day 134.	When Instruments Conquered Instruction	279
Day 135.	Choose Your Table Wisely	281
Day 136.	They Abandoned their Idols	283
Day 137.	Don't Be a Stranger	285
Day 138.	Strangers in God's House	287
Day 139.	Bark, For Heaven's Sake!	289
Day 140.	The Bread that Ends All Bread	291
Day 141.	Love is Always Crucified!	293
Day 142.	Fearers of Mirrors see Clearer	295
Day 143.	See God, Not Rome!	297
Day 144.	The Word Versus the World	299
Day 145.	If the World's Appealing, Heaven's Appalling	301
Day 146.	You are Treasure Too	303
Day 147.	What's in Your Temple?	305
Day 148.	Much in Prayer	307
Day 149.	No "If" About It	309
Day 150.	150 Days Behind the Wooden Door	311
Day 151.	When Peter Demanded Hell	313
Day 152.	Let's Go to Judea Again	315
Day 153.	It Must Be Broken	317
Day 154.	The Basket that Never Empties	319
Day 155.	The Habit of Listening and Responding	321
Day 156.	Are You a Burning Bush? (Part 1)	323

Day 157. Are You a Burning Bush? (Part 2) 325
Day 158. What is My Strength? 327
Day 159. When Jesus Stood Up 329
Day 160. The Good Soldier 331
Day 161. The Value of Living for Jesus 333
Day 162. The Grasping Hands of Faith 335
Day 163. All Alone and No One To Hide 338
Day 164. Do You Have the Passion? 340
Day 165. Raised to Make a Difference 342
Day 166. The Peril of Backsliding 344
Day 167. Hindered Prayer is Hazardous 346
Day 168. The Removal of Achan 348
Day 169. The Eternity of Abiding 350
Day 170. The Loyalty of Abiding 352
Day 171. God's Number One Hit Song 354
Day 172. Getting Alone with God 356
Day 173. Henotheism in God's House 358
Day 174. Self-Sufficiency Strikes Jesus Twice 360
Day 175. Are You Hungry? 362
Day 176. Revelation without Gethsemane Corrupts 364
Day 177. Washing Your Hands in Pilate's Sink 366
Day 178. Seeking God's Wisdom 368
Day 179. Is There Death in the Pot? 370
Day 180. Jesus, The Purpose of Life 372

Foreword

*D*evotion, as defined by God, is radical. God's command to love Him with all of our heart, mind, soul and strength seems radical because we often have other loves in our life and do not want to love God supremely. Devotion is only radical in this fallen world because we are rebels. Can you imagine the angels gathered around the Almighty's throne not loving Him with every fiber of their being? No, this idea is unthinkable.

An honest look at the Scriptures reveal there is only one kind of faith; that which is wholehearted devotion unto God. The early church understood this, therefore the testimony goes: *"They devoted themselves to the apostles' teaching, to the fellowship, to the breaking of bread and to prayer"* (Acts 2:42). This was wholehearted abandonment to God. Their understanding of devotion came from Christ's teaching on the subject: *"Any of you who does not give up everything he has cannot be my disciple"* (Luke 14:33). Notice that there was no middle ground, no compromise with the subject of devotion. It was designed by the founder of the true faith to be absolute and all consuming.

Any honest study of the book of Acts will reveal that God granted the church power to build Christ's kingdom. The verse following the devotion of the early church gives clear evidence to this fact: *"Everyone was filled with awe, and many wonders and miraculous signs were done by the apostles"* (Acts 2:42-43). Signs and wonders were not only done by the apostles but by lay people such as Stephen and Philip. All these men were given power through the working of the Holy Spirit because their devotion was Biblical. Today this level of devotion is considered radical and extreme to many self-professing Christians. But as Jesus said, *"Wisdom is justified of all her children"* (Luke 7:35; KJV).

Now if devotion is radical then should not our devotionals fan into flame the very desire that is God's will for every person? What a shame that so many devotionals teach people mediocrity and enable the readers to continue the practice of sin and remain lukewarm. With many of these, a random selection will often produce a response such as, "Wasn't that cute" or "What a sweet story." As an author and preacher, such a statement would make me want to bow my head in utter shame and beg God's forgiveness for producing such worthless rubbish. We don't need cute devotionals and sweet stories, but messages that stir the heart and provoke us to be more like Jesus.

David Frazier's devotional *180 Days Behind the Curtain* was written to do just this; to take people deeper into the life of Christ and to give us a fresh view of our wonderful Savior. His devotional is not cutesy or sweet. Each day's devotion was written to enlarge people's understanding of God and to encourage them to walk closer to the One who is the ultimate prize.

Set aside time each day to read this rich devotional. Next, pray over the lesson; allow the Lord to speak to you about what He wants you to receive from it. But don't stop there; meditate on the lesson throughout the day so its value may be fully grasped.

Don't read this book to do your "religious duty" or to fill some empty time on your hands. Invest in it that you might grow in Christ, so you would know Him a little better and be able to speak of Him to others with anointing on your life. I believe this is David's prayer for you and his purpose in writing *180 Days Behind the Curtain*. His desire is to create a greater longing in your heart to hear those most beautiful of words from the Savior, "Well done."

Glenn Meldrum, Evangelist/Revivalist, Pastor, and Author
Visit *In His Presence Ministries*, ihpministry.com

Preface

On the fields of war, lifelong bonds between brothers are formed through mutual suffering and camaraderie. There are countless stories during war that have trickled down to us like the blood of the men who fought, some of which tug on our heartstrings more than others. Below is one story in particular that wonderfully paints a picture of what devotion to Jesus looks like, and what it means to be "in His name." The story goes . . .

> One evening in late September, not long after the end of the Civil War, a man came knocking on the door of an old plantation house. As the master came to the door, he saw the shady appearance of the vagabond and in apprehension urged him to leave at once. The master began to shut the door on the strange visitor, but he put his foot between the door and the doorjamb and begged the master to give him just one minute.
>
> The master consented, and while he stood in the doorway with undivided attention, the disheveled man proceeded to pull out a bloodstained letter handwritten by the master's son who had died in the war. Quite puzzled, the master took the letter and began to read. The following is a portion of that letter: "Dear father, if this letter reaches you, the man who has come to call on you and deliver it has fought beside me with honor and courage throughout my entire assignment in the war. He and I have been over heavenly mountains and through hellish valleys together until just the other day when I took a blow from the enemy that laid me low. With the utmost of loving devotion, this man—who has become my dear brother and friend—has never left my side to care for my wounds until these late moments, which if you are reading this, have become my last. So please, father, receive him as you would receive me, as your son."
>
> Suddenly, in the eyes of the master, the disheveled, outcast appearance of the strange man was disregarded and evermore forgotten. Then the master eagerly reached out, pulled the

man to his chest and embraced him with overwhelming arms of love. For his son's namesake, and to honor his dying wish, the devoted man was forever welcomed into the father's home as a most beloved and devoted son.

As a former self-proclaimed Christian, my only evidence of devotion to Jesus was a pile of once soiled rags from Him always "cleaning me up." He was merely the washing machine to keep away the foul aromas of sin and preserve my outward image. Being a preacher's son, I was raised in the church. I believed in God, believed in Jesus, and got baptized at an early age. But the truth is I despised being disturbed from my self-centered agendas, self-prescribed ideas of God, and "comfortable Christianity." The last thing I desired was for anything, especially Truth, to disturb my kingdom-of-self. Later on in life, I did experience a taste of selfless service in the Marine Corps, but after my honorable discharge, I once again assumed the reign of my own fortress. On the outside walls was a handwritten sign that read, "I love God," while behind them the love of self and sin continued in blatant rebellion to the words on that sign. This is the living lie I played out on my own stage, scene after selfish scene. However, in 2008, I had a head-on collision with the real Jesus; I saw that one little fling with sin was equal to saying, "Just one more little whack at the nails in Jesus' hands!" With that revelation I broke and melted as the plastic I was. Through deep repentance and brokenness, I discovered what my problem was: It was a worship problem—I was my own little god—and all the coveted things of the world were just the elixirs for more self-devotion.

Since this life-transforming truth, I have gone on to complete a BACS, MA Biblical Counseling, two years of Greek, and am finishing a Th.D. I am currently an itinerant evangelist and biblical counselor, and have been counseling four years for an international ministry called Pure Life Ministries. However, I can say this does not necessarily define the meaning of devotion. It is quite possible to esteem the Word of God, even ministry, and still neglect the Author of both.

Nevertheless, these ministries have allowed me to peek under the rugs of hundreds of churches and their members from around the world. My analysis of the data gathered is that believers are extremely devoted, but for many, their devotion is grossly misdirected. Christians are being taught that the cross is just about escaping the "miseries" of hell and arriving in the "rewards" of heaven. If fellowship with God is not taught as the primary reason for Christ's agonizing removal of sin, then devotion to Him will continue to be viewed as optional, or even legalistic.

Heaven is an eternity of *fellowship with* and *devotion to* the Lord; if people willfully live their earthly lives absent of that, why would they want heaven? Our earthly fellowship and devotion honors God and declares to Him our love and gratitude for His Son Jesus who excruciatingly purchased us. You may have heard the foolish phrase, "Don't be so heavenly minded that you are of no earthly good." This is a lie, and generally used as a copout to justify spiritual apathy and sinful compromise. On the contrary, it is the most heavenly-minded people who do the most earthly good; Jesus, for one, proves this. Hearts that are dwelling in heaven change lives that are dwelling on earth.

> *"In Your presence is abundant joy; in Your right hand are eternal pleasures"* (Psalm 16:11).

Acknowledgements

Supremely to the Preeminent One—the eternal Word and worthy Lamb, Jesus Christ the Son of God—for rescuing me from the cesspits of sin, self, and pride and transforming me with His unmerited mercy; to my wife, best friend, and helpmate, Kim, who sacrificed more than I will ever know to help this book (two years in the making) come to fruition; to my dad, Dr. Ron Frazier, for his spiritual fortitude, Christ-like fatherly love, and biblical acumen; to Glenn Meldrum for his shepherding me and being my "Paul;" to Master's School of Divinity for their unparalleled biblical training and wonderful staff; to all at Pure Life Ministries; to Kyle Idleman for his endorsement and support; to Luke Gilkerson, community manager for Covenant Eyes, for his astute blog site and endorsement; to my mom, Jackie, and second dad, Dan; to my brother Scott, for his perseverance; to Steve Holloway and his mother for their spot-on editing help, and to all those who were voices and mirrors for each piece of the project . . .

Thank you! And may the Lord bless you with all the super-abundant mercies that come from His heavenly throne in glory.

Introduction

Before you begin the six-month journey of this devotional, you may need to understand the meaning of the terminology "behind the curtain." What in the world is behind the curtain? The answer is nothing! There is nothing *in the world* that can dwell behind the curtain. In fact, it is everything *in the world* that is hostile to who dwells there; no worldly (unholy) thing can come into the presence of God who is infinitely holy. This leads to the next question. What does "behind the curtain" mean?

The curtain (or veil) in reference is the one leading to the Most Holy Place where the Ark of the Covenant was placed. God commanded Moses to *hang* this curtain so that it would "separate the Holy Place from the Most Holy Place" (Exodus 26:33). The Ark was topped with a lid called the Mercy Seat where the High Priest would sprinkle the blood of the sacrificial lamb once a year to atone for the people's sins. On the Mercy Seat were two cherubim facing each other with their wings spread out and upward. Between them, God's holy and awesome presence was manifested to meet with Moses and speak to him in that Most Holy Place. Therefore, the terminology "behind the curtain" means coming into the holy presence of God to meet Him, communicate with Him, worship Him, learn from Him, and follow Him. This we can practically define as *devotion*.

The curtain symbolized separation from God. Before Adam and Eve sinned, they were sinless and walked with God in perfect fellowship. After they sinned that fellowship was separated, since God is too holy to look upon sin (Habakkuk 1:13). So when we talk of dwelling *behind the curtain*, we are forced to inquire and acknowledge what it is that allows us (being essentially unholy) the high privilege of entering such a holy place with God. It is none other than Christ's agonizing death on the cross that elevates us to such a standing. Sin's wages, which is death, was paid in full as the body of Jesus Christ the Lamb was pierced for our transgressions (Isaiah 53:5). When His body was *hung* and torn, the separating curtain was simultaneously torn once and for all (see Mark 15:37-38). Consider the following Scripture:

> "Therefore, brothers and sisters, since we have confidence to enter the Most Holy Place by the blood of Jesus, by a new and living way opened for us *through the curtain*, that is, *His body*, and since we have a great Priest over the house of God, let us draw near to God with a sincere heart and with the full assurance that faith brings, having our hearts sprinkled to cleanse us from a guilty conscience and having our bodies washed with pure water" (Hebrews 10: 19-22, italics mine).

This led me to the purpose of writing *180 Days behind the Curtain*. This devotional is meant to 1) be a magnifying glass for examining the Word of God, and 2) be a vehicle to daily transport you into that Most Holy Place behind the curtain. For most of the days, there is a section at the end called, "For Thought," that is designed to help you apply what was read and develop further insights from the content. Taking this part seriously will be the difference between being just another devotional, and bringing significant spiritual growth. *You should have your Bible open and ready for each day's devotion.*

I also envisioned a very interactive devotional that would fit both the individual and small group setting, while mining the depths of the fundamentals of faith and life principles along the journey (hopefully in a way that does not make people feel like they would rather go chew on aluminum). Why "180" days? It is the number of repentance ("a 180° turn"). It is also about half a year, which is a proven length of time for a habit to be deeply ingrained.

It is true that we become more like whatever we continuously fix our gaze upon. It is equally true that to whom we devote our life and affections we become more like that person. Dear reader, it is my prayer that *180 Days behind the Curtain* will usher in that "one hundred eighty degree turn" you have been praying for in your devotional life.—David Frazier, BACS, MABC, Th.D. (c)

The Beginning and the End

"May my prayer be set before you like incense; may the lifting up of my hands be like the evening sacrifice" (Psalm 141:2).

Do you have an evening offering of praise and prayer? Is the end of your day any less important or praiseworthy than the beginning? Should it not be all the more worthy of praise that God has sustained you with provision and all that is pertaining to life and godliness yet another day? What if there is un-confessed and un-repentant sin in your heart? Does not another evening represent yet another daylong opportunity granted for repentance and restoration by God in His mercy and long-suffering?

Jesus is the pre-existing God of creation. Since all things have their beginning in Him, then all things should equally have their end in Him as well (and they ultimately will one way or another). In the book of Revelation, Jesus said that He is "the Alpha and the Omega, the beginning and the end" (21:6). In Hebrews, He is the "author and finisher of our faith" (12:2, KJV). With these truths understood, should we not also begin and end every day with devotion to Him?

You say you have morning devotions, but what about in the evening? Is the time you now devote about as hurried and unfulfilling as the task of brushing your teeth? How loved would our spouses feel if we were always hurrying to leave their presence? David's prayers went up before God as a sweet smelling aroma (incense). The faith, love, and obedience that his prayers symbolized followed with sincerity. David was in awe of the *Shekinah* glory of God that filled the temple and longed to continually be in His presence.

There is no such thing as "your" time. All that you claim ownership of you will selfishly fight to maintain. However, once you realize the absolute truth that "your" day (and everything else) truly had its beginning in and through Jesus, you will find it easier to devote not only a small portion of it to Him, but also the entire portion as a living sacrifice. Then you should begin to see your need to lift up your hands to Him in worthy praise at the close of every day because you see it as nothing less than undeserved mercy. Let this be your evening sacrifice of prayer, as you also let everything else (every thought, deed, and word) have its beginning and end with Jesus.

For Thought:

What would be the significance of Jesus being the beginning and the end of everything you do? What would be the outcome in your actions, thoughts, and words? What about in your church?

The Curtain of Intercession; Not Separation

"Hang the curtain from the clasps and place the Ark of the Covenant law behind the curtain. The curtain will separate the Holy Place from the Most Holy Place" (Exodus 26:33, NIV).

If you were to hang a curtain or a veil in the entryway of another room, you could rightly say that the curtain is actually in both rooms at the same time. Although it separates both rooms, one side of it is in one room, and the other side in the other. We learn in the book of Hebrews that Jesus became the curtain/veil upon the cross: "We have confidence to enter the holy place by the blood of Jesus by a new and living way, which He inaugurated for us through the veil, that is, His flesh" (Hebrews 10:19-20). That means only Jesus can simultaneously be in both the Holy of holies where only God's perfect and holy presence can dwell, and the outer room where sinful man dwells. This is crucial to note, because it proclaims Christ's dual nature of being both God and man (a.k.a. "hypostatic union").

One side of Jesus (His divinity) is always in the Most Holy place, and the other side (His humanity) is always dwelling with us. Because of Him "a better hope is introduced, through which we draw near to God" (Hebrews 7:18). And because He and His Priesthood are eternal, He is always able to save all who come to God through Him, since He always lives to intercede for us (see Hebrews 7:24, 25). Although we cannot plug directly into God because He is too holy and infinite, we can plug into Jesus who alone connects us to the Father; that is why Jesus said He is the Gate for the sheep (John 10:7, 9). We plug into His human nature, while His divinity is in the Father.

We also read that the literal curtain was torn the moment Jesus breathed His last (Matthew 27:50-51). "Behind the curtain" was the room called the Most Holy Place (Exodus 26:34; Hebrews 9:3). That room was opened up for us by faith in Jesus' death on the cross. While His body was torn upon the cross, He became sin's substitute, and the curtain of separation (sin) was forever vanquished and removed. This declares that presently He is not a veil of separation, but rather a veil of intercession. He is only a veil of separation for those who stumble over this truth. Paul called it attempting to remove the "stumbling block of the cross" (Galatians 5:11). The Old Testament curtain was hung from clasps to separate; Jesus our Curtain of intercession was hung from the clasps of a cross to remove what separated us from God. Today the cross is increasingly being cleaned up, censored, watered-down, obscured, and removed (literally from the church, and spiritually from its members). People find it repulsive so they attempt to censor it. Do you know why the uncensored cross is so repulsive? You are seeing your sin up there!

For Thought:

Don't cover up what covers you. The cross changes everything! Look at it wide eyed in all its glorious vileness and it will change you.

Day 3

Repair the Altar First (Part 1)

"Elijah said to all the people, 'Come near to me.' And all the people came near to him. And he repaired the altar of the LORD that was broken down" (1 Kings 18:30).

Elijah had previously admonished the apostate people of Israel, "How long will you waver between two opinions? If the Lord is God, follow him; but if Baal is God, follow him." Needless to say, a showdown was necessary to determine the truth between the two. Both sides would put a bull on an altar, but the fire had to come down from the deity worshiped, which would prove who was true. In vain, the prophets of Baal had labored in ritual all day. When it came turn for Elijah, he told all the people to draw near, so they did. However, the Lord's altar was broken—in ruins—and needed repaired before Elijah could make a sacrifice.

The worship of God had so long been abandoned because of idolatry and sin that the altar was left in ruins. This nuance teaches a great spiritual truth once you know what the altar is. Your altar is not your church building, the steps in front of the podium, or a little Jesus shrine in your house. Dear saint, your altar is your heart. That is where you worship God. Notice the great commandment, "Love the Lord your God with all your heart" (Luke 10:27). However, you cannot sacrifice anything to God until your heart (your altar) has been repaired, which only the Lord can do. David said in his Psalm, "The LORD is near the brokenhearted" (34:18). Here the meaning of "broken heart" is a fragmented heart. It is fragmented because it has been divided by its worship of idols, just like the people of Israel. In other words, sin and idolatry break your altar, your heart. The "brokenhearted" are those who see and acknowledge this heart condition and cry out for mercy. The Lord is drawn like a magnet to the cry of sinners acknowledging their broken heart. Why? Because He knows it needs repaired and grieves over what sin and idolatry have done to it. But He also knows that once He repairs it you will give Him your life as a sacrifice out of thanksgiving rather than duty.

Let the Lord repair your altar; let Him mend your broken heart. Let Him wash your feet with His loving-kindness and tender mercies. This whole business about "having" to sacrifice everything to God in order to be a "true Christian" is hideously backwards. But once Jesus comes and makes your heart whole again by His saving grace and mercy, you will *want* to be a living sacrifice. That's why Paul said, "By the mercies of God" first, before he said be "a living sacrifice" (see Romans 12:1).

For Thought:

Elijah told the people to "come close." James said, Draw near to the Lord and He will draw near to you" (4:8). Draw near by crying out and Jesus will draw near in His mercy to repair what is broken. Have you ever acknowledged the ruinous, broken down condition of your heart and cried out to the Lord for His mercy? Has He repaired it?

Day 4

Repair the Altar First (Part 2)

"And he repaired the altar of the LORD that was broken down" (1 Kings 18:30).

How does the Lord repair the broken altar of your heart? Getting revelation from the *law of first mention* (see Day 7 for more on this), Jesus' first miracle was turning water into wine. Wine always symbolized "joy." The opposite of joy is sorrow, which is generally expressed in tears. What are tears made of but water? Put it all together and see that Christ's first miracle preaches His ultimate mission. The Lord came to turn tears of sorrow (water) into joy (wine).

Only a miracle can turn sorrow into lasting joy. Not one earthly comfort or sinful vice can offer lasting joy and eliminate grief. No, the root cause must be removed, otherwise sorrow will always return after the party and vacation is over. Since sin is the root cause of all grief and sorrow throughout all history, sin must be eliminated to bring lasting joy, and that took the greatest miracle in history, Calvary! Jesus' first miracle testifies to the first miracle He desires to work in the human heart, forgiveness and cleansing of sin. This repairs the human heart to a right relationship with the Lord, bringing wonderful relief, peace, and gratitude.

The first mention of an altar in the Bible was in Genesis 8:20. Without being told, Noah built an altar *after* he safely got out of the Ark that *saved* him from the floods of destruction. Receive the wonderful saving mercies of God first; sacrifice will naturally follow.

Abraham built the second altar in the Bible *after* God made him a promise concerning the land. Then Abraham leaves and goes to a mountain. Why? Perhaps to see the land he was promised. There, he observes and realizes what God has done for him by bringing him into His fold. The third altar mentioned in the Bible was built when Abraham was between Bethel the "house of God" and Hai, which at its root means, "Ruin, as if overturned." Here we see Abraham reminded of what his life could have been like without God. His life would have been an overturned heap of ruin. On the contrary, in the house of God, there is peace, mercy, grace, and blessings.

In our land, the land of our heart, we could have been *Hai*, but are instead *Bethel*. When we realize what ruinous end could have been ours, we will fall down in gratefulness first, and then build an altar to sacrifice our thanksgiving before God. We first receive His awesome mercy, and then we will thank him with our life for saving us from ruin, grafting us into Jesus the Vine, and making us into "The House of God."

For Thought:

Has the Lord destroyed the altar of idolatry and repaired His altar in your heart that once lay in ruins? Your unprovoked life of worship is the proof!

When the good news of the Gospel repairs your altar, sacrifices become thanksgiving, not duty!

Day 5

The Man behind the Curtain

"We have this hope as an anchor for our lives, safe and secure. It enters the inner sanctuary behind the curtain" (Hebrews 6:19).

One of the most famous lines from *The Wizard of Oz* is, "Pay no attention to that man behind the curtain!" Oz was just a little feeble man, all smoke and mirrors, and rightly deserved no attention. A sad truth today is that many believers treat God the same way. With shallow faith they view God as little and even feeble, and His biblical miracles are just smoke and mirrors. With love of this world and for themselves, they really do pay no attention to "The Man" behind the curtain.

If we truly understood who dwells behind that veil, we would surely not deem Him something in which to pay no attention. In fact, all our attention would be endlessly captivated because He is infinite in power, holiness, and glory. In the Old Testament, only the high priest could enter it once a year but not without blood. The dreadful outcome of Nadab and Abihu tells us that great attention and great care should be taken when entering behind the curtain: "They offered strange fire before the LORD, which He had not commanded them. And fire came out from the presence of the LORD and consumed them, and they died before the LORD" (Leviticus 10:1-2).

The Presence of the Lord is too holy for our unveiled exposure or for irreverent contempt. In the Old Testament, the Holy of holies was filled with the smoke of incense, which acted as a sort of veil within the veil. The Bible likens our prayers to be incense before God, so when we pray we enter that Most Holy Place to meet, fellowship, and communicate with God. Because Jesus intercedes for us, we can enter safely and boldly and make our petitions. "For Christ did not enter a holy place made with hands, a mere copy of the true one, but into heaven itself, now to appear in the presence of God for us" (Hebrews 9:24).

Are you paying attention to The Man behind the curtain? Do you take into account that when you pray it is only the precious blood of Jesus the Lamb that provides your access into the throne room of grace? This should begin to solve any problem of passionless prayer. When you pray, be conscious of the fact that you are in the Holy of Holies, and only by the slain Lamb of God. Be stirred, not deterred. Pay the closest attention to the Man behind the curtain; He is holy! He is worthy! And He died to give you all of His attention.

For Thought:

Read Amos 5:18-24. Israel's worship had deteriorated to ritual formalism. Today, machine-gun-like prayers are very prevalent in churches. Why? Do you think God is pleased with passionless praying?

Day 6

Hired and Qualified

"Therefore I urge you, brethren, by the mercies of God, to present your bodies a living and holy sacrifice, acceptable to God, which is your spiritual service of worship" (Romans 12:1-2).

As purchased property of God, all who call themselves "Christian" are by title and declaration ministers. The word *minister* in the Greek is *latrúō*, which means, "I serve" or "I worship." It comes from the root word *latris*—"someone *hired* to accomplish a technical task because *qualified*." Without a proper understanding of this definition, believers can fall prey to believing one of the most poisonous lies affronting evangelism ever spewed from the serpent's fangs. Under the delirious effects from the adversary's venomous bite they say, "I am neither hired nor qualified to minister; that is the task of the preacher, evangelist, or pastor!"

Dear believer, you most certainly have been *hired*, and that at the highest price—the precious blood of the worthy Lamb of God. *"Or do you not know that your body is a temple of the Holy Spirit who is in you, whom you have from God, and that you are not your own? For you have been bought with a price"* (1 Corinthians 6:19-20).

Do you call yourself Christian? If so, then know with faith that inseparable from that title is also the qualification. *"And these whom He predestined, He also called; and these whom He called, He also justified; and these whom He justified, He also glorified"* (Romans 8:30).

The questions are: Who is it that hires you? What is it that qualifies you? Are we only hired and qualified as ministers by man, the church, or the seminary? By the light of God's Word, I submit that we are not.

Therefore, if you are struggling with whether or not you are hired and qualified to do the worshipful work of *minister*, might I suggest that the problem you are facing may be that you have been looking to the wrong thing (or the wrong Person) that *hires* and *qualifies* you.

The same God that purchased (hires) us is the same God that qualifies us. When you see the blood of Christ Jesus you see the payment that *hired* you and the pardon that *qualified* you. When God sees the blood (Exodus 12:13), He passes over all that you say would be grounds to be fired and disqualified. What keeps us from ministering now? Excuses are skins of a reason stuffed with a lie! Jesus imperatively says to all His disciples *'Go into all the world and preach the gospel to all creation'"* (Mark 16:15).

For Thought:

If our fellowship with God was contingent upon our own qualifications and performance, we would all be in a heap of trouble!

Consider Jesus and His earthly payment for your heavenly employment.

Day 7

Have You Entered?

"Blessed are the poor in spirit, for theirs is the kingdom of heaven" (Matthew 5:3).

A hermeneutic (her-ma-'noo-tic) is an applied rule for the proper interpretation of Scripture. One hermeneutic of great value is known as "the law of first mention. Concerning a topic, you must find where it is first mentioned in the text. It is there you will discover the topic's primary essentials.

Jesus had been teaching, healing, and preaching all over Galilee (Matthew 4:23). However, there on the Mount, we have His first recorded sermon. Going by the law of first mention, we should have our hearts fixed upon this sermon. The first words from our Lord's lips are, "Blessed are the poor in spirit, for theirs is the Kingdom of heaven" In other words, in order to possess the Kingdom, you not only must come in this state of spiritual poverty; you also must remain in it. The door to the Kingdom is very small and very low.

Those who are poor are beggars. We live in a world that exploits the poor and belittles beggars. It is humiliating to beg for anything, so many people strive and labor to ensure against any possibility of experiencing such a wretchedly low position. Applied to the spiritual life, this is exactly the prideful attitude that keeps people alienated from Jesus. Poverty of spirit is the same as David's sacrificial "broken and contrite heart," which God will not despise (see Psalm 51:17). In another Psalm he says, "The LORD is near to the brokenhearted, and saves those who are crushed in spirit" (34:18).

The "crushed in spirit" are those who have truly had a sight of the wickedness of their own hearts, and acknowledged the hideous magnitude of their sin. Revealed by the Holy Spirit, they are crushed under the enormous weight of their guilt, and everything that was once gain becomes loss. They tremble at the sinful condition of their hearts and how they have been laid bare before a Holy God. They are broken at the understanding that their rebellion was spitting in the face of the wonderful Savior that came to rescue them. They have been made poor and cried out, "Jesus, Son of David, have mercy on me a sinner" (Luke 18:13). They come to Jesus as the most wretched beggar on earth, yet walk away the most blessed saint in heaven.

Nicodemus was the only person who came to Jesus privately; every other person in the Bible came to Him radically, openly, broken, and with full acknowledgment of their desperate and sick condition. In Luke 7:37-47, the harlot woman was so desperate for Jesus and poor that she completely disrupted the whole gathering, caring nothing for what anyone thought of her. Poverty of spirit was important enough for Jesus to say it first in His first recorded sermon. Have you entered?

For Thought:

Poverty of spirit is absolutely essential for devotion to Jesus

Teach Us to Pray Like That!

"Jesus was praying in a certain place, after He had finished, one of His disciples said to Him, 'Lord, teach us to pray'" (Luke 11:1).

*J*esus raised a man who was dead for four days back to life with three words, "Lazarus, come forth" (John 11:1); He made a paralyzed man walk with a seven-word command, "Rise, take up your pallet and walk" (John 5:8); He made a reckless disciple walk on water with a one-word call, "Come" (Matthew 14:29); He fed a vast multitude with five loaves, two fish, and five words, "Bring them here to Me" (Matthew 14:18); and He preached the most powerful ever preached; so powerful that if it were lived out in obedience by its hearers today it would turn the entire world upside down, again!

However, despite all these awe-inspiring miracles and wonders that Jesus performed in His disciples' presence, they never once asked Him to teach them how to raise the dead, walk on water, make the lame walk, feed a multitude, or preach a dynamite sermon; not to mention all the other amazing miracles He did.

What do these facts imply other than Jesus must have prayed in such a way that eclipsed every miracle and wonder? He prayed in such a way that His disciples were driven with deep desire to be taught how to pray like He did.

We do many things that when other people see they ask us to teach them. Some people, filled with selfish ambition, thrive on the envy of others as the fuel that ignites their arrogant engines. Often we hear, "Teach me how to earn money like that," or "Teach me how to sing like that," or even "Teach me how to preach like that!" But when is the last time (or the first time) that someone has heard us pray in such a way that they came to us pleading, "Teach me how to pray like that!"

Jesus prayed with heart-engaged passion, power, and longing for the presence of His Father, not with meandering drudgery or dreadful repetition, and it captured the longing of His bystanders. We can also rest assured that Jesus did not pray to His Father with a "Let's be hip" attitude. He sought the heart of God to receive the heart of God and pray with the heart of God! What do people see in you that they wish they could learn to do for the glory of God and His Kingdom? Whatever it is, it is nothing without being much in prayer!"

For Thought:

Do you have the desire to pray with such a passion that God is moved?

Glenn Meldrum wrote, "The Spirit moves the hearts of men to move the heart of God—a mystery indeed."[2] If people are moved without God's moving, it was merely emotionalism and fleshly work.

Cleansing the Temple

"He said to them . . . 'My Temple will be called a house of prayer, but you have turned it into a den of thieves!'" (Matthew 21:13).

What greed; what selfish thievery toward God; what defilement of His Temple; what treachery; what malicious intent; what affront of contemptuous pride; what scheming idolatry, to withhold in secret reserve one dark and shaded corner of my heart for a marketing table of self profit or profane pleasure. Do I not know that my body, specifically my heart, is the Temple of God? If I do know this, then I need to confess that it should be called a 'House of Prayer.' However, as long as this underground corner market exists, God's desire for intimacy and fellowship with me remains hindered and constrained. Thereby in His pure light and all-seeing eyes, the reality of my heart is exposed: I have been considering His temple with disdain and irreverence.

Jesus saw this same reality as He entered His literal Temple and saw it being used as a means for selfish gain. Moved with righteous indignation He radically cast down every vain thing that exalted itself against God (see 2 Corinthians 10:5). We see this seemingly rare side of Jesus and are stunned. However, when we open our spiritual eyes, we are shocked, not that Jesus did this, but that we had not seen the need for Him to do so beforehand.

Whenever God has to come because of our spiritual neglect or flagrant rebellion and do what is our responsibility to do—cleanse the temple—He will not come quietly. When God says to remove the accursed idols and we only hide them, like Achan, in the ground of our tent, He will come radically in His power shining like the sun, to raise them from dark secrecy and raze them to their proper place of desolation!

Have you been mistakenly waiting on Jesus to come enter His temple and turn over the tables of selfish gain you have allowed to remain operating in the shady corners of your heart? You must do it (see James 4:8). And you must do it with the same level of righteous indignation as He would, because of your love for Him and reverence for His dwelling place.

For Thought:

Read Leviticus 17:7, Deuteronomy 32:17, Psalm 106:36-37, and 1 Corinthians 10:20. Idolatry is likened to the worship of _____?

When you see the great cost of your salvation paid in full by Jesus on the cross, what should be your proper response?

What does it mean to cleanse your temple? Are there ways you are using His temple for selfish gain? How can you use your body to glorify God?

Day 10

Heart Melting Mercy

"Or do you think lightly of the riches of His kindness and tolerance and patience, not knowing that the kindness of God leads you to repentance?" (Romans 2:4).

The finished work of Jesus' death on the cross is intended to lead us to repentance (see Romans 2:4). However, this is only the beginning; fruit consistent with repentance is what Jesus is looking for (see Matthew 3:8). Many love to give Jesus their sins yet hate to give Him their lives. Jesus' sacrifice was not just to expunge our death penalty, deliver us from hell, and give us heaven; it tore the veil that separated us from God so that we could have fellowship with Him now, and for an eternity. If we could just see how passionately Jesus desires to fellowship with us behind the curtain in that Most Holy Place, we would cease to fall for the enemy's false portrayals of the Lord's character.

Many of us have experienced certain times in our lives where we were so "without excuse" for a wrongdoing that we gruelingly waited to take our punishment as they say, "Like a man." In other words, we were mortally guilty and we knew it, and our due penalty would be justice served.

However, something amazing happens to our heart when we are anticipating what we know we deserve for our sinful behavior, and yet receive not only unmerited forgiveness, but also an amazing outpouring of some lavished blessing. Jesus commanded, "Bless those who curse you" (Luke 6:28); He did not say if someone does curse you, "Don't curse them back and you're a good Christian." Not returning a curse for a curse is gracious in a small sense, but returning that curse with unmerited blessing is the love of God in action. This alone possesses the ability to melt the offender's sin-hardened heart like wax and win it over to Jesus. Mercy brings change where nothing else could.

Our Lord Jesus continuously responds to our spiteful attitudes and actions with blessing and longsuffering, therefore we are obligated to freely give that same unmerited mercy to others. If we refuse, we dishonor the cross, and enable them to remain in a place of darkness and separation from God. Merciless people need mercy; pour it out with joy and you may see them thanking you in heaven.

For Thought:

When everything else fails, what is it that will bring change every time?

Read Luke 6:27-38 and 1 Corinthians 4:11-13. How should we respond when we are mistreated?

A Life Hidden in Christ (Part 1)

"He must increase, but I must decrease" (John 3:30).

It is very popular in today's Christian (from lay person to preacher) to know much of what Jesus did, and yet know nothing of who He is and what His true nature is.

Imagine Jesus like a glass of pure clear water, and a person like a sugar cube. Only the sugar cube that gets inside the water and dissolves learns what Jesus is truly like. This is the mature believer who sincerely knows Christ's like-ness because they are in Him and have amalgamated with His character.

Many believers are content to just remain sugar cubes talking about what Jesus looks like on the outside, but never entering into the fellowship of his sufferings, They keep their own shape, clinging to their natural identity, hold to their comfortable squared-away form of life, and even love their own sweetness. They walk the landscape showing all their friends the only knowledge of Christ Jesus they have: A natural knowledge that points to an external Jesus and says, "I have Him in my life" The reply would be, "I did not realize it was your life and you just allowed Him in it."

> *"For you died, and your life is now hidden with Christ in God. When Christ, who is your life, appears, then you also will appear with him in glory"* (Colossians 2:3-4).

Even the world can see Jesus on the outside and point to Him from that perspective. However, only the true disciple of Christ knows what He is like on the inside! At first natural glance it seems it will cost him everything (and in fact it will), for what will a sugar cube do inside a glass of water other than dissolve? However, with a second spiritual gaze, like the Apostle Paul, he sees he is losing nothing and gaining everything. "I count all things to be loss in view of the surpassing value of knowing Christ Jesus my Lord" (Philippians 3:8).

When you want a cube of sugar to dissolve quicker in your tea you stir it to create the necessary turbulence for friction. This is desirable and good because you really want that sweet tea. Why then do you complain to God about the turbulence He has stirred up in your life to dissolve it into His drink? God has a stirring spoon and He always uses it for our ultimate good and to bring us into deeper intimate abiding with Him. The results will be you wondering why you resisted and an overflowing joy that you stopped. Let Him stir!

For Thought:

Are people seeing more of you or Jesus? Which appearance or likeness is growing?

Do you agree with what William Gurnall wrote, "The sweet bait of [Christianity] hath drawn many to nibble at it, who are offended with the hard service it calls to." [1]

Day 12

A Life Hidden in Christ (Part 2)

"He must increase, but I must decrease" (John 3:30).

As the sugar cube begins to dissolve inside the water its first natural reaction would likely be to resist. Therefore, God in His eagerness for us to dissolve does what we do when a sugar cube is not dissolving properly in our tea—He stirs it!

When we see turbulence and friction of life we often fail to see that God is stirring. Like Peter, we take our eyes off the Master, set our eyes on life's angry waves, and begin to sink in fear. What do many do here? They hop out of the water, all the while failing to realize what a sugar cube looks like after being in water for a time—it is a deformed lump that no one would ever think to use for his or her own tea. There is only one thing to do, get back in the water, *endure* ("abide under") the turbulence of God's stirring, and continue dissolving into Him.

Once the sugar cube dissolves it can hardly be seen any longer. Though it is still in there, only the pure water is really seen. The water and the sugar cube have amalgamated and are inseparable, and now it is even sweeter water. God created you to as a sweet sugar cube, not so you could remain unused and keep that form, but so you could dissolve into Jesus the Living Water and produce sweet water for others to drink through your spiritual union with Him.

Knowing what Jesus is like means dissolving into His inner world. No one can see you much anymore but they can undoubtedly see Jesus. You no longer have to describe Him from an outward perspective because you are no longer loving your life and protecting your own appearance. Jesus said, "If you cling to your life, you will lose it; but if you give up your life for Me, you will find it" (Matthew 10:39).

You will then become one who truly knows what His Savior is like from the inside out, rather than the person who remains bound to self-love and self-preservation. You and Christ Jesus will become just what He died for: Two becoming one with an unbroken fellowship. This is what it means to be married. Hop in the water, let Jesus stir, and enjoy your new spiritual marriage to the Jewel of heaven.

For Thought:

Are you decreasing so that Jesus may increase? Are you dissolving into His living water?

Many say they want to be like Jesus. Do you suffer to love those that hate and hurt you the most? Are you eager to surrender your most precious conveniences so they might benefit at your expense?

Is your discomfort too much for your neighbor's eternity? If so, let the stirring continue.

Day 13

Have You Been with Jesus?

"They were amazed, and began to recognize them as having been with Jesus" (Acts 4:13b).

Indeed the Sanhedrin marveled over the bold conviction of the Truth with which these unschooled men were speaking. Nonetheless, we know for certain these apostles had been filled with a Power not of their own at Pentecost, and spoke by an influential Presence wholly not of this world (see Acts 2:3-4). The Sanhedrin had often heard and felt the piercing words of Jesus, and the unearthly authority His teaching. And here they quickly recognized that same distinct power and voice speaking vicariously through these apostles.

Are you often astounded at the things you say and do? Is it mostly because of their God-inspired power and supernatural influence, or rather their ghastly and devilish nature? Take for example when we say, "I can't believe I acted that way," or, "I didn't really mean those awful words!" What about the horrifying deeds done in secret? Luke tells us the inescapable culprit: "The good man out of the good treasure of his heart brings forth what is good; and the evil man out of the evil treasure brings forth what is evil" (Luke 6:45).

We should do well to learn the following principle: We are like spiritual sponges. Therefore, when life squeezes us, what comes out is what we have been soaking in and absorbing the most. Jesus also gives us this same message, "If your eye is good, your whole body will be full of light. But if your eye is bad, your whole body will be full of darkness" (Matthew 6:22-23).

Jesus had spent three years teaching His apostles. They saw inexplicable miracles and were instilled with profound revelations, those of which no seminary could ever fully teach. However, right before Jesus ascended to the Father, He told them that the Holy Spirit would come and inundate them with Power from on high; and they must wait in Jerusalem until He came. Obediently, "They all joined together constantly in prayer" (Acts 1:14) until the fiftieth day, the Day of Pentecost. The Lord's disciples dwelt much in His earthly presence and even more in His earthly absence through prayer. Likewise, upon spending much time basking in the Lord's presence, you will be able to go about your everyday business radiating His light, stoked by His fire and speaking with His authority. Like the apostles, all those around you will unavoidably be amazed and recognize you as having been with Jesus too.

For Thought:

How much time do you spend with the Savior? Does prayer dictate your life or the other way around? Those who are weak in prayer are weak everywhere. Agree or disagree?

Day 14

Christ-like or Anti Christ-like?

"Do not be overcome by evil, but overcome evil with good" (Romans 12:21).

Those that have a gift of discernment are those who are able to distinguish between truth and error, light and darkness, sincerity and hypocrisy. We should never fall prey to the snare of squandering this precious gift. That means misusing it to be critical-spirited, faultfinding, and finger pointing. The gift of discernment is given with a probationary condition attached with it. It is given so that we may know how to pray. Once we use it to criticize, we defile the gift and make it a weapon of darkness. At this point, it loses all its illuminating light, and all that is good and holy about it departs. All that is left of it is selfish and evil.

Finger pointing and critical-spiritedness can be illustrated this way: We take a man and figuratively separate his good and bad character attributes with our discernment. We line up the good on his right side, and do the same with the bad on his left. At this point these attributes become sort of like people lined up on both sides. Now with our revolver of finger pointing we stealthily walk up behind each of the good and then one-by-one, execute them, until there are none. Therefore, all that is remaining is only what is bad. To satisfy our self-exalting ego, that is exactly how this man is presented to all others we know—a person of nothing but bad and fault. In other words, we overcame his good with our evil. The Apostle Paul writes in the book of Romans, "Do not be overcome by evil, but overcome evil with good" (12:21). Peter writes in his first Epistle, "Above all, keep loving one another earnestly, since love covers a multitude of sins" (4:8).

These two scriptures are admonishing us to exhibit the Christ-like behavior of forbearing the faults of others, not baring them. That means there is an element of suffering loss for their sake (see Matthew 5:4, "Blessed are those that mourn"). Many people take the meaning of this text to mean only the mourning of personal sin. However, mourning is so much more than this. Properly, the extended meaning is to suffer loss for the sake of doing what is good. It is good to suffer patiently alongside others' evils and faults.

Furthermore, knowing that the prefix *anti* means "opposite" or "opposed to," we must be extra diligent so as not to avoid the willingness to bear people's burdens. Anything opposite to or opposed to this type of Christ-like behavior could rightly be called "anti Christ-like" behavior. Suffering is inescapable with the truly merciful heart. Rex Andrews wrote, "Mercy takes the sins, evils, and faults of another as its own and frees the other by bearing them to God."[3] Anti Christ-like behavior frees self from the suffering of doing mercy and prides itself in baring the shortcomings of others, rather than forbearing them.

We should see that finger pointing, faultfinding, and critical-spiritedness destroy the good of our neighbor presenting only his sins, evils, and faults, and is nothing other than anti-Christ behavior? I believe this behavior has been glossed over and minimized far too well and far too long! The Lord suffered us long so we can be longsuffering to others. Let us truly repent and truly "love one another earnestly, cover a multitude of sins with love," and "overcome evil with good."

For Thought:

Is there someone in your life that you need to shower with love rather than with wrath? Are you carrying them or burying them?

Are you holding any captives or casualties of past wars? Who are you holding in debtor's prison?

Do you find the good qualities in a person and herald those, or do you drown them with floods of cynicism?

Day 15

Jesus Stopped!

"Many were sternly telling him to be quiet, but he kept crying out all the more, 'Son of David, have mercy on me!' And Jesus stopped and said, 'Call him here.'" (Mark 9:48-49).

Have you ever had a major revelation of the Lord Jesus Christ's divine eagerness and readiness to restore you? Whether it is forgiveness, healing, or deliverance, it is all about immediate restoration and reconciliation founded upon God's ever enduring mercy. How He hastens to the sincere heart cry for mercy. How He understands more than you or I ever could what we must be without it. "Give praise to the Lord, for He is good; His mercy is forever" (Psalm 118:1). Having our spiritual eyes enlightened, we can personally say, "I am the man full of leprosy; I am the blind beggar; I am the desperate tax collector, and Jesus has instantly restored and renewed me; O blessed thought!"

Many were telling him to be quiet. Anything or anyone that tells us to be quiet or compels us to remain silent when we should be crying out for mercy is in hostility toward God. We already have a three-fold enemy—the world, the flesh, and the Devil—set against us in that fashion. The world refuses to see its need for mercy and mocks us for doing so. The flesh heralds, "Unclean! Unfit!" in its own self-condemnation, which is no more than unbelief. The Devil whispers with his cunning and poison-filled words, "Don't bother God; it is too late for you and too much for Him." The last thing we need is our Christian family persuading us to be silent out of their own annoyance and false displays of piety.

It is the heart of the tax collector who, unable to lift his head, rents his garment and cries out for mercy because (1) he sees his desperate need for it, and (2) he fully understands his undeserved request. That is why the Word of God says, "come boldly . . . so that we may receive mercy" (Hebrews 4:16). It takes great boldness to beg for something we know we do not deserve, especially when we acknowledge the fact that we deserve the complete opposite. And if we, being in this same posture of spiritual poverty, recognize our desperate need for His mercy and what we are without it, God does infinitely more.

And Jesus stopped. It was not merely the sincere cry that halted Jesus in His steps, nor was it his mere belief in Jesus' divine power to heal him; it was the way he addressed Jesus. Bartimaeus "heard that it was Jesus the Nazarene," and he called Him not by His earthly title, "Jesus of Nazareth," but rather by His divine title, "Jesus, Son of David." Using the terminology *Son of David* meant that Bartimaeus was confessing with great faith that Jesus is the Messiah—the prophesied fulfillment of the Davidic Covenant and the everlasting King (see 2 Samuel 7:11-13, 1 Chronicles 17:11-12).

If you ever want to stop Jesus in His tracks, call Him Who and What He really is. If I desire to get Jesus to stop and minister His mercy to me, I must first come to Him as He is: The fully glorified Lamb of God, whose eyes are filled with fire; the One from whose mouth proceeds a two-edged sword; whose feet are like burning bronze superheated in a furnace; whose voice is like a thousand times a thousand waterfalls; whose face shines greater than the sun in all its power; the One whose countenance is so holy the angels must continually cover their feet and faces and cry out in prostrate worship, "Holy, Holy, Holy!" Praise is describing God to God, which tells Him we have had some revelation of Who He is and agree by faith.

Call him here to Me. I must also come to Him as I am: Blind, leprous, and desperate, falling at His feet as though dead. Only then will I feel His fear expelling hand upon me, and hear Him say, "Fear not! What do you want Me to do for you?" And I should respond, "Lord, give me eyes to see You. Remove the leprous things that separate me from You, so I can have the fellowship and devotion that You died to purchase for me. Quench my parched spirit with Your living water. I believe You have called me by name to come forth from the slumber of death like Lazarus, now raise me to newness of life with Your resurrection power. Amen."

Immediately he regained his sight and began following Him. The restoration is instantaneous; so should be our reckless devotion to follow the Lamb wherever He goes. No matter how feeble it may be, cry out to Him with sure faith in His divine eagerness to restore you. He not only hears you, He also stops to meet with you, so you can answer His question, "What do you want Me to do for you?" His restoration is immediate; let your devotion be.

For Thought:

Why did Jesus ask a man blind from birth what he wanted? What would your response be if Jesus asked what you wanted Him to do for you?

Day 16

Justice in Who's Hands? (Part 1)

"What have you done? The voice of your brother's blood is crying to Me from the ground" (Genesis 4:10).

Does justice usually rest in your own hands or in the Hands of the Savior? Adam's sin produced exactly what the Devil tempted him with, "being his own god, knowing the difference between good and evil" (a.k.a. judge). As a result, man has been judging apart from God ever since. Man says, "I declare what is righteous;" God says we are "declared righteous" by faith in the finished work of Christ, "Therefore we have peace" with Him (see Romans 5:1). If you do not have peace, it is because you are not seeking for it in the right place. Jesus gave us a clue when He said, "Come to Me . . . and I will give you rest" (Matthew 11:28).

The world's first murder was the result of Cain taking justice into his own hands. God's displeasure with Cain's sacrifice wounded his pride; big brother felt less accepted and overshadowed by little brother. Therefore, he was at war within himself and his outward expression declared it. God disciplined Cain, but it came with an encouraging promise as well as a warning, "If you do well, will not your countenance be lifted up? And if you do not do well, sin is crouching at the door; and its desire is for you" (4:7). Cain chose to remain at war with God, himself, and his brother rather than humbly receive God's offering of peace. In other words, Cain chose not to be forgiven all because of his pride. Because of this condition, the weight of guilt crushed his spirit. Cain had chosen sin and wrath as his justice. And since the wages of sin is death, the wages of Cain's sin was Abel's death. People who are at war on the outside are only that way because they are at war on the inside, because they have not received the peace that only God can provide. The opposite of peace is a fallen countenance from the inside out.

Both Cain's sin and God's wrath for it were not lifted up or satisfied, therefore Cain remained in an un-forgiven state by his own stubborn choice. God offered Cain His justice of repentance and restoration, but Cain chose his own justice of sin and wrath. Therefore, a victim of wrath was mandatory. Murder was inevitable because death is sin's full-grown conception, just look at the cross for proof. This is why Jesus said anyone that harbors anger towards his brother is subject to the same judgment as murder (see Matthew 5:21-22). God's justice was taken into the hands of His own Son nailed to the cross. Taking justice into your own hands makes Calvary cheap and dishonors the blood of Christ.

For Thought:

Do you have a hard time praying mercy for those you deem evil or enemies? Do you struggle with forgiveness, anger, or a critical spirit? Take those struggles to Calvary and find peace there.

Day 17

Justice in Who's Hands? (Part 2)

"What have you done? The voice of your brother's blood is crying to Me from the ground" (Genesis 4:10).

True Justice is seen only in the Hands of the "Lamb of God who takes away the sin of the world" (John 1:29). Those pierced Hands were fastened to Golgotha's tree of death to declare God's justice. The Greek word for "takes away" is *airo*, which properly means, "to lift up." The sin of the world was truly *lifted up* at Calvary that wonderfully cruel day, as God's wrath for sin was fully and forever satisfied upon His own Son, Jesus Christ.

People, who cannot accept God's forgiveness, either for others or for themselves, have exalted their own judgment above that of God. They, like Cain, have taken justice into their own hands and are in bondage. They are in debtor's prison! Forgiveness is the releasing of another from the grip of your chokehold. It amounts to agreeing with Christ's agonizing forgiveness for them. Forgiveness is a choice to plunge the offender into the blood of Jesus, rather than just trying to forget or overlook the offense!

Those who say they cannot forgive will not forgive, usually because there is some self-judged payment or stipulation upon which their forgiveness is hinged. However, by God's Standard, forgiveness has only one stipulation, the shedding of blood, and that has already happened through Christ once and for all. Unforgiveness of any sort demands more blood and more payment, which renders the cross of Christ insufficient or unfavorable. God's divine favor is disgraced by lack of forgiveness.

The sin of the world has already been paid for and lifted up once for all at Calvary through Jesus' precious blood. If you are having difficulty forgiving someone, including yourself, you have ignored, deliberately rejected, or never seen Jesus' immeasurable difficulty forgiving you. The Blood of Christ cries out from the ground the great injustice we do to His great justice when we harbor anger, bitterness and resentment, which are all classified as refusal to forgive. The only reason we are able to proclaim injustice of any kind is because we refuse to behold the Face of justice upon the Cross. Look upon Jesus and get peace through His forgiveness, and then give that to those you feel have treated you with injustice. True forgiveness means applying God's forgiveness to their injustice and sins, not your own forgiveness. God paid the highest price to declare you righteous. Do not cheapen the cost of Calvary another minute. Forgive and be free.

For Thought:

Is there an injustice that someone has done to you recently or in the past that you dwell upon?

Why do you think it is so difficult to apply God's mercy to others?

Day 18

Like His Unlikeness (Part 1)

"Woe to you when all men speak well of you, for their fathers used to treat the false prophets in the same way" (Luke 6:26).

God gives the command to all of His followers, "Be holy as I am holy" (Leviticus 11:45; 1 Peter 1:16). The holiness of God is none other than His infinite uniqueness. This can be explained as such: He is altogether unlike any person, any thing, any other god, or any other king; not only in His unique essence as the eternal First Cause of all life and existence, but in the way that is most relevant to us as humans—His absolute unlikeness of character.

Are you compatible with others based only on their compatibility with you; because their likes and dislikes are congruent with yours; because their tastes, behaviors, sense of humor, and personalities are very much like your own? In other words, are you more drawn to the development of friendships and relationships because they are a reflection of your self more than that of Jesus Christ?

Man's natural propensity is to love himself and for others to do the same. Man naturally loves himself more than anything or anyone else; and without an authentic transformation through the crucifixion of that old self, we will always default to loving the reflection of ourselves in others and err by calling it a godly friendship.

In the first person it sounds like this: "You remind me of myself, and the things you do coincide with my desires, actions, and gratifications. Therefore I am pleased with you because you remind me a lot of myself. You are my friend, and I'll be yours, at least until you start changing."

Keep this in mind: Apart from living out God's biblical Standard of love (which is always denying self for the benefit of another) all that is left is self-devotion, which is the root of every sin. Without discipline toward godliness (2 Timothy 4:7), man will favor himself at the expense of others, rather than favor others at his expense. He will only favor others as long as everything is going his way (see James 4:1-2).

Jesus Christ, who was fully man and fully God (see Colossians 2:9; John 14:7-9) was altogether unlike anyone the world had ever seen. This alone is much of the reason why He was so despised and rejected. That kind of action-oriented love is a walking rebuke to man's version of sentimental affection, as well as the Devil's counterfeits of covetousness and lust.

The more you desire to fit in with the crowd, the more like them you become. It is total folly to think you are supposed to be, act, and look like the world to win them over to your Christian beliefs (this is called "cheerleader Christianity"). If the world does not see the likeness of Jesus in you, then you have chosen to which likeness you will be conformed. Be careful that people do not like you apart from Jesus.

Unconverted people are prone to despise everything that is not like them. Unlikeness brings in new understanding. New understanding always ushers in new ways of living, which in turn demands change. This is why God's own people vehemently shouted, "Crucify Him!"

The more like Christ's unlikeness you are, the more unlike the world you become. "Be ye renewed . . . according to God's likeness in righteousness and purity of the truth" (Ephesians 4:23-24, KJV). The more unlike the rest of the world you become, the more likely they will oppose what they see because it demands change in them. This especially goes for certain relationships that you have previously called friendships based completely upon sentimental emotions and carnal delights. Being always well spoken of can cause a spiritual heart attack.

> *"For to you it has been granted for Christ's sake, not only to believe in Him, but also to suffer for His sake"* (Philippians 1:28-29).

For Thought:

Read Mark 8:38. Unless we are willing to be despised by those closest to and most like our natural (old) self, we are essentially saying we are ashamed of Christ. When we choose the likeness of the world we are hostile towards God (James 4:4), and speak to Jesus by our choices, "I love myself too much and others too little to suffer to be like You."

Day 19

Like His Unlikeness? (Part 2)

"Behold, I send you out as sheep in the midst of wolves; so be shrewd as serpents and innocent as doves" (Matthew 10:16).

We do not separate ourselves from the world; No, our unlikeness by being like Christ Jesus does that alone. In analogy, it is the willingness to drive the opposite direction down a one-way city street—where all other drivers are perturbed and curse you for your error—all in the hope that just one might see that it is not your error but rather his or her own, and then turn and follow you in the right direction.

You may have a tendency to set your eyes upon your own holiness and therefore corrupt the essence of God's holiness. Your holiness is never something to claim ownership of or take delight in, but rather is nothing more than the fruit (evidence) of your devotion to the Lord Jesus Christ. As soon as you lay a claim to ownership of anything that exclusively belongs to God, it immediately corrupts and begins to die.

It is others' benefit to see your Christ-like unlikeness, not yours. When you focus on your own holiness, you risk falling into great error. You can become guilty of doing the same thing the world does—seeing yourself as better than others because you are better or different. Immediately a wall of spiritual pride has separated you from a lost world, rather than the true holiness of God. We see our own unlikeness, see the contrast in others, and if left unchecked, we will begin to condemn, despise, and reject all those that do not look like "our unlikeness". Without repentance, this is nothing more than a refined self-love that will not properly mingle with those it has deemed "dregs." Believers like this never position themselves in the muddy trenches to bring out filth-laden souls to the cleansing of Calvary. Can you now see how self-love is the greatest enemy of the love of God?

Jesus said He is sending us out as sheep among the wolves. This charge from Jesus is not merely a warning of persecution. Wolves devour sheep, therefore we see Jesus warning us not to be devoured. He gives a clue when He also said, "In the world you have tribulation, but take courage; I have overcome the world" (John 16:33). To paraphrase, Jesus is saying 'I have overcome the world—the carnal mindset of man's wisdom that is hostile to all that I am, and that which will cause you much grief. Do not let it overcome you with its cunning lies and various lusts. Love Me and you will not be devoured." Being an overcomer means Jesus overcoming you.

Very plainly, it is the *compromise to* and *love of* the world that devours the sheep. Remember, persecution only made the early Christian church thrive and grow, not only in size, but also in maturity. Stated another way, persecution only proves if a sheep is truly a sheep. In the parable of the sower (Matthew 13:1-23), We see "the seed that fell among thorns," This is very similar to sheep that fall among the wolves. Nevertheless, the seed was devoured by "the cares of this world and the deceitfulness of wealth."

Yes, our Christ-like unlikeness sets us apart in separation from the world, but it does not isolate or segregate us. Jesus called the Apostles to follow Him and they followed, leaving successful lives, family businesses, homes, and lands forever behind. "We have left all we had to follow you" (Luke 18:28). What do we have here but Jesus separating His disciples for a length of time long enough to teach, train, and transform them more into His unlikeness?

Nearness produces attraction, and distance produces repulsion. The nearer you are to Jesus, the sweeter He becomes; meanwhile the further you are from your former lusts and lifestyles, the more bitter they grow. Jesus has separated you to transform you into His unlikeness, thereby purifying you of your love *of* this world. So when He sends you back out as a sheep among the wolves you will not be devoured, because He has filled you with His love *for* the world.

For Thought:

In Exodus 33:7, Moses took his tent and devoted it to God for the use of becoming the tabernacle. His tent became a holy tent because it was in full devotion to the Lord. God's presence filled it, dwelled within it, and made it unlike any other tent in the world.

Day 20

Loving Jesus Produces Hatred for Evil

"You who love the Lord, hate evil" (Psalm 98:10).

Keeping in mind that love is an action, love for the Lord, therefore, is what produces a growing hatred for evil. Righteous actions prohibit unrighteous actions, and as it is said, "The sweeter Jesus becomes the more bitter sin becomes."

Take for example you have precious little children. If a convicted child molester had moved across the street and knocked on your door one day asking to borrow some sugar, would you let him roam freely in your house? Would you say, "Oh yes, sugar is in the cupboard. I'll just head back to my project out back; help yourself neighbor. By the way, my children are in their rooms playing"? No! As far as you know, he is potentially hostile to what you value and treasure above all else in this world.

David writes in another Psalm, "Your Word I have treasured in my heart so that I might not sin against You" (119:11). When Jesus, who is the Living Word is truly treasured in your heart, all that is evil is regarded as a hostile enemy in need of being fervently defended. This is also what Paul meant when he exhorted Timothy, "Guard, through the Holy Spirit who dwells in us, the treasure which has been entrusted to you" (2 Timothy 1:14).

> *"Light dawns for the righteous; gladness for the upright in heart"* (Psalm 98: 11).

For those who are pure in heart and in right standing with God, light and gladness certainly dawn for them. Just like when the light of the sun dawns in the morning and all darkness is conquered—it is the light of our Lord Jesus that conquers the darkness for those who love and practice righteousness. By continuously aligning your heart to His Truth, you will increasingly take on the heart of the Lord. David wrote, "Delight yourself in the LORD, and He will give you the desires of your heart" (Psalm 37:4). He does not give you whatever your heart desires; He gives you what His heart desires because you have agreed that His will is best; because your actions have proven that he things you want are the things He wants you to want.

As you increase in the assurance of God's love toward you, so will your devotion to Jesus, and those old sinful habits and dark lusts will shrink in the rearview mirror. Loving the light means hating the darkness and all that lurks and slithers therein. Falling deeply in love with Jesus is rising out of deep sin and evil; the depth of devotion to Him determines the depth of deliverance from evil.

For Thought:

Why would it be irresponsible to ask God to zap you and just make you holy? (Hint: Think about the 10 lepers in Luke 17 that all got healed, *but only one came back* to pay homage to Jesus).

Day 21

Mocker or Beggar?

One of the criminals . . . was hurling abuse at Him, saying, 'Are You not the Christ?' But the other was saying, 'Jesus Remember me when You come into Your kingdom'" (Luke 23: 39-42).

Have you ever found yourself caught in a fluctuating pattern of mocking God and begging God? Have you found in the midst of your heart a mixture of these two attitudes, each of which are completely opposed one to the other? At Calvary we see the cross, driven as a wedge directly between these two attitudes. The Cross of Jesus Christ always separates—belief from unbelief, pride from humility, mocking from pleading, and judgment from mercy. It is no coincidence that we see this exact principle exhibited with Jesus being crucified between two guilty malefactors, one mocking in prideful unbelief, and the other begging in humble belief.

The obligation of a righteous earthly judge is to separate what is good from what is evil through his wisdom and discernment, thereby rendering his judgment. Likewise, but infinitely more at Calvary, the one righteous Judge sets His people apart, to make them holy as He is holy (Leviticus 20:7; 1 Peter 1:16). Through the cross, Jesus is continually accomplishing this task by separating those who live in mocking unbelief and disobedience from those who cry out in humble repentance, "Have mercy on me, a sinner" (Luke 18:13).

One of the thieves rightly confesses to Jesus, "We are receiving what our deeds deserve" (vs. 41). *Confess*, in the Greek means properly to come into agreement with God. The other thief would not confess; he only desired to escape his judgment. He cried "Save Yourself and us!"

One thief essentially said Jesus is the Christ and wanted to be a part of His Kingdom after death. The other said, 'If You were really the Christ, You would get us out of this mess!' Both petitioned the Lord to save them, but only one wanted to be a part of His Kingdom. The mocking thief only wanted to be saved from his punishment, probably so he could have more selfish life in this world. The begging thief wanted to be saved from his sins so he could have life in another world. Both were guilty and were receiving what all of us deserve, but only the begging thief confessed that fact. Jesus was crucified directly between the repentant and unrepentant, and there is only fellowship between the two through the cross.

The Word of God, which is the sharpest Sword in existence (see Hebrews 4:12), is to accomplish that same separation in believer's hearts. It is the winnower that sifts the wheat from the tares, the pure from the impure, faith from unbelief, the arrogant from the meek, the lofty from the humble, the ambitious striver from the suffering servant, the Pharisee from the tax collector, and the mocker from the beggar. The Word of God is not just God's Word in the Bible. It is Jesus Himself, whose "eyes are a flame of fire, and on His head are many diadems; and He has a name written on Him that no one knows except Himself. He is clothed in a robe dipped in blood, and His name is called The Word of God" (Revelation 19:13). Jesus, The Word of God, is the Judgment that separates the mocker from the beggar.

If our church is not filled with beggars declared righteous, it will become filled with self-righteous mockers. If our hearts are not filled with pleading for mercy and prayer for the lost, they will become filled with mocking selfishness. The cross of Jesus Christ will forever judge, separating those declared righteous from those who choose to remain unbroken and righteous in their own eyes. If you find yourself caught in a wishy-washy pattern of mocking and begging, meditate on the cross and talk with The Word of God who was fastened there. He judges the mocker and justifies the beggar; let Him separate the two once and for all.

For Thought:

Jesus revealed the difference between two thieves that otherwise looked identical; only He has that ability. What truths about yourself has He revealed that others could never have known otherwise?

Read James 5:16. Why is it important to confess our sins to one another?

Day 22

Caught off Guard

"Don't let Him find you sleeping when He arrives without warning . . . Watch for Him!"
(Mark 13:36-37, NLT)

Has God ever caught you off guard? God always does what He said He would do, and Jesus said He would return in His Father's glory (Matthew 16:27). We should be living in constant expectation of the coming of the Lord Jesus Christ, to the point that when He does show up we are only surprised by how He came, not *that* He came. To the ten virgins, His discipline was to keep oil in their lamps, and that Oil is the Holy Spirit. To the watching servants, his command was to keep the lamps burning, which signifies a warning against spiritual apathy and complacency. To the sensible steward, it was to keep his house in order with mercy and grace until the master's return.

God knows it is possible for deceitful and wicked servants to watch for His return only to quickly try and clean up their debauched living when the watchman spots the approaching master. But good and faithful servants long for their Master's return and mourn His departure. This is the reason surprise visits are imperative and good. Whenever God catches His servants by surprise it is always a great mercy of God to do so in this life as a sobering discipline. Woe to us if He finds us sleeping in a house of ill repute and living in disorder on the Day of the Lord.

One of the most amazing attributes of God's surprise visits in this life is the fact that although you may be faithfully watching for His return at the front door, He enters into your house through other openings that only He knows about. He does this to continue His refining work. He catches you busy guarding your walls against obvious enemies while He exposes cracks and fissures in other areas you otherwise never would have seen on your own. When God catches you off guard, you should be joyful that He calls you a true son by this merciful discipline (Hebrews 12:8). True sons of God are only surprised by the manner of His coming. "We were expecting You to show up Lord, but not like that!" As for His imminent return in all of His glory, the surprise will be with awestruck amazement in how He comes, not that He did! Devote yourself to Him and though He may often catch you off guard, you will not be caught in sin.

For Thought:

Are you living prepared for the Lord's arrival? Are there things in your life that He would condemn if He showed up unexpectedly?

When is the last time He caught you off your guard in a good way? What was it?

Day 23

The Balanced Walk of the Saint

"The laborers who carried the loads worked with one hand and held a weapon with the other" (Nehemiah 4:17, HCSV).

The greatest weapon of the child of God against the enemies of God and all their tactics is the prayer-life. Nehemiah and the returned exiles of Judah were doing a physical work of rebuilding and were continuously fighting off physical enemies. The Apostle Paul tells us, "Our struggle is not against flesh and blood, but against the spiritual forces of wickedness in the heavenly places" (see Ephesians 6:12). For such a spiritual battle we need a spiritual weapon.

The walk of the saint is balanced only when the prayer-life is at par with the work-life. If your physical work is greater than your spiritual work, you are vulnerable, unbalanced, and have a gap or a low place in your wall. It is there that the enemy can and will come upon you like a flood from a ruptured dam to destroy you, defeat you, plunder you, or at least stop the work. We read in Nehemiah 4:11, "Our enemies said, 'they will not know or see until we come upon them, kill them and put a stop to the work.'"

Are you praying as much as you are working? Are you in front of the altar of your prayer closet as much as you are in front of your computer screen, television, conference table, or shopping aisle? Are you standing in the gap as an intercessory prayer-warrior for your family as much as you are working to provide for them? As an elder, deacon, pastor or preacher, are you praying in equal proportion to the measure of your working? Have you replaced going to prayer with going to church? Are you reading God's Word without spending time prostrate before the God of the Word?

Many today are building their big churches whose praying in comparison is nearly absent; they have replaced the spiritual work with the physical. As with the spiritual condition of God's people in Jeremiah's time, their worship has deteriorated to mere physical ritualism and an outer "form of godliness" (see 2 Timothy 3:5).

Just like Nehemiah was commissioned to rebuild, we have been commissioned to rebuild. What is the rebuilding of a life squandered on selfish gain, self-centered agendas, and the lusts of the flesh but a desperate and deep spiritual work? What is the great commission to convert sinners to saints through the power of the Gospel but a great spiritual rebuilding? This is the rebuilding of a life from a *heaping mound of rubble*, and the very thing that the enemy is relentlessly going to come against with every cunning tactic he possesses.

If the people of God think for one second that their mission is accomplished through physical labor only, then that is the most tragically foolish second in time! Likewise, if you think that your own walk as a saint will successfully withstand the wiles of the enemy without a fervent prayer-life that is equal to the fervency of your work-life, that thought is one to shudder indeed.

The enemy taunted Nehemiah and the laboring rebuilders, "Can they bring these burnt stones back to life from the mounds of rubble?" They could and they did, and it was only because they did not get lost in the physical work to the point of neglecting the spiritual. "Our God will fight for us," they said (4:20). They were willing to fight for God because they were confident would fight for them. They were confident because He had countless times proven Himself as the unfailing, undefeated, and uncompromisingly trustworthy God. Therefore, they did their work with one hand and fought the enemy with the other.

Is your Christian walk balanced or unbalanced? Is your time spent behind the curtain in God's presence keeping the scales of life balanced? If you spend much time in the presence of God's enemies without bathing in the presence of God, you have no grounds for complaining about feeling unbalanced, discontent, dirty or depressed. In His presence "is fullness of joy" (Psalm 16:11b). Work with one hand while you pray with the other.

For Thought:

Why do you think so many American Christians are weary or unfaithful, when those in harsher environments willingly die for their faith?

Read Hosea 10: 6-8, James 4:4, and 1 John 1:6-8. Do you think love of the world, ease, and comfort is the culprit of the vast unbalance we see?

Day 24

The Crest and the Trough

"I will rather boast about my weaknesses, so that the power of Christ may dwell in me . . . for when I am weak, then I am strong" (2 Corinthians 12:9-10).

From our Lord Jesus' heavenly perspective, our valleys are His mountaintops. What is a valley turned upside down but a mountain? For example, when we look normally at a transverse wave we identify the high points as crests and the low points as troughs. However, if we could hang by our feet from heaven, the troughs would become crests and vice-versa. What does this proclaim other than that everything we know and see is turned upside down the moment we become heavenly-minded?

It is in the valleys of life where we come to know Jesus the most, because that is where He spent most of His life when He was upon the earth. Yes, we also come to know Him on the mountaintop, for we know Jesus called Peter, James, and John up with Him upon the Mount of Transfiguration to see something about Him that they would not come to understand until after His Resurrection from the dead. However, before this glorious history-changing event, Jesus' disciples still could not grasp the reality of His Divinity, let alone His dual nature (fully God and fully man).

This teaches us that the Lord shows us things today that we cannot fully grasp, but will eventually come to understand at some future point. This also teaches us that the temporarily incomprehensible revelations Jesus gives us on the spiritual heights of the mountain will serve a perfectly timed purpose in tomorrow's valleys. It is when we experience the blissful moments and the spiritual ecstasies on the mountaintop that we come to know more of Christ's Divinity; it is in the drudgery, labors, and lowliness of the valleys where we come to know more of His humanity. Our Mountaintops reveal Jesus' exalted Divinity; our valleys reveal His humbled humanity.

So the next time we are in the low ebbs of life we can thank Jesus kindly that He is teaching us what it is to be like Him—the One who assumed the *nature* of a humbled servant. And the next time we are enjoying the wonders of a spiritual mountaintop we can worship Him for giving us a fleeting glimpse of what it will be like to see Him in eternity—the one Lamb of God who is fully glorified and seated at the right hand of the Father.

For Thought:

Why are the valleys of life so important?

Read Matthew 17:1-9 and Mark 9: 2-10. What happened on the Mount of Transfiguration?

Think of the most lovely, blissful moment you have ever had. Multiply that times infinity. That is what heavenly eternity promises, because you will be in the presence of infinitely perfect Love.

Day 25

The *Winds* and *Fires* of God

"He makes winds his messengers; flames of fire his servants" (Psalm 104:4)

Stale and stagnant air cannot sustain life any more than it can move heavy objects. It eventually becomes putrefying to the olfactory receptors in our nose and suffocating to our breath. Without a fresh supply of air brought by the wind every living thing in the area will surely die. One of the plagues of Revelation (The Sixth Seal) is the restraining of the wind from blowing on the earth (7:1).

However, when the winds come, all suffering life drinks them in deeply as their refreshing power relieves, rescues, and restores. Wind stirs things that would otherwise be dismal and animates them into thought-provoking motion. Fields of wheat are transformed from stagnant ponds into golden life-filled seas as they are churned by the winds.

Winds in unrestrained power also move otherwise unmovable things. For instance, an EF5 tornado that was a mile and a half wide producing 200 mph winds recently moved an entire city, razing to the ground all that man has labored to build. Winds of this magnitude declare the eternal power of God and the temporal feebleness of man.

Now we should have a more sobering understanding of what God expects from those who call themselves "messengers" or "ministers." We have not even begun to talk about His "servants" being "flames of fire" yet! The Hebrew word for flames here is *lahat* (law-'hat), which means, "blazing." A *blazing* fire is a consuming fire (see Hebrews 12:29) that uncontrollably spreads and purifies that which is corrupt.

Stagnant, position-holding, motionless, chair-sitting, committee-forming ice cubes can call themselves *deacons* (servants) and *ministers* (messengers) if they so choose. But the evidence of surrounding lifelessness caused by their suffocating and frigid religion declares otherwise, especially to God.

To all of us who are considered servants and messengers: Are things moving? Burning? Being purified? Breathing? Refreshing? They would be if we were! "Therefore repent and return . . . in order that times of refreshing may come from the presence of the Lord" (Acts 3:19).

For Thought:

The Devil's Decoy

Let's build a nice meeting that people enjoy, we'll
thrill them with talent and calm them with coy

We'll warm them in sentiment and dynamic words
We'll jar them with jokes so our sermons are heard

We'll woo their self-interests and dress up a fake
With great sounding music we'll keep them awake

They'll fight over polls but not over souls
'Cause their building is all that's at stake

With positions and programs they'll be pacified
Behind old traditions God's absence we'll hide

We'll teach them to strive in strength of the flesh
We'll get them deceived like David Koresh

We'll hijack their vision by prompting self-gain
We'll sell them the Christ while usurping His reign

We'll promise them glory for what they have made
While a lost world is perishing for their charade

Their spiritual genocide unsparingly justified
With "At least we're drawing them in!"

To what, pray tell, or to whom are they drawn?
To Jesus, or just to mere men?

God only invites what His fire ignites
From this fire, they'll certainly flee

For fire exposes their decoy of roses
And from Him . . .

They'll run straight to me.

Day 26

The Discipline of Listening

"I told you about my life, and You listened to me; teach me Your statutes" (Psalm 119:26).

How often do we come before the Father taking full advantage of entering into His throne room of grace, pouring out our lives and endless petitions at His feet? How often is it just to relieve ourselves of our heavy burdens, but with no real intentions of taking up His yoke and learning from Him? We can judge it a great annoyance when others only seek our counsel to unload their refuse but have no purpose of listening or receiving direction or correction. Yet how many times have we exhibited the same behavior toward God?

Once our spiritual cataracts are removed we see like David and say, "Lord, all I have done is continually tell You about my life, and yet You still listened to me like a patient gentleman. Now teach me Your ways, I am ready to be still and know You" (see Psalm 46:10). If we would see with the right perception we would find out we have been too busy talking rather than listening. We would finally hear God speak, "You told Me about your life and I listened to you. Now let Me tell you about My life and you listen to Me!"

Mary sat down and listened to her Savior's teaching. Martha talked too much, was full of anxiety, and was troubled by a great many concerns (Luke 10:38-42). We make our endless petitions to God without sitting still and listening quietly with faithful patience and that makes us the same as Martha saying, "Lord, do you not care?"

For how will we know His care when we are unwilling to be still and just listen to Him? He wants to tell us about "His Life." Are we willing to be like Mary, who did the one necessary thing, and listen to Him? Are we willing to see *His Life* instead of our own? How can we hear

Him speak if we are too busy doing all the speaking? Many of my petitions and burdens are rendered as nothing when I stop telling Him about my life and begin to listen to Him tell me about Jesus, the Way, the Truth, and the Life. There I see the cause of most of my problems exist because of the vast difference between *His Life* and my life. Telling God about your life makes you seem big and God seem small. Listening to God and seeing His life in Jesus Christ makes Him huge and you insignificant. When you see how important you are to Him you will see less of your own importance and develop the discipline of listening.

For Thought:

Practice sitting completely quiet and still, dwelling intensely upon Jesus, or a passage of Scripture. Begin to do this for 15-30 minutes a day for six weeks without letting your thoughts wander. This will do wonders for scatterbrained habits, forgetfulness, and what the world deceptively calls "ADHD," and without pills! This will challenge even the most mature saint.

Day 27

The Joy of Suffering

"I will most gladly spend and be expended for your souls"
(2 Corinthians 12:15)

The trials, sufferings, hardships, persecutions, and challenges of a life spent ministering the Gospel to a world that abhors these things is to be expected, but also considered a worthy privilege. To a hedonistic society (secular and religious) that loves comforts and pleasures, forsaking these for a life of selfless hardship and labor for Jesus is anathema. Even for believers it is often rejected, regardless of the historical veracity of Jesus' finished work.

Therefore, the saint devoted to Jesus and His Gospel will do well to pledge his or her neck to the gallows, embrace the fact that he or she has already died (Romans 6:3-5), and know that the very essence of the Gospel message is willfully, but joyfully crucified life. Indeed all life is suffering, saved or unsaved, because all life is dying. However, servants of Christ suffer with a hope that unsaved people do not have. "Brothers and sisters, we do not want you to be uninformed about those who sleep in death, so that you do not grieve like the rest of mankind, who have no hope" (1 Thessalonians 4:13). God gave us His promise of hope before he asked us to suffer for His sake and a lost world.

The joy of knowing the Lord is pleased and glorified by honoring what He died to redeem—our life—makes it all worth it. He plucked us like brands out of the fire. This is not even mentioning the eternal glory of our rewards and crowns that are far beyond the scope of any finite mind or lofty imaginations of men. However, in this world, the ultimate joy of suffering is seeing others who are suffering find hope and joy in Jesus.

Illustrated through Mary of Bethany pouring out upon Jesus the entire contents of the ointment that cost a year's wages, our Lord Jesus is thoroughly pleased when we pour out our entire life for His sake and for others. When we truly are in love with someone, expense is immaterial, and the thought of holding something back for ourselves is foreign. We only have reservations in pouring out our entire lives to Jesus because our hearts are attached to what we withhold. True love does not ask what the cost will be or what the reward could be. True love for Jesus already has its joyful reward in Him, and is exhibited in a life expended for Him and His Kingdom. "Oh how I love Jesus, Oh how I love Jesus, Oh how I love Jesus, because He first loved me." [4]

For Thought:

Are you being spent for Jesus? What have you held back from Him? What about from your spouse?

Read 1 John 1:1-4. The greatest joy of suffering is helping others who are suffering find the joy of intimately knowing Jesus. Is this is your greatest joy?

Day 28

Trading Worthy For Worthless

"Turn my eyes from looking at what is worthless" (Psalm 119:37).

What is worthless according to God's standard is anything that does not glorify Him. It is not essentially sinful to see worthless things; this is inescapable. Furthermore, it is absurd to imagine not doing so in a world that is full of worthless things and vain lusts for the eyes. The Hebrew word for *looking* in this text is *Raah* (Raw-'aw), which means to gaze with musing intent, or more simply, "to keep on looking with gratification."

We only fix our gaze upon things in which we find value. Much like memory foam, where the heaviest objects make the deepest and longest-lasting impressions, our hearts are impressed by what we gaze upon the most. Herein lies the weight of this particular sin of *looking*—fixing our gaze upon what is worthless. It means looking with delight at what God sees as worthless, thereby seeing the thing as worthy. We render God's perfect judgment of worth below our own.

Simultaneously, we are looking away from God who alone is worthy of our gaze, and in our hearts declaring Him as unworthy. In other words, we deem the Lord (who alone is worthy) worthless, and what is worthless, worthy.

Our hearts were made and formed by Him (Psalm 119:73) and were meant to be impressed by Him alone. The more our hearts are impressed by godless and worthless things, the harder they become to be impressed by God. It is certainly true that whatever we are impressed by we tend to worship and idolize in our hearts. All throughout the Psalms, we see David musing upon God, "I muse on all your works and consider what your hands have done" (Psalm 143:5).

The more we meditate on what God can do and who He is, the less we are impressed by what man can do or what this world has to offer. Therefore, worldly treasures are rendered worthless, and like the Apostle Paul we will sincerely be able to "consider everything to be a loss in view of the surpassing value of knowing Christ Jesus" (Philippians 3:8). Like David, we will say, "Your Word, have I treasured in my heart, so that I might not sin against You" (Psalm 119:11). When Jesus Christ, the Living Word, is truly treasured in our hearts, sin loses its appeal. Practice turning your eyes from what is worthless by fixing them on Jesus the worthy Lamb of God. This will strengthen your worship. Neglect it, and you will become more convinced that idols are more worthy than Jesus.

For Thought:

Read Jonah 2:8.

What have you fixed your eyes upon today? Have you found worth in anything God finds unworthy? Disagreeing with God holds the ideal of saying He is a lower judge and you are the Supreme Court.

Day 29

Show Me the Coin

"'Show Me the coin used for the tax.' So they brought him a Roman coin. 'Whose image and inscription is this?' He asked them" (Matthew 22:20, HCS).

Jesus is questioning the Pharisees this time. It was usually the Pharisees asking Jesus questions in order to trap Him in an error. The Lord never asks a question because He needs the answer. He asks questions because He is looking for a confession. God asked Adam where He was, not because He lost Adam, but because Adam was lost, and He wanted him to recognize his true condition. Jesus asked Saul of Tarsus why he was persecuting Him to get Saul to and see that what he was so convinced was God's work was in fact the Devil's work.

Knowing the Pharisees were there only for deceptive purposes, Jesus first asked them to show Him the coin. This speaks of the Lord's desire to scrutinize everything with His eyes of blazing fire (Revelation 1:14). Then He asked them whose image was on the coin. Jesus had seen Roman coins before and knew quite well whose inscription was impressed upon them. Nevertheless, they answered, "Caesar's" (man's image). His response is filled with spiritual meaning and a crucial warning. He said, "Then render to Caesar the things that are Caesar's; and to God the things that are God's" (vs. 21).

In other words, all who insist on keeping their own human image rather than the new Christ image impressed by God; all who continue to be impressed by man rather than God; all who insist upon keeping their own lives and wills, rather than the life of Christ and the will of God; they all will certainly have it that way, and that for eternity. It is all about the image of man versus the image of God.

If you insist on keeping your image, the Lord would say, "Very well, keep it; I'll just keep Mine too!" He died to give you His life and His will in exchange for yours. If you want to keep your life, He will keep His; you cannot have them both. We are "the coin," and one day He will ask for us to be brought to Him and He will scrutinize us with His blazing eyes. We will either have the image of man or the image of Jesus impressed upon us. If the Lord asked for you to be shown before Him today would He recognize you as an impression of His holy image? Or would He say, "Whose image is this?"

For Thought:

Whatever you are impressed by you will worship. If you are impressed with what people can do, you will be less liable to be impressed with what God can do. If you are overwhelmed by the power and glory of God, people will not be able to sway you.

If you are a parent, you may want to watch what kinds of things your children are posting up on the walls of their room.

Day 30

What Makes You Unique? (Part 1)

"I have suffered the loss of all things, and count them but rubbish so that I may gain Christ, and may be found in Him" (Philippians 3:8-9).

There is much to consider when discussing the "life hidden with Christ in God" (Colossians 3:3). It is indeed very mysterious. One of the reasons why this is such a mystery is that what is hidden cannot be seen with natural eyes; and what cannot be naturally seen can only be spiritually experienced through an abiding faith.

We see much individuality and special identification in Christianity these days, especially in so-called "outstanding" preachers and Christian event speakers. The questions are, "What makes a person outstanding? Is it man's natural abilities, talents, uniqueness, and dynamic charisma?"

The sad answer is "Yes!" Since when is dying to self or fighting an unseen war in the bloody trenches of the intercessory prayer closet considered "outstanding?" Man's natural glory seeking radar picks up on highflying objects; low flying objects are rarely seen and therefore remain *hidden*.

Jesus was always in the low places washing feet, eating with wretched sinners and walking with lepers. This is the spiritual Man that would never be noticed in today's man-glorying, achievement worshiping society, let alone be heralded as "outstanding." This word *outstanding* has come to mean nothing more than "self standing out", based on the ability to succeed, achieve, and impress (a.k.a. vainglory and pride).

What man can do for God has also become a glorified error that radically needs to be reformed. It first must be what God can become to a person, and then what He can do through His emptied vessel—that which has truly been crucified and resurrected with Christ to be molded by Him alone.

One of the most tragically neglected teachings today is that there are essentially two levels of brokenness that we are called to experience as followers of Christ Jesus. We abundantly hear about the tyrannical reign of sin, which was broken at the cross. Many delightfully come to Christ broken over their sin and the consequences of its relentless grip; this is the first level of brokenness. However, many of these same individuals never enter into the second level of brokenness. Being broken of our individuality is accomplished by dwelling in the presence of Jesus, and devoting ourselves to His will. Nearness produces likeness and His likeness becomes our uniqueness.

For Thought:

A Christian can only spiritually mature through brokenness, surrender and devotion. Why is that the case?

When people stand out, Jesus fades out.

Day 31

What Makes You Unique? (Part 2)

"I have suffered the loss of all things, and count them but rubbish so that I may gain Christ, and may be found in Him" (Philippians 3:8-9).

When we were young children, to hide we would pull the blanket completely over us. There was the evidence in the shape of a person underneath, but all that others could see was the blanket that covered us. This somewhat illustrates the life "hidden with Christ" (Colossians 3:1-3).

To the reader: Your old life had become your identity, to such an extent, that when people mentioned your name, they immediately identified you with that outward thing for which you were most well known. For instance, mention Abraham Lincoln and we answer, "Sixteenth President of the United States;" mention the name of Ralph Waldo Emerson, and we might reply, "Transcendentalist poet." Here we see the natural man being identified by the natural.

What is of particular interest is how unspiritual people can only identify natural things, as with the identification of Jesus in Mark 6:3, "Isn't this the carpenter?" In contrast, only spiritual people can identify spiritual things as with Jesus' identity in Matthew 16:16, "You are the Christ, the Son of the living God." Natural people identify themselves by what they are; spiritual people are identified by "Whose" they are.

> *"I will also give him a white stone with a new name written on it, known only to him who receives it"* (Revelation 2:17).

Our name is our overarching identification in this world—more than an occupation, a birth certificate, or a blood type. Being given a "new name" by God is His way of emphasizing our new hidden identity in Him that must become progressively foreign to all that once identified us.

Take for example Apostle Paul's natural identification before his Damascus conversion: "Circumcised the eighth day, of the nation of Israel, of the tribe of Benjamin, a Hebrew of Hebrews; as to the Law, a Pharisee" (Philippians 3:5). However, after the transformation of Paul's natural identity into a spiritual one, Paul' new hidden identity in Christ is made crystal clear at the forefront of every letter He wrote:

1. "Paul, a bond servant of Jesus Christ, set apart for the Gospel" (Romans 1:1).
2. "Paul, called an apostle of Jesus Christ by the will of God" (1 Corinthians 1:1)
3. "Paul, called an apostle of Christ Jesus by the will of God" (2 Corinthians 1:1).
4. "Paul, an apostle—not *sent* from men nor through the agency of man, but through Jesus Christ and God the Father, who raised Him from the dead" (Galatians 1:1).
5. "Paul, an apostle of Christ Jesus by the will of God" (Ephesians 1:1).
6. "Paul and Timothy, bond servants of Christ Jesus" (Philippians 1:1).
7. "Paul, an apostle of Jesus Christ by the will of God" (Colossians 1:1).
8. "Paul . . . in God the Father and the Lord Jesus Christ" (1 & 2 Thessalonians 1:1).
9. "Paul, an apostle of Christ Jesus according to the commandment of God our Savior" (1 Timothy 1:1).
10. "Paul, an apostle of Christ Jesus by the will of God, according to the promise of life in Christ Jesus" (2 Timothy 1:1).
11. "Paul, a bond servant of God and an apostle of Jesus Christ" (Titus 1:1).
12. "Paul, a prisoner of Christ Jesus" (Philemon 1:1).

For Thought:

Because of Christ's cross and Paul's carrying his own, he experienced his own daily crucifixion to the old natural man and a resurrection to a new spiritual one. Paul was hidden and Christ was made known so people could come to know Jesus not Paul.

Paul was identified by whose he was, rather than what he was. He was the Lord's property and he wanted the world to know who had purchased him.

Day 32

What Makes You Unique? (Part 3)

"I have suffered the loss of all things, and count them but rubbish so that I may gain Christ, and may be found in Him" (Philippians 3:8-9).

When the name of the apostle Paul is mentioned, most would immediately think, "Great saint and author of two-thirds of the New Testament." However, I propose that Paul would not have taken too kindly to this identification. Again, even with such an impressive and pious sounding identity as this, it still identifies Paul by what He did, and is nowhere to be found in how Paul identified himself.

Honestly, "Paul, a bond servant, prisoner, and apostle of Christ Jesus" does not have any fireworks behind it. But this was Paul's new God-given identification, and the only thing whatsoever that set him apart as unique. He only cared whether or not others saw Jesus completely covering and hiding him like a blanket.

To the reader: Do you still have a strong tendency to cling to your natural abilities, achievements, appearance, credentials and successes—all of which make up your own self-portfolio? This is the individuality of your natural man that has become most important to you, and even more, that by which others still identify you. This is the old natural man that needs to be put on the altar of sacrifice, crucified, and resurrected to something not of this world.

God is a jealous God and will not compete with your own self-uniqueness (natural individuality). He paid too high a price to set you apart to Himself. His desire for you is to be holy as He is holy, and this comes through devotion to Him. It is nothing less than the precious blood of Jesus that makes us different than the world, and love-based obedience that progressively transforms us into His unlikeness.

God has already uniquely created you in His own unique image; He sent His Son to initiate and perfect that holy work (Hebrews 12:1). For you to continue delighting in the identification of your old uniqueness, based on any natural thing you have done, would be an attitude in dire need of repentance. These selfish ambitions are high places in need of being demolished and brought to the obedience of Jesus Christ, the only one who is truly set apart.

Christ Jesus, the Son of God, is the One who willingly left the glory of heaven and exchanged His robes of Majesty for the filthy rags of man's feeble flesh to purchase you as His holy possession. He righteously thunders from His Throne, "I alone am your uniqueness! Live it out and tell it to every creature with your very life; I died for it!"

For Thought:

Read Colossians 2:3. It is a wonderful thing to be hidden in Christ; you do not have to perform any longer.

Day 33

Love without Hypocrisy

"Let love be without hypocrisy" (Romans 12:9a).

Evil always comes to the front door of the heart with a seemingly irresistible payoff in its hand and a pleasurable mask on its face. You will only cling to what is good and abhor what evil offers if your love is without hypocrisy. Evil offers only what pleases and benefits the self-life. All that evil offers is perishable—it must be consumed entirely by its partaker. *Self* can be defined with an acronym: *Seeing Everything Like Food*. The order is to crave, chase, capture, consume, and cast out. However, "Love is not self-seeking" (1 Corinthians 13:5).

Clinging to what is good is the Christ-like attribute of gracious contentment (gratitude) in action. The same as it takes two arms to physically cling to something heavy; it also takes two arms to cling to what is good spiritually. These two spiritual arms are gratitude and thanksgiving.

Selfish desire is the poisonous venom that demobilizes the strength of gratitude and thankfulness, to the point they lose all grasping ability and ultimately drop what is good. An ungrateful and unthankful heart cannot hold onto goodness because it is full of Truth. Selfish desire's two mangled arms, ingratitude and un-thankfulness, can only hold evil because evil's promises are empty. This is why a person will drop Jesus to reach out for what is evil.

Evil can be held with one arm, but goodness must be held with two. Evil does not care about your half-hearted devotion, it only cares that you are not fully devoted to Jesus. Evil is content to be held with one arm, but Jesus abhors it; in fact He rebukes it as the double-minded treachery it is; "No one can serve two masters" (Luke 16:13).

Do all you can to maintain gratitude and thankfulness, directing them both worshipfully toward the Lord. This will not only keep those two spiritual arms strong enough to cling to what is good, but also strengthen them further just as lifting weights builds muscle. The longer you grasp Jesus with two arms the more you will love Him; the more you love Him the more you will detest evil, seeing that it only promises one thing, separation from God. "Give thanks to the Lord, for He is good, His love endures forever" (Psalm 106:1). Cling to Him and He will become the treasure of your heart, thereby rendering all evil as unappealing. This is love without hypocrisy. The world *says* it's grateful and thankful; a devoted saint *lives* thankful and grateful. Let your life say thank you, not just your lips.

For Thought:

This is day thirty-three of your 180-day journey behind the curtain. Jesus was roughly the age of thirty-three when He fully exhibited love without hypocrisy on the cross.

Day 34

Clinging is Two-Handed

"Abhor what is evil; cling to what is good" (Romans 12:9b).

To cling to something means to grasp it with both hands and with the strength of both arms. We cling to something with both hands and with the strength of both arms because we are desperate for it and are not about to let it go for anything!

We cling to what is good with gratitude and thankfulness. Gratitude is the overflowing joy of being granted something you know you do not deserve, not just being glad you have it. Thankfulness is the action of proving your gratitude for something by how it is devoted to God. Stated another way, gratitude is gracious contentment for something undeserved from God; thankfulness is something you do with it for Him; that is why it was called a "thank offering" in the Old Testament. We thank the Lord with gratitude-filled actions of selfless love for Him and for others.

If the arm of gratitude fails, so will the arm of thankfulness; without one the other cannot function; you cannot continue to hold what is good, because according to God anything "good" is weighty—it is full, not empty and vain. Therefore, it must be grasped with both arms. If you let go of what is good with one arm to reach out for something evil, the whole thing will fall. One-handed grasping is absolute error. Grasping what is good with only one hand declares it is not good enough to cling to with both.

Hypocrisy's twin brother in the Bible is double-mindedness (*dípsūkos*), which literally means "two souled." It carries with it the notion of spiritual schizophrenia. Wherever you see hypocrisy, double-mindedness is also there lurking in the shady areas—that's where they love to dwell. It can accurately be said that double-mindedness grasps something with the right hand and something different with the left.

Adam and Eve ceased to cling to what is good as they reached out for something else. Read Genesis 3 and see how it was the arm of gratitude that failed first, as "good" became not good enough, and God became not God enough! Jesus said, "No one can serve two masters" (Matthew 6:24). Are you grasping Jesus with one hand and His opposite with the other? If so, you betray them both. Reach out and grasp Him with both hands. He stretched out both of His to grasp you.

For Thought:

Imagine two train engines facing opposite directions on the same track. You then stand in the middle holding onto the back end of each with one hand. What would happen to you if you fastened your hands to both engines while they both start off in their different direction?

With this word-picture, can you understand why so many Christian lives are torn apart?

Day 35

Godly Relief or Ungodly Release?

"LORD, blessed is the man You discipline and teach from Your law to give him relief from troubled times" (Psalm 94:12-13, HCS).

When the jaws of trouble have clamped down and are ever tightening as a vice, relief becomes a most preoccupying desire, to say the least. To the godly, times of trouble caused by the un-triggered trials of life—such as misfortune, tragedy, calamity, or being sinned against by our neighbor—produce spiritual maturity and enduring patience because of their tried and tested faith.

The Greek word for *endure* is hūpŏménō. It comes from combining two words, hūpŏ ("under authority") and ménō ("to abide or remain"). Therefore, *endure* means "to remain under trials or difficulties as authorized by God." We do this in faith, understanding that they will accomplish the good for which they have been allowed. In times of trial, see to it that patience, not passion, is set to work. Do not pray for the removal, but for the wisdom to make right use of it. Relief to the godly comes from the implanted Word of God because they have been taught, chastened, and blessed by it.

To the ungodly, like the mouse caught in the snap-trap, relief comes in the form of releasing his tail from the hammer he triggered. They see the coveted object, but do not see it as bait on the catch, either through willfully suppressing the truth or through sheer ignorance. You smell the cheese, your mouth waters, you imagine the pleasure, and set forth to seize it and "SNAP!" You are painfully caught! Immediately you cry out for help. The Lord who is the "ever-present help in trouble" comes and lifts the hammer off your tail, and "Ah!" Instant relief! There are certain injuries incurred, but relief is like an opiate that blocks out the pain. You involuntarily respond with reflex action, "Oh, thank You,

Lord. I would have died if it weren't for Y . . . Hey! Is that cheese over there?" SNAP!

True godly relief in times of trouble comes in the form of godly discipline and godly teaching, not merely being delivered out of trouble. In this sense, godly discipline does not mean being disciplined by God; it means being disciplined to God. When you focus on the joy of your salvation, it brings comforting relief. Therefore you can have comforting joy *in* our trials, not *for* our trials because you have Jesus. If you have Jesus, the Bread from heaven, you will not go looking for crumbs on the enemy's trap. This is preventative relief.

For Thought:

We all love to be released from our troubles. But true relief comes from true devotion. Do you think a reason so many Christians today are defeated by their troubles is because they desire only release, not relationship?

What is the difference between help and change?

Day 36

Merciful Contempt

"He pours contempt upon princes, and makes them wander in a pathless waste" (Psalm 107:40).

A prince is an heir to the throne and a child of the king. The Apostle Paul clearly tells us that we as Christians are indeed princes, "Now if we are children, then we are heirs—heirs of God and co-heirs with Christ" (Romans 8:17). What would be the act of a prince boasting in his power, though he was raised from nothing, but utter foolishness? The same God that raised man from a heap of ashes can just as easily reduce him back to ashes.

Ruling princes of the heathen nations were hostile threats to the people of God, to the will of God, to the glory of God, and to His holy intentions. The Prophet Isaiah warns, "For a day belonging to the Lord of Hosts is coming against all that is proud and lofty, against all that is lifted up—it will be humbled . . . the Lord alone will be exalted on that day" (Isaiah 2:12-17).

This is the heart of God toward heathen princes who set themselves in rebellion toward Him even though it was He that set them up. How much more is He provoked by His own princely heirs that continue in willful rebellion and wicked pride, using their title for license to sin? Peter warns against such error, "Do not use your freedom as a covering for evil, but use it as bondservants of God" (1 Peter 2:16). Albert Barnes, pastor of the First Presbyterian Church in Philadelphia (1830-1868) adds that Christians who live this way are like princes that live above being ruled by anyone other than themselves; they believe that:

"The freedom of the gospel implied deliverance from all kinds of restraint; that they were under no yoke . . . that, being the children of God, they had a right to all kinds of enjoyment and indulgence." [5]

Think of Manasseh's disgraceful consequences being led captive for hundreds of miles by a rope strung through a ring pierced into his septum; think of Nebuchadnezzar grazing like an animal for seven years; what about Herod's putrid and deplorable end of having his living flesh eaten by worms? Are these not God's mercy in the form of chastening that could lead them to repentance? How is it that God would be so gracious to pour out His contempt and degrade them in this world rather than allow them to suffer the everlasting degradation of eternal disgrace—all for the chance to repent? This He will do when all previous acts of kindness have failed. Many call this "wrathful." How blind they are to not see that this is merciful contempt!

For Thought:

Compare 2 Peter 3:9 with Hebrews 12:7. Are you equally thankful for God's chastening in your life, as you are His gracious patience?

David said in Psalm 119:71, "It was good for me to be afflicted so that I could learn Your statutes."

Staying in Light or Playing with Wax?

"Let love be without hypocrisy [sincere]" (Romans 12:9a).

In Bible times the marketplace was riddled with pottery retailers. In greedy competition with one another, there was much temptation to produce quantity ultimately at the expense of quality (as it still is today). In order to get more pottery on the sales counter, potters would cut the time spent refining the clay of its impurities. Therefore, the clay's impurities when hardened in the furnace would form cracks in the vessel. The potter would dip the cracked vessel in paraffin, which took little time, then paint over it. Wax filled the cracks and paint covered the tracks.

However, there were potters who were more concerned about the quality of their products rather than the quantity because they were driven by a passion for their work rather than a passion for money. These potters would allow the potential customer to take the vessel and place it out in the heat of the blazing sun. The sun would melt any wax used to disguise the flawed product. The retailer who would allow such a thing was called "sincere" as was his product. Those who disallowed the customer this privilege were said to be insincere, or "hypocrites." The word *hypocrite* means "mask-wearer, or an actor who wears a costume or plays the role of another." If insincere vessels were cracked and ugly underneath but masked with a costume of attractiveness, the sun would expose the fraud of its veneer.

Likewise, only Jesus the Son can expose the ugly cracks that we have filled in with wax and painted over with nice-looking colors to fool others. No wonder so many believers become rabidly angry when the fiery Truth of God gets too close and begins to melt and expose what is false. King David was sincere when he prayed the fiery prayer, "Search me, God, and know my heart; test me and know my anxious thoughts.

See if there is any offensive way in me" (Psalm 139:23-24). He knew what he was like apart from the sin exposing, darkness expelling, wax-melting light of God.

Whatever you cover up, He will uncover; whatever you uncover, He will cover. Do not censor what He reveals just because you cannot bear to see it. If you do, you will never come to hate it and repent of it. Are you staying in light or playing with wax?

For Thought:

Plastic means counterfeit. The heat of the sun melts plastic, as does the light and fire of the Son of God. Plastic Christianity implies the neglect or absence of God's presence.

Are you living in the light or filling in the cracks?

Day 38

Sacrificing Idols or Isaacs?

"Present your bodies a living and holy sacrifice, acceptable to God, which is your spiritual service of worship" (Romans 12:1b).

There was a recent leader of a large church that told his fellow constituents he wanted to sacrifice his leadership "position" on the altar and lay it down at the feet of Jesus for a while. Days later, he was fired from his position because they claimed that he did not value it. They said, "We want someone who takes this prestigious position seriously and cherishes it like we do!" What they failed to see is that this man absolutely cherished his position, and that is why he knew he needed to put in on the sacrificial altar. He brought to God what he felt was his most valuable possession.

Churches today have become very used to its members willingly offering things upon the altar that have no value. In other words, we have so habituated ourselves to giving God our surplus—bringing Him our blemished sacrifices—that only things like sinful vices are brought there.

What are the things we know we need to put on the altar and lay at the feet of Jesus but the things we care about the most? Is God after our sins or is He after our selves? What is it that needs to be turned to ashes as a burnt offering to the Lord but what we love more than Him? Moreover, what is it that man loves more than God other than himself? God is not just after the idols *in* our lives; He is after the idols *of* our lives. He does not desire valueless idols; He desires valuable Isaacs. If we would see this spiritual principle with enlightened hearts, the altar would be flooded not with sinful vices or dollar bills, but rather with His people's lives—their prestigious positions, self ambitions, and vainglorious images. Many desire to give

Jesus their sins that refuse to give Him their lives. Devote yourself to Him because He fully devoted Himself to you and raised you from death. "Abraham reasoned that God could even raise the dead, and so in a manner of speaking he did receive Isaac back from death" (Hebrews 11:19). Have you taken your Isaac up Moriah's hill for sacrifice? What is it? Whatever it is, once you lay it down, it becomes the Lord's; and when He raises it back up, it will be full of everlasting life and triumphant purpose.

For Thought:

We are each *a penny in the basket* (a "mite") in Christ's economy. We should not try to split a penny in half and give half to God; half a penny will not spend!

On her wedding day, the Bride typically wears a beautiful white dress. What is the last thing she wants to happen to that dress? Why?

Once you see how white the robe is that Christ purchased for you, you will cherish it with devotion.

Day 39

Make the Eternal Exchange

"Are not five sparrows sold for two assárion? Don't be afraid; you are worth more than many sparrows" (Luke 12:6-7, HCS).

An *assárion* was a brass coin of the littlest value. It was basically the Roman equivalent of the mite (*lépton*), which was not Roman currency. One *assárion* or *mite* is very close to one penny. In the above passage, Jesus is saying that we are worth abundantly more than that to Him. At first glance this seems to be in contradiction to the teaching of seeing ourselves as "just a penny/mite in the basket of Christ's economy" (see Day 38 and Day 90). This is not the case at all.

First, there are quite a few who inaccurately take the principle of being just a penny in worth to cultish extremes, that which is known as "Worm Theology." Many destructive doctrines such as flagellation, self-asceticism, human holiness, and mysticism have their foundations in that. The psychologized world would call it "low self-esteem." Yes, we must see our depravity, but we err greatly if we fail to acknowledge our Christ-imparted dignity. The truth is that "low self-esteem" is a big problem because it is nothing more than what the Bible teaches as "self-pity." However, where many blunder here is declaring "high self esteem" to be the solution.

Second, there are many believers who just as improperly adhere to high self-esteem, and because of this they see their own self-assessed value. The Bible calls this "the pride of life" (1 John 2:16). High self-esteem is just a devil-inspired euphemism to obscure pride from the believer. So, if both low self-esteem and high self-esteem are wrong, what is right? The answer is no self-esteem—"Stop looking at yourself and fix your eyes upon Jesus and loving others."

We are worth an infinite amount to God, so much that He came to purchase us through Jesus' death on the cross. The proper application is that our value is purely in God's perspective of worth, not our own perspective. Only God can truly declare the worth of something. Therefore, we must come to Calvary and make an eternal exchange. We must drop our own self-assessed worth and accept His. We will only see our true value once we confess our own self-assessment as valueless. We will then say, "My life has tremendous value only in Your economy, Lord."

For Thought:

God's very best and man's very best were both present at Calvary. What did man's very best do to God's? Our best always kills His best.

We desperately cling to earthly value because we fail to see from God's perspective that He is offering us the most infinite treasure in the universe—Himself!

Day 40

The White Squirrel

"For we are His creation, created in Christ Jesus for good works, which God prepared ahead of time so that we should walk in them" (Ephesians 2:10, HCS).

If you have ever seen a White Squirrel you have had the pleasure of seeing an amazingly beautiful creation of God to say the least. Also known as the Albino Squirrel, this heart-melting animal is indigenous to just a select few localities and is treasured and revered by all who see it.

One day, a particular gentleman was walking along a trail in the woods. Viciously wrestling with the reality of his own wretched and sullied heart, he sat down upon an old wooden bench next to a rustling stream to pray. Seated with his face buried in his hands, he cried out to God, "Lord, Your Word says that I am cleansed by the blood of the Lamb, and my sins, though scarlet, have been made whiter than snow. I certainly don't feel like that's true of me. I know I recently fell into the mire of sin again, but help me understand why I constantly feel so filthy. If I continue on despairing like this I'll die!"

Immediately after praying this, the man lifted his face from the tomb-like darkness of his hands and right before his eyes was something he had never seen before—a white squirrel. It was sitting on a tree branch less than three feet away from his face and staring right at him. The man was so enamored by the creature that he began to wonder if this were some divine visitation. He could not get over the beauty of its majestic white coat. But before he could ponder too long, the squirrel suddenly slipped and fell into a filthy mud puddle.

The squirrel was fine, though not without being a little flustered, and not without crawling out a filthy black mess. Relieved at the squirrel's safety, the man thought to himself, "That is exactly how I feel all the time, little squirrel!"

Then a still small whisper seemed to speak to the man's heart, "Is that squirrel, so beautiful and white to your eyes a minute ago, so filthy and black to you now?" The man contemplated for a moment and then reasoned, "It is; and surely it must feel that way too." The whisper continued, "Although it fell and its coat is now stained with black mud, is it a black squirrel and no longer a white squirrel?" The man silently puzzled this question.

An epiphany is unmistakable, and this man's face suddenly began to radiate with one. Welling up with tears, the man said out loud, "That squirrel is white because God made it white; there is not a puddle or stain on earth that could change that!"

The Whisper said with affirmation and with a seeming decibel increase, "That's right, child; and just as the white squirrel in all its beauty can suddenly fall into the mud and stain its coat with the filthy mud of this earth, so can you; and just as the white squirrel is white because I made it that way, so are you. The difference between the two of you is the squirrel doesn't look at itself when it falls in the mud and then call itself a filthy black squirrel. It never questions what it is! Therefore, it lives like a white squirrel, not in order to be one, but because it is one.

After a pause the Whisper said with finality, "You are white because I have made you white. Now, go and live like it!" Joyfully, the man leapt up from the bench, and marched away with the whitest of purpose and with the purest of heart he had ever known.

A man that does not question what he is lives like what he knows himself to be. For instance, if a man believes he is a duck he will act like a duck, "For as he thinks within himself, so he is" (Proverbs 23:7). Many Christians fall into the mud and then continue to live filthy lives because they view themselves as filthy.

However, like the man with the white squirrel, once you begin to see your God-made whiteness as something you could never do for yourself, and something you could never change no matter how filthy of a mud pit you have fallen into, you will stop jumping into the mud on purpose. You will begin to live white because you are assured you have been made white by the blood of the Lamb (see Revelation 7:9-14).

For Thought:

Faith in Jesus' finished work produces faithfulness.

What is the last thing a bride-to-be wants to happen to her white wedding gown? Why?

Does she have to be coerced to stay away from mud puddles or things that could stain her dress?

We abstain from sin because we value Christ's blood-bought righteousness. Are you wearing His white wedding gown? How valuable does your life declare it?

A Worship-full Heart is not Noisy to God

"Take away from Me the noise of your songs. (Amos 5:23).

An extremely gifted singer can impress us with their singing talent, but we are bowled over with delight when we see one who is lost in a state of sincere intimacy with the essence of the song. When the singer is thoroughly engaged from the heart it is unmistakable and wonderful. When the heart is disengaged it is obvious, and the song is stale and greatly disappointing, no matter how talented the singer or well performed the song.

The Old Testament Prophet (Amos) is writing to reveal God's heart to His people whose worship had deteriorated to well-performed formalism and stale ritualism. Their hearts were completely disengaged from the act. God called it "noise" because it was devoid of true, heart-felt love. This should remind us of Paul's similar words, "If I do not have love, I have become a noisy gong or a clanging cymbal" (1 Corinthians 13:1).

God deplores our acts of service where the heart is disconnected or disengaged, and performed with stale formalism. Faith and obedience are love-driven, but when the faith and obedience that our religious exercises symbolize never follow, God is so disgusted by this hypocrisy that He says He despises them, disregards them, and "will not smell" them (see Amos 5:21). In the Old Testament, the burnt offering was totally consumed by fire and regarded as a pleasing aroma to God as it ascended to Him. In clearer terms, empty worship is an offensive stench in His nostrils.

God had been long trying to get His people to return to His true worship, and it took seventy years of exile to do it. However, it had been less than one hundred years since their return and they had again lost their first love. Although they had not returned to their pagan idolatry, they merely traded it for self-idolatry. God had commanded them to rebuild His Temple, but they instead labored to build their own "paneled houses" while God's house still lay in ruin (Haggai 1:2-4).

Just like then, hearts are disengaged from true worship today because they are captivated by the selfish affections for other things; yet they continue to *perform* their services. Empty worship reflects an empty heart. True worship declares one's salvation and devotion. The sincerity of your worship will prove itself by how enraptured you are with the Savior that rescued you. It is unmistakable!

For Thought:

Many popular songs in churches today have lyrics making serious vows to God. Many come and sing those words living in direct opposition to what they sing. Would you consider that empty worship?

On Sunday you may sing, "All to Jesus I surrender, all to Him I freely give."[6] Are you surrendering Monday through Saturday?

Victory is Losing (Part 1)

Read: (Matthew 16:25) and (2 Timothy 3:1-4).

It has been supposed that there is nothing more righteous than pure righteousness, and nothing more evil than pure evil. The former is true but the latter is false. There is one thing in this world that is more evil than pure evil and that is evil refined and polished. Evil disguised is repetitively discussed and warned against in Scripture.

An anonymous person recently came to me and confessed, "God touches me and I can walk in victory for a time, but then I am tempted and fall again. Sometimes I am victorious, but I want to be able to stay in victory when victory is experienced. My greatest fear is not overcoming my lust!" This seems to be a noble statement but is filled with selfish error (see Proverbs 16:25).

To expose this error, allow me to personalize two questions for you, dear reader: 1) "What is victory?" and 2) "Why do you desire it?" Also, I might propose the following insight to help you in answering: The sincere answer to the second question is the key to answering the first truly. For instance, if the reason I desire victory is because it separates me from Jesus, then to me "victory" is an intimate relationship with Jesus, and therefore it is Christ-centered and sure.

If, on the other hand, I desire victory because I hate defeat and the way it makes me feel, then victory to me is merely a "victorious image" on display for myself (and others) to admire. This meaning of victory is self-centered. It intensely desires to say, "Look how good and victorious I am. I haven't committed that sin in quite some time!" This person's "greatest fear" will always be defeat because his greatest fear is not based on what it should be—fear of being separated from and displeasing the Lord. The Lord emptied Himself and excruciatingly died to rescue you from the tyranny of not only sin, but also that of yourself. If you see your need for salvation from sin, but remain blind to your need of being saved from the most deadly idol, self-love, then the root of defeat remains, your desire for victory is selfish, and your efforts will continue to be misspent.

For Thought:

A person comes to church filled with sin, self, and pride. He is told he is going to hell if he does not get saved. With concern, he inquires about salvation. He is told to say "the sinner's prayer" (unbiblical), then to get baptized. So he does both. He comes up out of the water with his sin issue "taken care of." Now he is filled with self and pride in the church. His self-life is never crucified and his pride is never dealt with, and for that matter, never even mentioned. He continues to live a life defeated by sin and pride and so he must pretend to be victorious to maintain his outward Christian image. He never wanted to lose His life for Jesus, but only wanted Jesus to enhance it. Who is this?

Victory is Losing (Part 2)

Read: (Matthew 16:25) and (2 Timothy 3:1-4).

People who are self-loving are always looking for ways to feel more righteous and love themselves more. Therefore, "victory" becomes their new refined idolatry. They set their aims on the improved self. Believers with this mindset set sail for victory because of the deemed ugliness of sin and lust and the taboo label that gets stamped upon their consciences because of it. They love themselves so much that they become severely agitated when they fall into that sin they deem to be so wretchedly offensive. Because the way they *want* to see themselves is in conflict with the way they really do, "victory" becomes the coveted idol that will end their inner conflict and bring reconciliation with themselves (not God). In this context, any claim of "being for God" is generally a ruse to medicate their consciences and put on a front for others. They are—and will remain—the object of their own worship unless God intervenes in a mighty way.

These people generally hate those slum dwelling sins because they hinder their ability to see themselves as good as they would like, or as righteous as they pretend to be. Self-improvement becomes the aristocratic sin that moved from the ghetto into the palace, and is even praised for its appearance of nobility.

Self-love is most cunning. It reasons within itself, "I love me, and I really want to be able to do it more. But every time I fall into that old sinful lust it ruins my ability to do so." In other words, defeat is the hindrance to the real idol—self-love.

It goes like this: You already love to see yourself in the most favorable light, and for others to see you the way you do; to the point that when they fail to do so you are confused or even bitter. You then immediately set out to fix this "problem" through crafty self-improvement tactics, thereby quenching your thirst to be looked upon favorably. Equally, when you fail to live up to your own lofty view of yourself because of sinful defeat, you seek victory over lust and sin as a means to better serve your idol of self. Victory, in its truest spiritual sense, is only possible by your self-love being conquered. Lust is not the hindering factor to your loving God; your love for yourself is.

Never fall into this pit; and if you are in it, the way out is to 1) see victory as completed and paid for by Jesus, and 2) seek it because sinful defeat separates you from Him.

For Thought:

What is victory? Why do you desire it?

Sin separates us from God and cost the mutilation and humiliation of Jesus. Do you hate sin for the same reasons God does?

"Remind us of why sin is so detestable to God, not just why it is troublesome to us."[7]—Luke Gilkerson

Day 44

What is Your Recharging Base?

"I am the vine, you are the branches; he who abides in Me and I in him, he bears much fruit, for apart from Me you can do nothing" (John 15:5).

Cordless phones work best when they remain on their recharging base and only detached for their necessary use. The phone is efficient when it spends the majority of its life on its base; it is useless and frustrating when it is dead because it has been used too much and irresponsibly left off its base.

The fruitful and unexhausted minister dwells much in the prayer closet, *then* enters the world of ministry as moved by the inspiration of God. The frustrated and wearied minister is always toiling in the world of ministry and enters the prayer closet moved by the exasperation of self.

Someone once asked a quite successful minister, "Preacher, what do you do when you are not preaching?" He replied, "I am ministering to people, first to my wife and family." The inquirer continued to press him, "Yes, but what do you do when you are not preaching or ministering?" The preacher responded, "I'm studying God's Word." The interviewer pried further, "Okay, besides preaching, ministering, and studying the Bible, what do you do for retreat?" The man of God responded with ease, "I pray!"

If Jesus dwelled in the secret place communing with His Father whenever He was not pouring Himself out to a lost and dying world, how much more do we need to dwell in that most Holy Place behind the curtain?

If prayer is not our base upon which we return after long hard days at work, ministering for the Master, or going through heavy trials, then we mistakenly believe we can do many things apart from Christ! To abide means to live in response to the knowledge of God's love for you revealed at Calvary.

When you come home from a hard day does your heart yearn for Jesus, the one who alone can replenish the vitality of your life? You cannot stand up for Jesus until you learn how to sit at His feet. You cannot minister for the Master without first being ministered to by Him. Be a mere garden hose—tapped into the Source. You will always be full as the water flows through you as a conduit to nourish the thirsty. The Lord is your fountain of Living Water; you should never need to draw water from your own sources or polluted wells.

For Thought:

"My people have committed two sins: They have forsaken me, the spring of living water, and have dug their own cisterns, broken cisterns that cannot hold water" (Jeremiah 2:13).

Day 45

Whose are You?

"From now on let no one cause trouble for me, for I bear on my body the brand-marks of Jesus" (Galatians 6:17).

The Apostle Paul used the Greek word (*stigmata*), which is translated "brand-marks" or sometimes "scars." It is plural, and this fact is important. The Greek word for *slave* in the Bible is *doulos*—meaning a "bondservant" who surrendered all his rights and willingly served under his master. Slaves gladly allowed themselves to be brand-marked by their owners to identify who exclusively owned them. This branding was performed only once per slave. Typically, most slaves had only one brand, and no owner marked his slave more than once.

The use of the plural *stigmata* should bring to our perception that Paul's owner, the Lord Jesus, allowed Paul to be marked more than once. He was beaten by the rods of Roman magistrates in Antioch, stoned by unbelieving rulers at Lystra, and whipped by a Philippian mob, just to mention a few. Paul was certainly not a spectator of Christ's sufferings; he was a participator in them. Paul wrote that his goal was to know Christ "and the fellowship of His sufferings, being conformed to His death" (Philippians 3:10). Are you a spectator or participator?

When we go through a scar-producing trial for Christ, do we say, "I should never have to go through that again"? Paul went through it multiple times, and said that it was part of his "goal." Our scar-producing trials for Christ identify us as to "Whose" we are, not just what we are.

Paul's "trouble" was not his suffering; his trouble was the opposition to the truth of his Gospel message and the skeptical questioning of

His Apostleship. He could therefore easily write, "From now on let no one cause me trouble" because he possessed indisputable evidence as to the Authority of his message and the fact of his being sent of God to deliver it. He bore the plural brand-marks of His Master. What troubles you? Are you more troubled by your branding, or by the eternity of those who hate what the branding means? Your sufferings are temporary; theirs are eternal. Be troubled *for* them rather than *by* them.

For Thought:

Do you bear the marks of a bondservant to the Master, to whom you have surrendered all rights to yourself?

Are the scars of Jesus fresher than the scars of the world, the flesh, or the Devil?

Do others see the cross of Christ in your life? If so, do they see it as a trophy of vanity hanging on your neck, or as a brand of love carried on your back?

Suffering your will to please yourself in order to please the Lord may not make brand-marks, but it certainly marks you as the Lord's property.

Day 46

The Day the Earth Swallowed the Son (Part 1)

"For God, who said, 'Let light shine out of darkness,' made his light shine in our hearts to give us the light of the knowledge of God's glory displayed in the face of Christ" (2 Corinthians 4:6).

Let us imagine a time machine. You get into it and set the date for Golgotha. Upon arriving, you emerge from the capsule and see off in the distance the fateful site—three silhouetted crosses upon an increasingly ominous backdrop. You cannot make out the images in detail yet, but you have resolved to get as close as possible. The nearer you get, the louder the commotion. As you proceed, jumbled chatter slowly turns to discernable sounds, which then turn to audible insults and grief-stricken groans.

Upward you climb, and as your own shortness of breath suddenly catches your attention, you are prompted to think of the difficulty even a physically fit person would have carrying a heavy object up this hill, let alone one suffering near hypovolemic shock from massive blood loss. Nevertheless, upward you climb.

Finally, at the plateau, you gather your breath and collect your thoughts and set your sights upon the malady of the scene. The mere act of someone spitting in public has always repulsed you, and yet this repulsive act is being performed repetitively from multiple persons. Your stomach turns and your throat tightens with that notorious bitter taste, and you have yet to even look to Jesus of Nazareth, the recipient of all those vile projectiles of hatred and pride. However, when you finally do, unbelievably the spittle loses its revolting rank; it actually seems to have somewhat of a cleansing effect as it washes away some of the dried blood from His face. Just a bit heavenward, above His head, is a makeshift sign carved in haste and carelessness with the inscribed words of mocking truth, "The King of the Jews."

A cacophony of mad barking draws your eyes back to the earth and there you see men-like figures who look more like snarling dogs dressed in priestly garb. Some in particular are provoking Jesus to prove He is the Messiah by detaching Himself from the cross. Others are spitefully gambling for His belongings. A man on a cross to His left is mocking Him, and another on His right is begging Him for a place in His Kingdom. You approach even closer and come up next to a man whose appearance is distressingly humble and peculiarly saint-like. It seems you may have even slightly interrupted a conversation between this man and Jesus on the cross. There is a weeping woman standing adjacent to this apostle-like man and you begin to have much reason to assume this must be the "beloved" John and Jesus' mother. Nonetheless, you continue even nearer. (Stop! Pray, and then meditate upon Jesus taking care of John and His mother from the cross).

Day 47

The Day the Earth Swallowed the Son (Part 2)

"For God, who said, 'Let light shine out of darkness,' made his light shine in our hearts to give us the light of the knowledge of God's glory displayed in the face of Christ" (2 Corinthians 4:6).

Suddenly, as you glance down, you realize you are standing in a puddle of blood that has gathered directly below Jesus' feet. Your gaze then shifts upward as you step back two paces, and there you make unforgettable eye contact with God in shredded human flesh, Jesus Christ of Nazareth. You also notice how the Romans placed the nail in His feet precisely where the most pain would be felt as the victim pushes up with them just to gain one agonizing breath. You understand their cruel intelligence employed to prolong the suffering of a crucifixion. By autonomous reflex the victim will push up with his feet so not to asphyxiate and also because the pain caused by relaxing the leg muscles is so intense.

As you are pondering the brutal methodology of a Roman crucifixion, the blood-dripping feet in front of you begin to stir and your attention is once again captivated toward Jesus as He excruciatingly pushes upward with what little energy He has left. With one large breath gained in unfathomable pain, He cries out, "My God, My God, why have You forsaken Me?"

His voice is loud to your ears but deafening thunder to your soul! You begin to reflect on the man standing next to you and recall what he wrote in His Revelation about this same deafening voice that thunders "like many waters." You get it now; it is not about decibels. Just as the thunder usually follows the flash of lightning, hanging before you is the Light of the world whose thirty-three years worth of a life poured out seems as but a flash of time; but oh what matchless power that Flash of Lightning possesses, and now rolls His thunder—"It is finished!" He trundles with His final grasp for man's attention, and in that finality He breathes His last human breath, for every subsequent breath would be inhaled and exhaled in His resurrected and exclusive Divinity. (Ponder this thought prayerfully and worshipfully).

For Thought:

Because of the incredible trauma and massive loss of blood and sweat, Jesus throat would have been swollen with His tongue cleaving to the roof of His mouth. This was the fulfillment of Psalm 22:15, "My strength is dried up like baked clay; my tongue sticks to the roof of my mouth." Jesus knew what He was about to speak were the most important words in the history of mankind, "It is finished!" And in order to make this divine declaration, He would need something for the wetting of His mouth. His "thirst" was a selfless thirst. What do your thirst for?

Day 48

The Day the Earth Swallowed the Son (Part 3)

"For God, who said, 'Let light shine out of darkness,' made his light shine in our hearts to give us the light of the knowledge of God's glory displayed in the face of Christ" (2 Corinthians 4:6).

His feet have ceased to stir but yours begin, and with one careful step you stagger backward. Your legs start to buckle under the weight of sorrow and awe that has suddenly flooded your heart. All you can recall now is your pride, your lusts, your self-worship and vain arrogance, and what all of it looks like at the foot of the cross. What ridiculous mockery it would be to turn around right now to the present crowd and boast about what you can do! What absurdity it would be to begin performing a song or do a juggling act and say, "Hey everyone, look what I can do. Look at me; don't look at Him!" What provoking arrogance it would be to drink from the poisonous cup of your devil-inspired lusts right beneath those holy eyes of eternal purity, and then look directly into them to ask Him to remove the poison you blatantly consumed! This you now understand is what your pride and rebellion is, and what it looks like in God's sight and in His holy presence. (Can you ponder sinning in the presence of Jesus hanging on the cross?)

Day 49

The Day the Earth Swallowed the Son (Part 4)

"For God, who said, 'Let light shine out of darkness,' made his light shine in our hearts to give us the light of the knowledge of God's glory displayed in the face of Christ" (2 Corinthians 4:6).

Your inner-world is shaken as you shudder to think of practicing sin with Jesus hanging there. But then you notice your outer-world is shaking all the more. The rocks are splitting and people are panicking with fear. "Earthquake!" they shout. One of your favorite Psalms has always been Psalm 46, and its verses begin echoing in your mind in only choppy relevant pieces: "We will not fear though the earth give way . . . and the mountains quake with their surging . . . The holy place where the Most High dwells—God is within her . . . The Lord Almighty is with us." Knowing that the Lord is in your midst is the only thing that can bring peace in the middle of earth-quaking terror, and His presence has just been removed by murderous request. With deepest dread you consider, "There will be no refuge in this earthquake; the Lord Almighty is no longer here! The Light of the world has departed."

In the blackest darkness of the most horror-filled nights, the coming dawn is often your only hope of reprieve. Like every day, the sun rose in the east this morning and will descend into the earth of the western horizon. But now it seems the earth will forever swallow the sun! And in this gruesome stretch of night, you think in tears: The Son of God rose in the east in the morning of His human life. But now, on this predestined evening, He has retired to descend into the darkness of the earth. In despairing anguish of soul, you look not to your time machine for escape, but instead you look eastward with anticipation. Because you know in less than three full revolutions of its axis, the earth will yawn, and in yielding submission release the Son it swallowed. The Son will rise again—Oh blessed hope—the Light that conquers the darkness. The Son of God will rise to save the earth that tried to swallow Him.

For Thought:

Is Calvary a place you often visit in your heart? Do you see pride as turning your back on Jesus to "juggle like a jester" (perform) for a crowd?

As Hebrews 12:2 portrays, "For the joy set before Him, He endured the cross despising the shame." Many do the exact opposite and despise the cross to endure shameful behaviors.

Has Christ's dying love become your undying love? Has your gratitude for Jesus increased after reading this four-part devotion?

Practical atheism is the practice of people who believe in God, but live their lives as if He does not exist. Which one is worse: An atheist, or a practical atheist?

Day 50

The Only Eyewitness on Earth

"God has resurrected this Jesus and we are all witnesses of this" (Acts 2:32).

The disciples had just been filled with the promised Holy Spirit in the upper room, but they did not come out preaching their experience of this spiritual phenomenon. They victoriously preached with boldness and divine authority the Gospel of Jesus Christ and His Resurrection, of which they were all eyewitnesses. *How* they preached was the result of what happened in the upper room; *what* and *why* they preached was the result of what happened at Calvary. They had witnessed the victory of Christ with their own eyes before the upper room, but afterward they preached *with* the victory of Christ because they were filled with the Holy Spirit who is exactly like Him.

The Holy Spirit alone leads us through to Christ's victory, so He must be able to demonstrate the victory of Christ through us as intercessors to a lost world. "The Spirit helps us in our weakness. We do not know what we ought to pray for, but the Spirit himself intercedes for us" (Romans 8:26). The Holy Spirit is the difference between victory and defeat for the Christian. The disciples had seen the Gospel of Jesus Christ with their own eyes and still needed the Holy Spirit, enough for Jesus to command them to wait for His outpouring and do nothing until then.

Victorious living, powerful preaching, and effective ministry depend on the Holy Spirit. He is the only Person on earth today who was an eyewitness of Christ's victory through His crucifixion and resurrection. There is power in the testimony of an eyewitness. Are you experiencing power and victory in your spiritual life? What about in your church meetings . . . your prayer-life . . . your ministry?

The Holy Spirit wrote God's Word, and He used the pens of men. In the same way He speaks God's Word, and He uses the mouths of men. He inhabits the temple of God, and He uses the hearts of men. The Holy Spirit witnessed the Gospel and He used men broken of their own wills and filled with His to live it first, and then proclaim it with authority, power, and victory. "Do not quench the Spirit" (1 Thessalonians 5:19), He is the only absolutely victorious Person on earth!

For Thought:

Have you ever heard that inner Voice say, "Don't!" or "Run!" or "Go tell that person about Jesus?" Did you ever proceed to do the opposite anyway?

Read 1 Corinthians 10:13. Do you think that Voice warning you to stop was the Holy Spirit providing you with God's provided way of escape?

The disciples had spent roughly seven days behind the curtain in the upper room, exactly "fifty days" after Jesus the Passover Lamb was crucified. Notice what day you are on.

Day 51

Walking Forward Backwards

"Trust in the Lord with all your heart and lean not on your own understanding" (Proverbs 3:5).

Why is it that the One who is infinitely and perfectly trustworthy—Almighty God—is many times the One we trust the least; and the one who is consistently letting us down with grievous disappointment—our self—is the one that we end up trusting the most? If this is not a declaration of the spiritual backwardness so prevalent in Christian circles today, I have missed something.

Naturally, if we saw someone walking backwards everywhere they went, we would certainly be apt to believe that person could be quite unbalanced. Furthermore, what if we experimentally attempted this ourselves just for amusement purposes? Would we not at least be a laughing stock for onlookers when we fall over every obstacle, and at worst, endanger ourselves with the possibility of serious or even fatal injury?

Thoughts such as "God may ask me to do something I do not like," or "He may send me somewhere that will cost me much suffering" are generally the culprit to our lack of trust. It is not that we believe ourselves to be trustworthy and God not to be; it is that trusting in God requires walking by faith and not by sight, which in turn requires us to cease trying to save and control our own lives. Trusting God means recklessly devoting the control of your life to Him as an empty vessel for His use.

With great error, the majority of behavior and attitude problems in Christians today are described by the popular phrase, "Out of control!" For instance, someone might say of John Doe, "Johnny's anger is out of control," when in fact it is exactly the opposite. Johnny is very much in control; anger is his learned way of either maintaining control or reclaiming it through his fear tactics of manipulation.

It is safe to say that our problems stem mostly from our insistence upon controlling and ruling our own lives. We are thereby imprisoned to ourselves, and devotion to Jesus is the only key to the cell doors. Either Jesus is worthy of our devotion or He is not. If He is worth anything, He is worth everything! It is only when we surrender to Him that we begin to walk straight and normal once again. Are you trying to navigate God's vessel, or is He taking you where He desires?

For Thought:

If God had designed Noah's Ark with a helm and a rudder, what do you think Noah would have tried to do?

Is your praying to God essentially running things by Him, asking Him to bless what you want? Or is it sincere surrender? How much of your praying is self-centered? How much is Kingdom-centered?

Day 52

Be Careful What You Love

"But they went to Baal-peor, consecrated themselves to Shame, and became detestable—like the thing they loved" (Hosea 9:10).

We have heard the clichés such as "One bad apple spoils the whole bushel," "Evil Company corrupts good morals," and "That person is rubbing off on me." These expressions do carry an element of accuracy when discussing the power of physical or natural influences. However, one of the most overlooked spiritual principles is that we take on the likeness of what consumes our devotion. Ask any spouse in a healthy marriage and they will tell you about the many ways they have taken on the likenesses of their partner, to such an extent that they become like them in many nuances.

Applying this principle, what if the person you are devoted to the most is yourself? Bearing the title Christian, this is exactly why Paul admonished us to put off the old unconverted lifestyle, which was devoted only to self, and put on the new lifestyle of devotion to the Lord. "Put off the old self that is corrupted by deceitful desires . . . put on the new self, the one created according to God's likeness" (Ephesians 4:22-24).

Whatever or whoever you worship will be what has your devotion. Whatever or whomever that is, you will become like it. The thing that the rebellious Israelites devoted themselves to was detestable and full of shame, and so they likewise became. What is it that captivates the largest portions of your affections, thinking, and time?

Be devoted to yourself and you will become like yourself more and more, thereby becoming less and less like Jesus. Consecrate yourself to worthless idols and not only does the same outcome apply, but you also forsake the Lord's mercy (see Jonah 2:8). Become like Jesus by devoting yourself to Him. Be careful what or who you love.

For Thought:

To what or who are you most devoted? Answer this question prayerfully.

What influences you the most: Television, sports, media, entertainment, or God's Word?

Lack of prayer always declares love for self.

Read Acts 2:41-42. To what four things did the new Christians devote themselves? Are these things present in your life? Are any absent?

Day 53

Righteous or Rebellious?

"For the ways of the Lord are right, and the righteous walk in them, but the rebellious stumble in them" (Hosea 14:9).

Solomon, the wisest man in the Bible, wrote about how to avoid stumbling: "Listen my son . . . I am teaching you the way of wisdom; I am guiding you on straight paths. When you walk, your steps will not be hindered; when you run, you will not stumble" (Proverbs 4:10-12). In the New Testament Peter also teaches us how to avoid stumbling in his second epistle, "If you do these things you will never stumble" (1:10). What "things" are we to "do" to avoid ever stumbling? According to Peter, the answer is, increasing in faith and godly love for others because we have obtained a faith of equal privilege with the apostles through the righteousness of Christ Jesus (1:1).

In Solomon's teaching it begins with a son listening, then walking in the paths his father has laid out for him, and ends with him "running without stumbling." In Peter's teaching it starts with the Divine power of our Heavenly Father's instruction to us as sons, then with our faith to walk in obedience to it, and ends with "never stumbling."

"There are thorns and snares on the path of the wicked; the one who guards himself stays far from them" (Proverbs 22:8). The righteous man walks without stumbling because of his obedience to stay on the snare-free path of righteousness, but the rebellious man stumbles because he chooses to tread the thorn and snare-infested path of wickedness.

Moreover, sin and rebellion are shackling bondage. Have you ever tried to run with shackles on your ankles? If you are attempting to walk on the righteous paths of the Lord, yet continue to remain in un-confessed and un-repentant sin, your ankles are shackled and you will continue to stumble and fall. If you are stumbling through life, check your heart, there is rebellion to be found there. Put it off at once! Put on righteous obedience, and enjoy the freedom to run and finish the race without falling on your face.

For Thought:

Read 1 Peter 1:1-10. The first verse starts with a provision, and the last verse (vs. 10) ends with a promise of "never stumbling," contingent upon whether or not we do the verses in between (2-9).

We stumble because we do not "follow" God's Word. If a tightrope trainer said, "If you do it like this you will never fall," would you follow his instruction with all your ability at 2000 feet up? Would you try to do it your own way? Why or why not?

Day 54

Beware what Makes a Lot of Sense!

"Has not God made foolish the wisdom of the world?"
(1 Corinthians 1:20)

It is normal and good, and even called common sense, to like pretty things. In our human nature we are greatly inclined to move toward things that are pretty, especially if they "make a lot of sense." Think for a moment; when was the last time one of your senses led you into trouble (your eyes, or your feelings, for instance)? More than likely it has not been that long ago. It just made sense to curse your brother in your fit of anger; it just made sense to stand up for yourself by slandering the coworker who slandered you; it just made sense to pursue that adulterous affair; to lust after that woman; to indulge in that evil desire. It also just makes sense to covet that great looking ministry and take the high or cozy position it offers, all the while justifying it with righteous sounding notions such as, "Look at all the good this big ministry could do for the Kingdom," or, "I need that big salary for the well-being of my family."

It "made a lot of sense" to David's men when they tried to convince him to rise up and kill Saul; "This is the day the Lord spoke of when he said to you, 'I will give your enemy into your hands for you to deal with as you wish'" (1 Samuel 24:4). Driven by the cunning temptation of the serpent, what "made sense" to those men was in direct hostility to God, diametrically opposed to His wisdom and justice.

Look at some examples of what utterly does not make sense: Jesus being both fully God and fully man (Colossians 2:9 and Hebrews 1:3); an infinite and absolutely perfect God leaving perfect heaven to hang on a tree that He created (John 1:14); the greatest Blessing to the earth (Jesus) willfully becoming the greatest curse on the earth (sin), to make the earth's greatest curse (sinful man) become the earth's greatest blessing (Galatians 3:13); The Messiah being Jesus *of Nazareth*—Nathanael said, "Can any good thing come out of Nazareth?" (John 1:46); Jesus, the only Person worthy of being served, becoming a servant of all (Philippians 2:6-8); Jesus saying, "Whoever wants to be first among you must be your slave" (Matthew 20:28); Jesus saying He "must go to Jerusalem" to suffer many things and be excruciatingly murdered (Matthew 16:21); the Lord sending Paul to Jerusalem where bonds and afflictions awaited him (Acts 20:22; 21:7-13); God commanding Hosea to marry a harlot who would commit adultery against him, then tell him to go and buy her back like a customer. (Daniel 3:27); An empty tomb (Matthew 28:6). And finally, "Love your enemies, do good to those who hate you, bless those who curse you, pray for those who mistreat you. If someone slaps you on one cheek, give also the other cheek. If someone takes your coat, do not withhold your shirt from them" (Luke 6:28-30).

If it "makes sense" to you, beware! More than likely you are leaning on your own understanding and not acknowledging God (see Proverbs 3:5-6). Once you resolve to abandon yourself to God's will, to disappear into the trenches of selfless love, the devil will always come dressed in light to derail you, making his presentation look remarkable and very sensible. Jesus is exactly opposite: "He had no beauty or majesty to attract us to Him, nothing in His appearance that we should desire Him. He was despised and rejected by mankind, a Man of suffering, and familiar with pain. Like one from whom people hide their faces He was despised, and we held Him in low esteem" (Isaiah 53:2-3).

To the natural man and his common sense, the Spirit-taught things of God seem foolish. To the spiritually reborn man, he will find choices that once made no sense—what seemed utterly absurd to him and the rest of the world—led him straight to Jesus and produced an eternal reward for himself and for others. The devil's traps are not always gross sins or dark dead ends; they are often sensible and comfortable, but designed to detour you from the course that would do the most damage to his demonic kingdom. Be careful of what you hold in high esteem; beware of what makes a lot of sense; if it does not begin and end with Jesus, it is most likely a trap!

For Thought:

With this teaching, do you see your desperate need to pray and wait upon God? When faced with decisions, many believers pray, but in reality are only "running it by" God with no intention of waiting for His wisdom and guidance. Does *that* "make sense"?

Day 55

"Abba, Father" Not Abracadabra (Part 1)

"All those who are led by God's Spirit are God's sons. For you did not receive a spirit of slavery . . . but you received the Spirit of adoption, by Whom we cry out, 'Abba, Father'" (Galatians 4:6).

To take a Scripture out of context and expect it to have life-filled meaning is about as absurd as taking a fish out of water and expecting it to breathe. The Prophet Joel wrote, "Everyone who calls on the Name of the Lord will be saved" (Joel 2:32), and this is just one of those. The rest of this passage gives us the context we need to rightly understand: "For there will be an escape . . . among the survivors the Lord calls." A textual clue is the second use of the word *calls*.

Those who *call* upon the name of the Lord leading to salvation are those that hear (and follow) His call to them. There are many who call upon the Lord in crisis with neither any intention of following His calling, nor any desire for His intimate Presence; they will not be saved (see Matthew 7:21-23). Calling on His name does not mean saying His name as if it were some magical "abracadabra" word. The third commandment is, "Do not take the name of the Lord for an unworthy purpose" (Exodus 20:7). That means using the name of the Lord as a manipulative device to reach some selfish agenda, or merely escape some unfavorable consequence with no real intention of Him being your Lord. Our call to God must be essentially the same in meaning as His call to us. The Greek word for *call* (*klātós*) means, "to summon for intimate and personal interaction" as a judge summons a person to appear before him for thorough examination. Our calling upon the Lord must possess the same meaning—to summons the Presence of God for intimate and personal interaction so we can thoroughly examine Him (see Deuteronomy 4:29 and 1 Chronicles 22:19).

God is pleased when you call Him "Abba" (daddy); it declares you have received by faith that which Jesus labored in anguish to give you. Jesus loves it when you call upon Him for personal interaction and examination. He knows the more you examine Him the more you will learn of Him, therefore the more you will ultimately trust Him. You have been freed from a life of slavery to sin, have His Spirit, and are His adopted child. Let your call to Him be one for devotion not just deliverance.

For Thought:

Have you ever heard of a "foxhole prayer"? What is it? God will answer such a prayer even if not reciprocated with devotion; He does this so there can be no claim of never receiving from Him.

Day 56

"Abba, Father" Not Abracadabra (Part 2)

"All those who are led by God's Spirit are God's sons. For you did not receive a spirit of slavery . . . but you received the Spirit of adoption, by Whom we cry out, 'Abba, Father'" (Galatians 4:6).

Those who are true sheep hear the call of the true Shepherd; they follow Him, and they know His voice. Since we have been saved because of Jesus our eternally interceding High Priest (see Hebrews 7:25), we also have the immensely merciful gift of the spirit of adoption—the heavenly ability to humbly call God our "daddy."

A true call issues from true love. Jesus called upon God His Father in perfectly abandoned love, "Abba, Father! All things are possible for You . . . nevertheless, not what I will, but what You will" (Mark 14:36). We only call upon those whom we truly love. We call upon them because we know that they love us, or better yet, loved us first. Jesus selflessly called upon His Father because He intimately knew the Father's selfless love. Equally, when we truly call upon the name of the Lord, we are revealing to Him that we trust in His selfless and unfailing love.

Jesus also called to us, "If you abide in Me and My words abide in you, ask whatever you want and it will be done for you" (John 15:5). We ask in words, and if His words are in us, what we ask will be what He wants us to ask. By so doing, we as adopted children are devoted to His perfect will, and He will accomplish our desire because it is His desire. In other words, God always accomplishes His will for His children when they are resolved and abandoned to do it. David wrote the same exact spiritual principle, "Delight in the Lord and He will give you the desires of your heart" (Psalm 37:4). Since we delight in Him, His desires become our desires. For example, I once had no desire for holiness, but since I now delight in Him, I desire holiness above all knowing that without it I cannot see Him (Hebrews 12:14).

For Thought:

The Lord is not our washing machine or genie; He is the One who suffered excruciating death to adopt us as sons and daughters, so we can forever call Him "Abba (daddy) Father."

There is a false doctrine growing today that is fundamentally hedonistic. It says man and his pursuit of worldly pleasures and carnal delights are what God wants to freely grant him; all man has to do is "A, B, and C." What is this false doctrine popularly called?

Day 57

Seeing is Not Necessarily Believing

"Peace I leave with you; my peace I give you. I do not give to you as the world gives. Do not let your hearts be troubled and do not be afraid" (John 14:27).

The natural man can see only what is natural. However, the spiritual man can see both what is natural and what is spiritual; he merely chooses to use his spiritual sight because he has learned through the life of faith, all that is natural must submit to that which is spiritual. For instance, when Peter stepped out of a boat battered by angry waves and walked upon them to come to Jesus, he could see the waves but he could also see Jesus. The waves naturally could have drowned Peter had not Jesus been there. To the natural man, it seems completely ridiculous to willingly exit the only safety and salvation from drowning (in this case a boat) and enter what is deemed impossible (surviving an angry sea). To the spiritual man, all that is natural—the laws of logic and physics—must submit to Jesus, because He created it. Jesus' peace is the natural submitting to the spiritual, and the impossible surrendering to the supernatural.

When faced with the choice between focusing on the boisterous waves that promised natural death, or Jesus who promises resurrection life, Peter chose Jesus, and his choice resulted in a supernatural walk of faith that no man has walked since. Peter is the only man in recorded history that walked on water, and it was only possible because he was absolutely focused on Jesus, the Lord of the impossible. But once Peter's spiritual attention was stolen by the natural, all that was spiritually miraculous was overruled by what the natural continually propagates—"This is impossible!" And he immediately began to sink.

As saints, we have two sights, "natural seeing" and "spiritual seeing". The natural will remain stuck at the Red Sea, but the spiritual will see its miraculous division. The natural sees the impossible and says, "It's all over for us," but the spiritual says, "It is just the beginning of a new revelation of God." One might ask, "You mean to tell me, the same type of peace that sleeps soundly in a battered and sinking boat, in the midst of one of the worst squalls in the biblical record, is the peace I can have?" The Lord would answer, "Yes! I died to give it to you. Consider the cost, and perceive the treasure of it. If I am in the boat, stay in it, there is peace there. If I am outside of the boat, get out, do not mind the waves, and walk to Me. Let your unbelief drown rather than faith!

For Thought:

Read John 14:1, 27. Notice Jesus said twice, "Do not let your hearts be troubled". Do you think He was redundant or emphatic? The word, "be" is in the Greek continuous tense, meaning to not let your hearts *continue to be* troubled. Meditate on this.

Day 58

Fire of Redeeming Love

"For love is strong as death; jealousy is cruel as the grave: the coals thereof are coals of fire" (Song of Solomon 8:6, KJV).

The Lord had been brutally removed from the earth and the disciples were bewildered. Sometimes when people are uncertain of how to move forward after a traumatic event, they default to something they are familiar with and comfortable doing. This was the case for Peter when he said, "I'm going fishing" (John 21:3). What else was there to do? His hopes of becoming a fisher of men seemed dashed to pieces, so why not go back to fishing for something he could catch?

They had fished all night without a bite. Peter must have silently thought, "If only Jesus were here to give us a miraculous catch like He did the day I first met Him." Suddenly, a faint voice echoes from the east, "Children, you do not have any fish, do you?" How could anyone from the shore know that? "Cast the net on the right-hand side of the boat and you will find a catch" (21:6). Now how could anyone say such a thing so surely? Nevertheless, they consented, and that miraculous catch Peter imagined was realized. No man could know they had no catch; no man could assure them of one; and only one Man had done something similar to this. John put it all together and cried out, "It is the Lord!" And in reckless zeal, Peter jumps in and swims to Jesus.

Why did Peter do this? In John 20:3-4, on Resurrection morning, John and Peter got into a racing match to the tomb and John won. Peter could have thought, "Not this time, John! You might be the faster runner, but I'm the better swimmer." Truth is, John went to the cross with Jesus but Peter had denied it, and was undoubtedly filled with guilt. What a miraculous opportunity this was for Peter. There was Jesus, resurrected and cooking fish. What is vital to notice is the "charcoal fire." We have heard about Peter's three-fold redemption from his three-fold denial, but we usually miss the fact that Peter denied Jesus while he was warming himself by a "charcoal fire" (John 18:18). In the near future, Peter would travel countless miles on foot as an evangelist. Charcoal fires were common instruments to keep warm, so each time Peter would gather around one, he would have had to remember the bitterness of his denial of Jesus. But because of the Lord, Peter would instead remember every charcoal fire with joy rather than painful regret. Here we see the absolute thoroughness of Jesus' desire to redeem us.

For Thought:

Don't be surprised when the Lord asks you to repeat something you failed in the past. Very likely He is purposing to redeem every nuance of it. He wants nothing of yesterday to fill you with sorrowful regret. Let His radiant glory redeem all the darkness of the past, like the diamond that shines brighter upon the blackest velvet.

"But" Does Not Follow God

"With man this is impossible, but with God all things are possible" (Matthew 19:26).

Jesus' obedience is what caused Him to experience separation from His Father. It is utterly impossible to fathom our obedience ever separating us from God. Aside from all miracles, this is truly evidence of Jesus being the God of the impossible. With our human natures we have the bad habit of making a list of our seemingly irresolvable problems and circumstances. God's Word tells us love does not keep record of wrongs (1 Corinthians 15:5). When it comes to the wrongs that normal life serves, make your petitions to God rather than record them on lists. Fix your gaze upon God's Love through His Son Jesus, devote yourself fully to Him, and you will not be busy making lists of unfortunate or unresolved events. God's Word is forever the final Word, and whenever we create lists of our giants or give people reports of our insurmountable problems, we begin to put our word after His, which says, "God, yes, but this circumstance." *But* cannot follow God, it must always precede Him. In other words, all things, including all circumstances and problems must come before God, never after!

What happened when ten out of twelve spies reported back to Moses, 'God, yes, but these giants?' It sent the entire nation of Israel into dark despair and unbelief, near mutiny, and caused them to wander for forty more years in the wilderness. Joshua and Caleb correctly said, 'These giants, yes, but God.' The Israelites had allowed the enemy to get a foothold through their disobedience and became so full of his darkness that they desired to stone Joshua and Caleb to death for attempting to defend the truth and power of God. That is what unbelief ultimately does; it desires to murder the Truth of God with the lies of the Devil. Look at Calvary and test this fact. Unbelief kills Jesus!

Throughout scripture we see the word "but" precede God. It should always be circumstance first, then God. For example, "We were . . . objects of God's Wrath. *But God*, being rich in mercy . . . made us alive with the Messiah" (Ephesians 2:3-4). Here we see the most impossible and hopeless situation and God having the final word. An impossible or hopeless situation is fertile soil for God's delivering hand of Mercy. Never take a snapshot of your circumstances and then call that reality. Learn to say, "But God!"

For Thought:

Read Job 38. God had patiently listened to the unresolvable cases and opinions of all the characters. Then it says, "And then the LORD speaks" (38:1). God has the last word because He is the first and last. When He fails have the last word, our problems remain because they are all we have chosen to see. Remember, it is circumstances, *but God*, not God, but circumstances.

Day 60

Tear Down the Wall!

"I tell you what I am going to do to my vineyard: I will take away its hedge, and it will be destroyed; I will break down its wall, and it will be trampled" (Isaiah 5:5).

Idolatry and self-worship thrives and prospers behind mighty walls and man-made coverings. Generally, people detest being disturbed from their self-centered agendas, self-prescribed ideas of God, and their comfortable Christianity laced with the opiate of easy-belief. The last thing that they desire is for anything to disturb their peaceful little kingdoms. Confrontation disturbs people, just like Jesus disturbed the religious people, and Jeremiah disturbed the religious soothsayers.

Religious frauds man their walls with fiery arrows, aiming to kill all that threatens to penetrate the fortress walls of their miniature kingdoms. On the outside of their walls are inscribed the words, "We love God," but on the inner courts of those same walls they sit on their thrones sanctioning the very things God hates. They set up stages for actors to act out scene after scene atrocious things in God's sight, not omitting the one most deplorable to God—Heart-disengaged ritual! As it was for the post-exilic Jews during Amos' ministry, though they had not returned to pagan idolatry, they merely substituted it for something worse. Its proper name is formalism. We call it "religion!" Pagan Rome did the same thing when she changed into a prettier gown and became Papal Rome.

There is also the formalism of today which leads many believers to feel as though by their regular maintenance of it they are bestowing a favor upon God. It is called "church-going." God desires not our favors; he desires our heart and our gratitude! With meetings so cold you can see your breath, and people so lifeless you want to check their pulse, we need bold, fiery, and confrontational preaching; eternities depend on it!

Whatever fortress you build to protect your garden of idolatry—whether it is the love of the world, hidden sin, or just being your own little god—God will tear it down and lay the whole garden to waste if you will not! Keep in mind; God's standards are only as hostile to you as you are to them. To those living in God's Truth, His approach is welcomed with open joy rather than defended from high walls with grief and panic. Tear down what has separated you from the Lord, or be assured that He will, hopefully in this life!

For Thought:

John Owen wrote, "Be killing sin or it will be killing you." [8]

Read Genesis 4:7 and Romans 8:13-14. Is this congruent with Owen's statement? Why or why not?

Day 61

The Fullness of Forsaking Sin

"Nor shall he cause the people to return to Egypt . . . the LORD has said to you, 'You shall never again return that way'"(Deuteronomy 17:16).

The exodus of God's people from the tyranny of Egypt typifies Christ delivering us out of sin's tyranny. God solemnly forbid the Israelites to ever go back to Egypt. That means once God delivers us out of bondage to a sinful stronghold we should shudder to think of returning back to it! Jesus told a parable demonstrating the same principle, but added to it a portrayal of the consequences should we not take heed to His warning. Consider Jesus' words:

> *"When an impure spirit comes out of a person, it goes through arid places seeking rest and does not find it. Then it says, 'I will return to the house I left.' When it arrives, it finds the house unoccupied, swept clean and put in order. Then it goes and takes with it seven other spirits more wicked than itself, and they go in and live there. And the final condition of that person is worse than the first. That is how it will be with this wicked generation"* (Matthew 12:44-45).

The spiritual thrust of the idea is this: Whatever the Lord has delivered you out of, you must never return to it, not even for a fleeting visit. If this command is not regarded, the end result will be seven times (completely) worse. To support this idea, Jesus said, "Behold, you have become well; do not sin anymore, so that nothing worse happens to you" (John 5:14). The theological and contextual thrust is this: Although Jesus (who the religious treated like an unclean spirit) was momentarily cast out of their comfortable and religion-infested lives, His Gospel would return inevitably to their land and their lives and eventually wreak a seven-fold (complete) havoc rendering them utterly desolate.

Leave nothing behind for an occasional return visit to your former lusts. They were swallowed up in the Red Sea (the blood of Jesus) and the way back has been closed. The way must remain closed. Neither should you mimic the Israelites in the fact that although God indeed got them out of Egypt, He could not get Egypt out of them. Forsake, abandon, and renounce (F.A.R.) all appearances of sin and evil and you will be *far* from its bondage and nearer to your eternal Deliverer, Jesus Christ the worthy Lamb of God. The nearer you are to Jesus the farther you will want to be from sin.

For Thought:

Imagine being an Israelite looking back upon the Red Sea having swallowed up all your fearful enemies. What should this tell you about what God can do to the enemies ahead of you?

Read Deuteronomy 28:65-68. The more you insist on going back to Egypt (sin's bondage), be warned, the Lord just may ship you back Himself in a sort of "reverse exodus." Now that's a sobering thought!

Day 62

When You See War

"God said, 'The people might change their minds when they see war, and return to Egypt'" (Exodus 13:17).

When the Christian life is realized as the war declaration against the enemy that it is, many see the enormous cost along with the level of perseverance it takes, without realizing the Holy Spirit they have to empower them. So their hearts faint and they turn back to their former lifestyles of sin and bondage.

Before the Exodus, the Israelites had spent a very lengthy period of time in bondage to the tyranny of Egypt. Generations of Israelites had long been removed from even the idea of fighting a battle. The feel and weight of a sword was remembered only in shadows and stories. They were about as fit and tuned for war, as a single lit match would be for a spelunking expedition. The fact that they were unprepared, unfit, and untrained for war, especially against the fierce Philistines was true. However, 430 years of being battered into submission had also deeply ingrained a spirit of timidity and defeat into their hearts. Being tyrannically beaten as slaves for that long would drain the vitality and dignity out of anyone.

Knowing their timorous hearts were riddled with defeat, God would certainly not lead them the shortest route through Philistia because they would have surely faced war there. Instead, He mercifully led them the longer route, which would take them through the Red Sea, the very instrument He would use to 1) reveal His divine power and mercy to them by parting the waters, making a way where there was no way, and 2) swallow up the pursuing enemy of tyranny and bondage in a watery grave. These Israelites had yet to witness the miracle working hand of God, nor had they seen His absolute power and authority; they were powerless and God-dependent.

Many fear fighting because they are afraid of dying. They do this because they disbelieve or forget that God that "goes with them to fight for them to give them victory." Return to Egypt and you will surely die . . . in your sin. Nevertheless, the war against evil and sin will be fierce at times, but remember who and what you are fighting for (Jesus, and His honor). Remember also "why" you fight (Jesus forgave your sins). Face and fight the war with faith and the Lord will bring you home a victor. That is His Promise!

For Thought:

If you are coming out of a long season of bondage to sin, very likely you are habituated to defeat. However, one thing you have that these Israelites did not yet have is the full revelation of God in His Word and His Son Jesus who conquered every foe through His finished work.

For Study:

Read Genesis 20:4.

Day 63

When God Stops Paying

"I count all things to be loss in view of the surpassing value of knowing Christ Jesus my Lord" (Philippians 3:8b)

In today's career arena, most of us choose our place of employment based upon whichever promises the best benefits and offers the most bonuses. In the career arena this method of choosing is wise and good. However, a great error is presented when this same methodology carries over into our spiritual lives.

If the idea of what God will do *for you* or *through you* is more important than what He can become to you, then knowing Jesus has ceased to be the surpassing value of your heart. You have fallen prey to one of the enemy's most cunning tactics—tempting God's people to set their gaze upon the effects rather than the Source of their salvation. When the gifts of the Spirit are the focal point rather than Jesus the giver and Lord of all grace, His value has been surpassed. When the ministry vision God has given you is the predominating factor in your thinking rather than the vision of the revelation of Jesus Christ, then He has taken second place. The Lord will not take second place, not even to His gifts and graces!

Too many of God's people are too preoccupied with what they are doing rather than with the One for whom they are doing it; where Jesus is taking them rather than just walking with Him; how He can "use them" rather than being in awe that He even does, or actually can. They have replaced the "Who" with the "what." The following evidence will give away those who only desire benefits: When God's divine favor and blessings digress, so does their devotion to Him. When God stops paying, the people stop praying, and start playing.

Very few can sincerely say with Job, "Though he slay me, yet will I trust in Him" (13:15). Many come to Jesus for blessings and rewards, yet are offended when all He offers is a cross to carry and Himself as the reward. On the contrary, if the desire of knowing Jesus is your all-surpassing value, even if His blessings are withheld or removed you feel no void and gain no offense. His blessings are to you what they really are, bonuses and benefits, not the employment. When Jesus is all you desire and value, then if all else is stripped away and He is all you have, no person on earth and no devil of hell would ever be able to tell by your response.

For Thought:

What would happen if you went for an interview at a large company, and said, "I am only applying for the benefits, but I don't want to work for your company"?

Would you give the great benefits of your company to someone who did not want to be an employee?

Day 64

Come to Jesus Like a Dead Person

"And when I saw him, I fell at his feet like a dead man" (Revelation 1:17).

John the Apostle walked closer to Jesus than anyone on earth ever has or will. He had seen the Lord miraculously transfigured on a mountaintop, and was the only disciple present at His crucifixion. Yet in his Revelation vision, the sight of the Lord was so immense and awe-inspiring that John did not even recognize Him, and he "fell at His feet like a dead man."

This response of prostrate worship has very similar language to Matthew's account of the Roman tomb guards on resurrection morning: "And behold, there was a great earthquake; for an angel of the Lord descended from heaven, and came and rolled away the stone, and sat upon it . . . and for fear of him the watchers did quake, and became as dead men" (28:2-4). Although it is true that what the Roman guards saw was not Jesus, it was indeed His power manifested through the angel/messenger that was unmistakable and fearsome, to the point that they could not continue to stand.

Whatever posture or nuances this dead-like fear portrayed itself in the guards, we do not know. But we can be absolutely sure that this will be the inescapable response of every person in the presence of an infinitely holy and powerful God—if not willfully and joyfully in this world, then irresistibly and terribly in the next!

John wrote these words from the Isle of Patmos (traditionally known to be a Roman salt-mine and slave camp). He was well along in years. He had selflessly labored for the Gospel, suffered great hardship and persecution for that Gospel, and seen many of his dearest brothers and friends brutally martyred for their steadfast testimony. He was cut-off from fellowship with all the churches he painstakingly founded. And what is he doing in the midst of all this? Worshiping Jesus caught up in the Spirit on the Lord's Day. What is most remarkable is his response to the One he saw. If anyone were to recognize Jesus it should have been John, but he did not. Jesus was fully glorified and John could not stand in His presence. How much more should we be the same? Have you gotten too used to "standing" in His presence, remaining unchanged? John could not! Every living person will ultimately come to Jesus like a dead man.

For Thought:

There is not one incident in the biblical record where someone came in contact with the Living God and remained unchanged.

"If you are stagnant in your spiritual growth; if you have never fallen prostrate like a dead man before Jesus, then you have not dwelled in the Presence of the Living God." Are these true words?

Day 65

The Evil of Motivational Manipulation

"They are enthusiastic about you, but not for any good. Instead, they want to isolate you so you will be enthusiastic about them" (Galatians 4:17, HCS).

We live in a culture that is inundated by motivational speakers and the largest percentage of our churches are flooded with them. Their sole agenda is to get people to do what the speaker wants. They do this generally by their charming personality, pleasing folks with eloquent speech, and promising temporal rewards. The sin of pleasing people may at first glance seem to be no big deal but when it is seen with its pretty mask ripped off, it is revealed as the morbid and devilish monster it truly is. The flattery of people-pleasing pride is most cunning and is engineered to win people over to a selfish agenda.

The Devil remains the most cunning beast of the field (Genesis 3:1). As the serpent, he is the greatest and most successful motivational speaker ever to slither the earth. The success and greatness of a motivational speaker is based on his ability to move an otherwise unmovable person, much like the world's strongest man is the one that moves the most unmovable object. The Devil was able to motivate a perfect man (Adam), living in a perfect paradise (Eden), to sin against an infinitely perfect God. There will never be a greater motivational feat to outshine that. Better stated, there will never be anything more evil, selfish, or malicious . . . ever!

Flattery, motivational manipulation, and the pride of people pleasing exist only to incite a responsive outcome from those whom it targets—a responsive outcome that benefits a personal agenda. Quite often we only flatter others because we ultimately want them to please and favor us. Flattery is selfish manipulation shrouded with good intent, and is devilish in nature. Flattery rules the pulpits of seeker sensitive churches.

The signs, miracles, and wonders of Jesus drew many people, but the majority of those people were not interested in Him at all. Nonetheless, He never motivated anyone with cunning personality, eloquent speech, flattery, or prosperity promises of temporal amenities. No. He lived thirty-three years of a crucified life that had its absolutely surrendered end with a crucified death. He meekly calls you to mimic Him (see Philippians 2:5-8), and this is His only motivation. If the Lord's call tolerated selfish ambition, His Kingdom would be full of disorder, and every evil thing (see James 3:14-16).

For Thought:

Famous speakers are praised for their motivational abilities and dynamic charisma. Are they stressing sin, repentance, and the crucified life for Jesus? Are they motivating you to find paradise on earth? Jesus said heavenly paradise must be our focus.

Day 66

The Futility of Solomon's Futility

"There is a futility that is done on the earth: there are righteous people who get what the actions of the wicked deserve, and there are wicked people who get what the actions of the righteous deserve" (Ecclesiastes 8:14).

The age-old question, "Why do bad things happen to good people?" plagues the thoughts of many people. On the other hand, we could just as easily ask, "Why do good things happen to bad people?" The solution to this unexpected conundrum can be found by examining our corrupted assumptions. In simpler terms, we wrongly expect justice (righteous people receiving righteous things and wicked people receiving wicked things) even though life itself has continuously proven this preconceived notion to be pure fantasy. Solomon saw this injustice of life and called it futility.

First, you might expect that bad things should happen to bad people (wicked outcomes for wicked people, etc.). Be careful here not to agree to swiftly; if this "justice" of yours were the case, we would all be doomed to be under God's wrath forever. Jonah had this problem of desiring wicked people to get what they deserved. For this God was extremely displeased, to the point that He allowed Jonah a three-day taste of what he was wishing upon the people of Nineveh—God's wrath (in Jonah's case it was death). Our hearts should be overflowing with worship and gratitude that God has not given any of us what we really deserve (death) and has given what we never would deserve (eternal life). The "futility" that Solomon saw was the real futility.

The solution to this seemingly futile problem is found at the cross: Jesus, the only One who is righteous, getting what the wicked deserve, so we who are all wicked could get what only He deserves. The next time you are plagued by the foolish question, "Why do bad things happen to good people?" you need to ask the right question: "Why do good things happen to bad people" Better stated, "Why did the best thing in history happen to me? What did I do so good to get Jesus to save me?" If you are demanding justice, be careful, you just might get what you demand! Get into the habit of saying this: "Death was mine and Jesus took it; Life is mine and He lost it."

For Thought:

Read Mark 10:18. Why is it incorrect to ask, "Why do bad things happen to good people"?

Q: Why did the worst thing in history happen to the most righteous Person in history?

A: To conquer the reason "bad things" happen to people (sin).

Day 67

How Could a Good God Allow Evil?

"Let Us make man as Our image, according to Our likeness" (Genesis 2:26).

God would not and does not allow evil. If so, then He is not God and He is not good. God, being infinitely good could only create what which is good. And as we read in the creation, everything was "good," including mankind. But mankind chose to reject the goodness of God. They listened to the Devil convince them that God was the cruel tyrant withholding good, which implied His allowing of evil. Believing the lie that God allows evil is what moved the first man and woman to judge rebellion to be good. No wonder this same old tactic of the Devil continues so strongly today. It works!

Why would a good God put something so desirable in the garden and then forbid Adam and Eve to eat it? Understand that God, infinite and overflowing in love, created man as the receptacle in which He could pour out His uncontainable love. If you had a container that was spilling over with its content, wouldn't you look to find something that could catch the overflow? When overwhelmed joy or love, do you not look for someone with whom you can share it? How painful is it when that love is not returned? How blessed would you feel if people only loved you because they were "programmed" to love you? How would you ever know anyone truly loved you unless there was a choice not to love you? We are a people who want to be loved by choice are we not? Now do you understand why God would give man a choice? God desires, like we do, to be chosen out of the myriads of other "alternatives," and when we choose to love Him in response to His love, we are doing what we were created for, and are thoroughly pleasing to Him.

Why would God allow evil? He would not. As soon as Adam and Eve sinned and the curse of sin and evil entered the world, we read in Genesis 3:15 how God immediately set out to redeem man. God promised He would permanently solve the problem of evil that the serpent inspired by crushing his head with a descendant of Eve (Jesus the Messiah who would fulfill that promise on the cross). God also temporarily covered Adam and Eve with animal skin, which means that an animal was sacrificed. Remember, God said if they ate of the fruit they would surely die. If not punished with death, then God would be a liar and an unjust Judge. God who is eternal, perfect, and infinitely wise could only be immutable (unchanging). He can only fulfill all He says because He is true, and He "spoke" us into existence. Since we came into being through God's true and spoken Word, if He changed the Word He spoke, all existence would change too.

Adam and Eve listened to the lying words of the serpent as he convinced them that God was the evil tyrant. Therefore, what the Devil had to offer—"You can be your own sovereign ruler apart from God"—seemed good, and they chose to rebel against God's Word. However, for God to be both merciful and just, He punished their sin with physical death but covered their spiritual death with both a temporal solution (animals), and a permanent Solution (Jesus, the Messiah). Through both, we all would have to face the ugliness of sin, but also the goodness of God, who would mercifully provide the means to keep us from suffering an eternal death apart from Him.

Why would God allow evil? He would not! He solved the problem of evil when He sent His Son Jesus to be the final sacrifice for sin on the cross. Calvary solved the problem of sin and evil. All who complain about evil or sin refuse to go there and receive the most wonderful Gift that God has ever given, His only Son! You should be very glad that God did not come and just obliterate evil, because you (and I) would have been counted in that number and eternally cut-off from God with no hope, left with only evil forever! Let's say God came down right now to remove evil from the world and left all those who are "good." When is the last time "good" people never did anything evil? Has history not proven that "good people" corrupt? So that means God would have to continually come down over and over to remove the evil people that had corrupted from their former "goodness." An infinitely wise God would never have such an absurd and foolish solution as this!

He would come once and for all to solve this dilemma we call evil. Praise Jesus!

For Thought:

As soon as you think God is not good, the serpent's venom courses through your veins, and his foul perversions will soon go from seeming logical to seeming very good to you.

Day 68

Spirit-Filled Equals Sin-Restrained

"For the mystery of lawlessness is already at work. Only he who now restrains it will do so until he is out of the way" (2 Thessalonians 2:7).

As the story of Roman Emperor Constantine outlawing the persecution of Christians unfolded in history, we see the tragic outcome of what happens when adversity against God's people is removed, when His Spirit is also removed. For the first 312 years of Christendom, being a Christian, especially a leader, meant there was a death sentence attached to your life. The words "follower of Christ" being proclaimed from your mouth would very likely put you in the mouth of a lion.

With the removal of persecution by Constantine in 312 A.D, the leadership of the church of Christ immediately went from being behind the crosshairs of torture and death to being behind the rear sight aperture of selfish ambition and avarice. The Holy Spirit was squelched, if not gone entirely. Leadership changed from being lived out to preserve the Gospel at the cost of one's life, to being sought out as a position to adorn one's life. A holy and consecrated platform on which God's fiery love reigned became a defiled and desecrated platform where man's lust for power and prestige burned. They were self-appointed elders rather than "Holy Spirit" appointed.

The mystery of lawlessness was already at work, meaning that the early church had already begun to apostate (depart from the true faith). Paul warned that this would indeed happen not long after his death: "Take heed unto yourselves, and to all the flock, in which the Holy Spirit has made you overseers . . . I know that after my departure grievous wolves shall enter in among you, not sparing the flock; and from among your own selves shall men arise, speaking perverse things, to draw away the disciples" (Acts 20:28-31).

Pagan Rome and all her emperors eventually fell, which enabled the complete removal of what restrained *the man of sin*. Now there was no Holy Spirit to lead and no Roman adversity to suppress! This left nothing but open and unrestrained pride and rebellion. Notice that Paul said, "The Holy Spirit has made you overseers." Apostasy can only begin when the Restrainer (The Holy Spirit) is removed. This takes place through either purposed usurpation, the repetitive squelching of His voice, or by the continuance of rebellion—It ripens through maneuvering to escape suffering for the love of pleasure.

A Spirit-filled Christian is a sin-restrained Christian; the same goes for the church. But a sin-filled church is a Spirit-restrained church and headed for departure from the true faith, and ultimately for barrenness and desolation.

For Thought:

Read Proverbs 29:18 and Ephesians 4:19.

Day 69

The Smiling Scowl

> *"Prove yourselves to be blameless and innocent, children of God above reproach"* (Philippians 2:15).

A "wolf in sheep's clothing," we have heard this common saying tossed around to the point of banality, like the store clerk who smiles with insincerity and says the canned response, "Have a nice day!" How do we know whether or not the clerk is genuine? How can we spot a wolf if it looks exactly like a sheep? The answer is, if you watch it long enough it will do wolf-like things—habits native only to a wolf. For instance, sheep do not prance, prowl, or drool, etc. The same principle goes for the clerk; if insincere, the smile returns to its original state when we turn around—a scowl.

If people watch you long enough, will they see wolf-like habits, or will they see habits becoming of a sheep? Will they see behavior that follows the Shepherd? True children of God do not act like wolves when not being watched because they are not wolves. Have you ever seen a sheep trying to behave like a wolf? If you did, the actions would certainly look unnatural, and peculiar, therefore easily seen to be "a fraud." A child of God trying to behave like a child of the Devil should be more and more difficult as time spent at the feet of Jesus increases; just as a wolf has a difficult time maintaining its sheep-like act as time passes by.

To be "above reproach" means to live in such a way that no blatant error can be seen. "Reproach" is essentially something that exposes error because of its opposite contrast—it makes the error more apparent and obvious, just as a true dollar bill reproaches a counterfeit when juxtaposed. Light reproaches dirt, etc.

If you are a wolf trying to behave like a sheep you will be exposed just as Jesus promised, "For nothing is hidden that will not become evident, nor anything secret that will not be known and come to light" (Luke 8:17). If you are a sheep behaving like a wolf, you should be warned to take extreme heed that someone does not mistake you for a wolf, and then follow your lead. Historically, there are endless stories of actors who acted their part so well that they almost became the part. Be careful that you do not become the part you might be acting.

For Thought:

Read I Timothy 3:2-7. What does it mean to live "above reproach"?

Are you a sincere sheep or a wanton wolf?

Read Luke 12:1. What did Jesus say was the leaven of the Pharisees?

Day 70

Turn Cope into Hope

"They turn, but not to what is above" (Hosea 7:16).

When dealing with the myriads of life's problems and sinful behavior patterns, there is a foul tragedy in those who claim to be the people of God today. Whether it is a remedy to their afflictions, or relief from their distresses, many persistently seek everything and anything but God. They temporarily medicate their sin-caused problems and would ingest any available opiate to numb themselves from their own self-inflicted wounds. Rather than turn from their sin and turn to God, they are complacent to cope with the poisonous results of their sin and rebellion, so long as they can continue to alleviate the unpleasant side effects. It is the person that says, "I know lying with dogs gets me fleas, but I refuse to stop because I love doing it; I will just continue applying the anti-itch fleabite medication. Who cares if my whole body is hideously covered with bites? Besides, I can cover that with clothing and makeup."

There are also some who continue to believe the lie that there are some problems of life God and His Word just cannot fix; they think that psychology, psychiatry, self-help therapies, and dangerous drugs capable of producing irreparable harm are the answers. This is in direct opposition to God's breathed-out Word that says, "His divine power has given us everything required for life and godliness" (2 Peter 1:3). It is illogical and false to claim that God created life, revealed Himself through His Word, and yet that Word not have the solutions to life's problems. No! God, the creator of life must also possess the solutions to all of life's problems, or else He is not God! If one problem of life were able to perplex the Creator of life then we would all instantaneously cease to exist.

God already solved life's two greatest problems—sin and its outcome (eternal death)—when He poured out all of His hatred for sin upon His own Son at Calvary. It is absurd to assume He cannot or would not solve all of the lesser problems of life. Just like you cannot satisfy your thirst unless you go to the faucet and drink in the water, you cannot find the solutions to your problems unless you turn to the only One who possesses them. No matter how strange a problem you may be facing, turn to Jesus and find more than just the ability to cope, find hope. The world says, "We must teach you how to *cope with strange*;" God says, "Turn to Me and find *hope for change*."

For Thought:

Jesus said, "If anyone is thirsty, let him come to Me and drink" (John 7:37). Do I have grounds to complain about being thirsty if I refuse to go to Him and drink?

Just as thirst is the outcome of refusing to drink, life-dominating problems are the outcome of refusing their Solution. Do we have grounds to complain about what we have demanded to keep?

Day 71

Seek and Find, Not Hide and Seek

"Or what woman, if she has ten silver coins and loses one coin, does not light a lamp and sweep the house and search carefully until she finds it?" (Luke 15:8).

Lost things remain lost because they evade our sight, either by hiding behind other objects, residing in dark places, or sometimes both. In order to find what has been lost, it takes *lighting* the dark areas, *sweeping* away all the clutter, and thoroughly *searching* the obscure and unusual places.

First, those who do not habitually clean their houses generally prefer to keep them dimly lit, because too much light exposes the layers of dust and dirt that otherwise go unnoticed.

Second, if you have ever tried to sweep your house you know how impractical and difficult it is to accomplish—at least to any degree of satisfaction—when it is cluttered (usually with unnecessary things).

Finally, most people who live in dim and cluttered homes are super-reluctant for anyone to carefully search the inside. Out of fear or embarrassment of what might be found, their resistance will prevail and many times with increasing intensity.

In this "parable of the lost coin," Jesus personifies Himself as the woman possessing three significant methods to find what has been lost: *Lighting a lamp* (The Holy Spirit illuminating the Word of God to our heart), *sweeping the house* (the removal of idols, lusts, and ungodly attitudes exposed by His light), and *carefully searching* (the Omniscient God overturning every unturned stone, combing through every nook and cranny of our being, disturbing our false sense of comfort, and picking the locks to all our secret chambers of sin and pride). All this He does to truly find us, so we can truly know Him and how passionately He desires our fellowship.

Oh how desperate He is to expose, clean, and search you. He will not let you hide behind objects or continue to dwell in darkness. He longs for fellowship with you, but He can only have intimacy with the real you. When God found Adam, He got him to see and confess where he truly was—hiding in fear and shame, completely exposed as a helpless sinner before a Holy God (see Genesis 3:9-10). Has He truly found the real you, or have you only let Him search and find self-chosen parts? Can you say like David, "You have searched me Lord, and You know me" (Psalm 139:1)? Do not play hide and seek with the Lord. Instead, let Him seek and find you every day. He will cover with love what is uncovered by His light, transforming you into His glorious image.

Day 72

Don't Settle for 'Only Human' (Part 1)

"What is the source of wars and fights among you? Don't they come from the sinful desires that are at war within you?" (James 4:1, HCV).

This great spiritual truth of James should produce in us the great need to continuously dwell in God's light, and to be continuously at peace by yielding to the Holy Spirit rather than to our fleshly desires. All the little fleshly and peevish annoyances that get us perturbed and riled up at people must go. But they will never go if we do not put them out, and we will never put them out if we fail or refuse to see them as greatly needing to be expelled.

If we were dwelling in the light of God's holy presence—the One who hates all manifestations of selfishness—we would know that our peevish annoyances are extremely selfish. We would know this because He who is the discerner of our hearts would not fail to tell us. We would cease to call them "little" because God does not see them as little at all, but rather as big and deadly (Remember, the littlest scorpion is the most poisonous and the tiniest jellyfish in the world has the most deadly sting). They are poisonous attitudes that we endlessly justify and minimize to make them tolerable. These dubbed "little" annoyances that get us all riled up and perturbed at people are not love. They are reactions to not getting our way. They are the shoots (young branches) of offense, bitterness, resentment, hatred, and if left unchecked, possibly even rage or murder. If they are allowed to grow they will surely become mature.

A great tragedy is that many Christians allow sinful attitudes to mature but do not mature in holiness and love. You may think these attitudes can be swept under the rug and forgotten as no big deal, but this thinking is laced with Satan's lying opiate because he knows the following truth: They build up and grow up if you continually neglect to deal with them. And the only successful way to deal with them is by yielding to the Holy Spirit, thereby replacing them with mercy and love.

For Thought:

"Love covers a multitude of offenses" (Proverbs 10:12; 1 Peter 4:8).

Mortifying sin is properly motivated only by the foundational love of Christ Jesus and His cross. [9]

Pray often, "Search me, God, and know my heart; test me and know my anxious thoughts. See if there is any offensive way in me, and lead me in the way everlasting" (Psalm 139:23-24).

Have you ever prayed this prayer? Do you think it should be a persistent practice? How many ongoing problems could be solved if you did?

Day 73

Don't Settle for 'Only Human' (Part 2)

"What is the source of wars and fights among you? Don't they come from the sinful desires that are at war within you?" (James 4:1, HCV).

*H*atred for anything other than sin is not love. To hate sin means to love what is not sin, and that means people. People are sinful because they are bound to it, but they are not sin itself. The way you respond to people who do sin against you determines whether or not you hate or love sin. If you are offended with sin you will love people, but if you love sin you will be offended with people. The same way I cannot love two masters (Luke 16:13), I cannot hate both sin and not sin at the same time; I must choose, and *there* is the war.

So in essence those "little" annoyances are only evidences that our fleshly nature is still very much alive and our pride is being injured. What is dead does not react when it is poked. Pride is at the root of all sin, and those offenses are the surfacing of that pride. We must see these manifestations like dashboard indicators telling us that something is wrong under the hood; that there are areas of selfishness and pride that God the Master heart mechanic has His finger upon for us to put to death. To allow them to live by justifying or minimizing them is rebellious and risky. They keep us in great bondage to our old sinful (human) nature and discourage our maturing in love.

We hear it said, "It is only human to get offended!" What is really being said is, "It is only fleshly to be that way and I personally do not desire to be anything other than that." Paul exhorted, "For this is the will of God, your sanctification" (1 Thessalonians 4:3). What is sanctification but having less of the fleshly (human-like) nature, and more of the spiritual (Christ-like) nature? We are ambassadors of

Christ and His will is to reproduce Himself in us. Our selfish words and attitudes while under the brandishing title, "Christian," grieve the Lord. Furthermore, they inform others that this is acceptable behavior and part of today's Christian standard, thereby encouraging them to sin by our consenting approval (see Romans 1:32).

For Thought:

Read Romans 8:13. We will only desire to mortify what we hate and our own sinful nature must be the subject. We must not be content or comfortable with being "only human." Jesus set the standard for humanity and He gave us His Holy Spirit to empower us to meet it. That standard is more than just human; it is Christ-like. Paul imperatively exhorted, "Make your own attitude that of Christ Jesus" (Philippians 2:5). However, be motivated by your love for Him, or do not be motivated at all.

Day 74

Would You Be Blessed?

"You have placed our iniquities before You, Our secret sins in the light of Your presence" (Psalm 90:8).

Supplemental Reading
(Psalm 68:1-3)

It sounds pretty and ornamental for Christians to pray at their meetings, "Bless us, Oh Lord, with the light of Your presence." But the reality is that the majority of the biblical persons who truly came in contact with the actual light and Presence of God hated and despised it. More than this, all the biblical persons who did not hate or despise it were utterly undone, and most certainly did not feel very *blessed* ("enviably favored") at first.

This is because His Light is an all-exposing light and His fiery presence an idol-destroying fire. I could comfortably say that the same effect would apply today—Most would not feel very *blessed* with an actual visitation of the light of God's Presence. He is a sin-exposing, darkness-expelling, heart melting, idol-destroying light. If the true light of God's presence showed up in the average church meeting today, many would despise it, reject it, mock it, or flee from it.

Am I "blessed" when His presence turns me inside out and purges to ashes? Only as much as I hate my sin and selfishness in the light of the cross do am I blessed by God's presence. Those who are "blessed" by this otherworldly light are the sin-hating saints who truly seek to live the crucified life of holiness for Jesus and His Gospel. The blessing contained in His light and presence is the purifying separation and removal of tares from the wheat (evil from the good, false from the true). This blessing may come in the form of a church of four hundred immediately plummeting to forty. "Bless us, Oh Lord, with the light of Your presence?"

Read (Psalm 68:1-3)

If you love numbers in your church, and are preoccupied with them, the light of God's presence will likely not be a blessing. If you love secret sin, it will not be a blessing. If you love pomp and circumstance, shows and programs that have replaced the presence of God, it will certainly not be a blessing to you. It will instead be a heavy rebuke and an unwelcomed nuisance. However, if you habitually "walk in the light as He is in the light" (1 John 1:7) you will be blessed that He has come and overjoyed with its result.

For Thought:

Are you used to being in the presence and holiness of God? Are you used to having your will crossed by Him? If you hate change and love tradition, chances are the answer is "No." Agree?

Day 75

A Baptism of Prayer and Faith

Then Jesus said to her, "O woman, your faith is great; it shall be done for you as you wish." And her daughter was healed at once" (from Matthew 15:22-28).

*H*ave you been rescued, restored, and released by Jesus from the vexation of the devil through a baptism of unceasing prayer and unyielding faith by either that of a parent or a loved one? If so, your entire life should be consumed by and occupied with the unrelenting mercy of intercession for others.

Since we were the "daughter grievously vexed with a devil" whose *mother* (any parent or loved one) relentlessly pursued Jesus in hopes to receive just one tiny crumb of His mercy . . .

The *mother* who also not for one instant back-peddled at the seemingly brass heavens;

The *mother* who also wearied not in the persistence of pleading in the face of delay;

The *mother* who also at the risk of humiliation remained in lowliness and faith to seek, knock, and find;

The *mother* who also dropped anchor in the harbor of the Master's feet with utter refusal to sail on until the words were spoken, "It shall be done for you as you wish;"

It is through this baptism of prayer and of faith that we realize our lives have been spared, saved, and made white purely as a means to another end and purpose—"to become like the mother by taking on her role." We are to become the unrelenting intercessor for our children, our neighbor, and our brother that *she* was for us.

For Thought:

Have you ever pondered the possibility that the reason God saved you was not because He had some lavish plan or ministry for your life; but rather because unknowingly, someone was desperately praying for you?

Many can testify in agreement with this, that the reason they were not left to die in their sin is because of a loved one who was faithful and unrelenting in prayer. Can you too say that?

Are you someone's answered prayer?

Day 76

A Large Heart Means a Little You

"For You will enlarge my heart" (Psalm 119:32b).

In this Psalm, David petitions the Lord to enlarge his heart. Do you see the enlarging of your heart as a desperate need? What thought first comes to mind, making your heart larger or cleaning out the one you have to make more room? Typically, when we think of the enlarging of something our first thought is making it bigger in size rather than creating more room. If we need more room in our home, which is easier, looking for a bigger home, adding on to the one we have, or cleaning it out by getting rid of all the clutter and unnecessary things?

The answer is rhetorical, and David knew the meaning of it: Expelling the selfish clutter to make more room. But making more room for what? More room for the infilling of the Holy Spirit and God's Word, and more room for loving others is the correct answer, but is it our sincere answer? With an honest-to-God assessment, we would acknowledge the clutter consists not of the things in our life. No, the clutter is self; *we* take up too much room!

Therefore, in order to have an enlarged heart I must shrink and dissolve, and like John the Baptist, decrease so Jesus and others can increase. Samuel reminded king Saul who eventually became corrupted with pride, "When you were little in your own sight, were you not made the head of the tribes of Israel, and the LORD anointed you king over Israel" (1 Samuel 15:17). Maybe the reason our hearts seem so small and in need of enlargement is because we are so big in our own eyes and take up most of the room. Love is not full *of* itself; love is full *in* itself. Love never runs out of resources to pour out for others or the willing ability to take them in. We only look down upon, condemn, or shut out others because we deem ourselves better and more important than they are (see Philippians 2:3-4). Therefore, the work is not in the increasing of our heart size, it is in the decreasing our self-size.

For Thought:

The smaller we are, the larger our heart is. Do we daily see the desperate need to shrink and dissolve more and more?

What can you do to make more room today? Ask the Lord for His empowering grace, and then commit to do it.

Day 77

The Hand and the Glove (Part 1)

"All of them were filled with the Holy Spirit" (Acts 2:4).

When I was young I played a prank on my brother. He had gotten a pair of new snow gloves for Christmas and I took the right hand glove and sewed two of its fingers shut with my mom's sewing machine. It seemed to take forever to snow because of my eager anticipation to experience the payoff of my prank—his reaction. In late February there was finally a large snow, and my long awaited day had come. Filled with excitement he got out his gloves and I watched with even more excitement as he tried on the right one. Even though three fingers of the glove were open his hand could not fit into the glove because of the two sewn shut. He was severely frustrated as he tried unsuccessfully to make it fit. Needless to say, he was not very happy, but I sure was; at least until he told on me.

Jesus spoke with peculiar wording in John's gospel, "If anyone loves Me, he will keep My word; and My Father will love him, and We will come to him and make Our abode with him" (John 14:23). Mere guests are generally not allowed to roam freely about every corridor of our house. On the contrary, the person to whom you sign over the title of your home comes to fill it completely. At that point you no longer have the right to disallow that person access to any place therein, and if agreed upon that you stay, you become the guest.

Have you made the Holy Spirit the owner of your temporary home (your body)? He serves as the right Hand of God and you are the glove. A glove cannot move without a hand, and He has come to spread Himself out through every finger and fully animate you from the inside out. Do you have fingers sewn shut to Him because you believe you are doing well enough in those areas on your own? If yes, then you are essentially saying, "These two areas of my life I can handle and with them I am in no need of assistance. But these three over here aren't functioning to my liking, so they are open to you, Holy Spirit, to pick up that slack."

He cannot fill you properly if you have fingers of self-sufficiency or rebellion. He is severely frustrated and His desire to fill you fully is unsuccessful.

For Thought:

Are you still the owner of your "home" and He is just a mere guest? Sign over the title to Him and become the guest in His house. Then you can begin to be controlled by the Holy Spirit. Much fruit will come of it if you do.

Read Amos 3:3. Compare that with what A.B. Simpson wrote: "There is no blessing so great as that which comes when our hearts are lifted out of self and become one with Christ in intercession for others and for His cause." [10]

Day 78

The Hand and the Glove (Part 2)

"For from now on there shall be five in one house divided, three against two, and two against three" (Luke 12:52).

Jesus is the great line of demarcation; He always divides before He unites. Jesus first has to separate sons of peace (those open to Kingdom Truth) from those who are sealed shut by the hardness of their hearts. That is when the uniting takes place—the recipients of God being added to the recipients of God. Truth separated eight people from the entire world immediately before Noah's flood and united them together in the ark. Truth separated two seemingly identical thieves at Calvary and revealed their opposing qualities. If not for Jesus being crucified directly between them, no man could have told the difference between the two on the outside. But after He came in their midst they were seen as diametrically opposed on the inside. Only one of the two was united with Him in eternity.

Only Jesus can judge righteously and that means separating the sincere from the counterfeit, the believer from the unbeliever, and the good from the evil. Houses are not divided by any injustice of God, but rather by the obstinate rebellion of their residents against Him. Jesus would rather three be saved than see the entire house be lost in Hell forever.

What about the house of your own heart? Is it divided? Are there, like the hand and glove illustration, "three divided against two," because two fingers are sewn shut to the Lord? Ask Him to come in and make His home fully within you (see John 14:23). Then let Him do it by signing the title of yourself over to Him, and become a guest in your old house. Let your heart continuously resonate with the words of the

Savior, "Not My will, but Your will be done" (Luke 22:42). He will unite your entire being to Himself.

For Thought:

The life of prayer "is the intercourse of an inseparable divine companionship."[11]—A.B. Simpson, *The Life of Prayer*

"Many have accepted the gift of eternal life, but instead of realizing that their life belongs to the One who died for it, they keep it to themselves—They are like the man in the parable who hid his talent in the earth instead of gaining on it." [12]—Rees Howells

Day 79

Self-Love Multiplies Sorrows

"The sorrows of those who have bartered for another god will be multiplied" (Psalm 16:4).

We have heard it said that we hurt those we love the most. This also means that we are hurt the worst by those we love the most. When a stranger sins against us it hurts to an extent, but the pain is intense when the sin comes from someone we deeply love. The question we need to ponder here is, "What if the one we love the most is ourselves?" When I sin I am certainly hurting myself, and the same principle applies. Since I am most affected by the one I love the most, my sorrows are multiplied when I love myself the most (self-worship)—I have bartered for another god. Below is the process unfolded:

You may have heard someone say, "I am my own worst enemy." Oh, how true and profound that is! The reason we are our own worst enemy is not because we are greatly opposed to ourselves, but rather because we love ourselves too much. Who is it that hurts, wounds, disappoints, and torments us the most but self? We disappoint and hurt ourselves much more than other people do. When others sin against us, the natural reaction is to demand justice and recompense, either through their punishment or our retaliation. Therefore, logically, if I love myself the most, when I do something sinful, I am extremely affected by it because I have hurt my self greatly. Therefore, I must demand justice. When self is on the throne, the same way we are inclined to heap condemnation upon others' sins and faults, we will be inclined to heap condemnation upon ourselves for our own sinful, faulty behavior. This is why the sorrows of self-idolatry multiply. This is also why many fall into the error of self-mutilation, self-condemnation, and penitence.

Here is the principle: Self-love is a lofty view of self. A lofty view of self is displayed as self-righteousness and self-love. If you worship yourself, then *you* must render your own punishment. Self-righteousness and self-love always produce self-condemnation.

God will never hurt us or harm us (see Jeremiah 29:11). And if He is the One we love the most, we will not experience the multiplication of sorrows. "Therefore, there is now no condemnation for those who are in Christ Jesus" (Romans 8:1). If you are constantly experiencing the multiplying sorrows of self-condemnation, self-pity, or depression, your worship is misdirected and maligned. A true worshiper of God may be attacked by, but cannot remain in these self-centered attitudes.

For Thought:

Self-pity is unachieved lust. With self-ambition, driven by the spirit of the world, you set out to achieve all that promises pleasure. When you fail, you drown in your own missed achievements.

Day 80

The Way Out

"But with the temptation will provide the way of escape also, so that you will be able to endure it." (1 Corinthians 10:13b).

This is God's way of saying, "Whatever the problem, there is a solution, and I am giving it to you. But you must choose to take it and follow Me." In the Exodus, the Israelites were stuck at the Red Sea with Pharaoh and his chariots (symbolizing the Devil, his demonic cohorts, and his worldly manipulations), and they were closing in fast to kill them. There was no way out it seemed. The mountains on both sides were impassable, and the sea ahead was un-crossable. They were "stuck." Do you "feel" stuck? God revealed Himself in a brand new way to them, and in all His power and glory He opened the Sea making a way of escape where there was none. He did this while they were screaming, "There's no way out! We're going to die!" The Israelites could have said, "No way, we're not going through that," and resultantly would have been destroyed. But instead they followed their shepherd Moses (who represents Jesus our Shepherd) and once the last Israelite came out safely on the other side, God swallowed up their enemies behind them once and for all!

Look for God's provided way of escape and take it, follow Jesus recklessly and faithfully, and go through the formidable Sea. Only then will you come out on the other side, look back, and see that God victoriously swallowed up every foe in His Almighty power. In error, believers say, "God, if you deliver me I will follow you through the fearful places." "I'll stay in this marriage if; I'll quit this sinful habit if . . ." God would say, "What do you mean, 'If;' I already have delivered you!" God first delivered them out of bondage, but the Red Sea was a long fearful walk of faith opened by the Lord, led of Him, and allowed by Him. But look what happened on the other side: Every enemy behind them was swallowed up in victory, and they came to know the Lord in a way they could never have fathomed! This is the Lord's desire for every person, and this is the only way that He will have you know Him—Personally, experientially, and intimately! He died for it. He is the "Way" out!

For Thought:

If you're stuck, you're in the perfect position for a powerful move of God! You will experience God's solution, and see that man's attempts are foolish and vain? Will people change? Maybe. But if not, *you will*. And, your intimacy with Jesus will be sweeter than you could ever know. Through that, Christ in you and shining through you will truly affect more people than you could have ever dreamed or done in your own effort, adamancy, or striving.

"Be still and know that I am God" (Psalm 46:10).

Day 81

God's Dwelling Place

"How awesome is this place! This is none other than the house of God" (Genesis 28:17).

With a blessing and a charge from his father, Jacob was on his way to Paddan Aram to find a wife. It was on this peculiar trip that Jacob saw in a dream the stairway connecting earth to heaven, popularly known as "Jacob's Ladder." Without going in detail about all the theological and spiritual significances connected with this holy vision, we will examine Jacob's response here. Jacob's exclamatory remarks, "Surely the Lord is in this place," and "What an awesome place," reveal that he was extraordinarily moved by this revelation of God. He was moved to such an extent that he took the stone he had used for a pillow and set it up as a memorial and then poured oil upon it as an anointing to set it apart as holy. He then renamed the place *Bethel*, which means, "Dwelling place of God."

Stones do not make nice resting places to lay our gentle heads any more than stone hearts make favorable resting places for the gentle Holy Spirit. The Lord longs for his people to set apart their hearts as a memorial upon which He can pour out His Holy Spirit. Should we desire anything less?

The Holy Spirit, when poured out upon a stony heart, should continually soften it. If not, then He cannot rest upon it; and there is why so many—claiming to be people and churches of God—are not really dwelling places of God at all, but only stone buildings.

Will you cry out to God continually for Him to pour His oil upon your heart and make it an unmistakable dwelling place of His Spirit? Because of His mercy to you, set apart the altar of your heart to Him and let no unclean thing be welcome there. He will fill you with His

Holy Presence and you will come to say, as well as the people around you, "How awesome is this place! This is none other than the dwelling place of God."

For Thought:

Church leaders call their churches the house of God but maintain the prerogative to tell Him when He can come and go. They dictate how long He can speak ("Keep your sermon to 20 minutes, there preacher!"). Then while He is speaking, they rudely yawn and look at their watches like people do when they really want someone to hurry it up already! Do they have the evidence to call it "God's house?"

People are slaves to their watches because they are slaves to themselves; elders are slaves to the people who are slaves to their watches who are slaves to themselves; pastors are slaves to the elders who are slaves to the people who are slaves to their watches who are slaves to themselves. Authority-despising people are leading the church . . . Madness! The tail is wagging the God.

Prayer-paration

"Blessed are the pure in heart, for they shall see God" (Matthew 5:8).

The next time you face a trial, how you respond will be affected greatly not by how you prepare for their reoccurrence, but rather by your time spent dwelling at the feet of Jesus in prayer. Unceasing prayer purifies the heart, and a purified heart responds to trials with wisdom and grace.

Our reactions to the unpleasant circumstances that life dishes out reveal the truest condition of our hearts. It is deceptive and misleading to say, "Oh! I cannot believe I reacted that way, because that is so unlike me." No, that was the *real you* alright; it was only shocking because everything had been going your way up until that point. The circumstances just caught you off your guard and pierced the real you, leaving no time to disguise it.

The other reason a man's reactions seem so unbelievable to him is because of the infrequency of his inner-person truly being pierced. Christians who are much in prayerful exposure to God are used to having His sharp two-edged Sword pierce through to the remote recesses of their heart. They will not be very surprised by their inordinate reactions to the ill-favored spurs of life. In other words, God has disillusioned them, and they come to grips with what they are like apart from Him. This produces the tremendous need to continuously be in God's presence through prayer.

We react mainly with words, and as Jesus made clear, "That which proceeds out of the man, that is what defiles the man. For from within, out of the heart of men, proceed the evil thoughts" (Mark 7:20-21). If you are in constant communication with God, dwelling in His presence through unceasing prayer you will become pure in heart. And when he has purified your heart, you will continue in this holy practice because a pure heart longs to be close to the heart of God who purifies it. That is why the formerly demon-possessed and forgiven prostitutes loved to be near Jesus. Therefore, when the tremors of life shake your tree, your reaction will be shocking only because of its Christ-like transformation. Prayer trains us for life's knockout punches; it does not plead to evade them. This is "prayer-paration."

For Thought:

Jesus said, "Apart from Me you can do nothing" (John 15:5). Is it fair to say that if I neglect prayer I am basically declaring to the Lord, "I don't need You; I can handle life and all its various trials without Your help today?"

When we pray without ceasing, we proclaim our weakness (poverty of spirit, in-action). At the same time, we proclaim His mighty power and wonderful grace to sustain us through another day, and He enables us to continue walking in a manner worthy of the calling we have received.

Day 83

Fearful and Amazed

"And He said to them, 'Where is your faith?' They were fearful and amazed, saying to one another, 'Who then is this, that He commands even the winds and the water, and they obey Him?'" (Luke 8:25)

*I*n Genesis 1:2, the Spirit of God was brooding over the waters He had created. He then performed His first display of Sovereignty and power over all His creation by dividing the waters with an expanse (vs.7). His second display was dividing the waters on the earth by making dry land to appear. Many years later, one of the most crucial times in history was at hand for God's people (stuck at the Red Sea with impending death approaching from behind). They needed a revelation of this God of their fathers, so He performed the very same display of Sovereignty over His creation by dividing the waters and making dry land to appear. This *amazing* and yet *fearful* act of God should have instilled into them a steadfast faith in an All-capable, All-powerful, and All-merciful God in the midst of any storm of life. However, it was not too long afterward they were fretting once again over their seemingly insurmountable situation. Man's insurmountable situation becomes the horse that God victoriously rides in all His glory.

Jesus had been sleeping in the storm-tossed boat so soundly that the disciples had to awaken Him. With their fear-laden words, "Master, Master, we're going to die," they were including Jesus in the word "we." That's what fear does; it not only drowns our faith, it also drowns Jesus with it. When the threatening waves of life look bigger than the Lord, the result is fear, which fails to notice that He is never worried (the Creator cannot be drowned by what He created). Jesus speaks to the waves and they submit to Him, and this is to display to us that

He is the same God who commanded the waters in the beginning, at the Red Sea, and commands them still today. In fact, He not only conquers them, He also utilizes them for His glory and His purposes for us. The disciples were undoubtedly fearful before the waves were stilled, but afterward they were "fearful *and* amazed." Their fear was transformed from the fear of death to fear of God.

For Thought:

When we see the giants of trouble, do we see the Slayer of giants?

Do we see God as the utilizer of giants—the One able to make right use of their affliction?

What about the storm of hurried living? Do not let that be the only storm He cannot calm. "Be still and know" that He is God (Psalm 46:10). Be fearful and amazed only of Him.

Day 84

Disillusioned but Not Disappointed

"Within your temple, O God, we meditate on your unfailing love" (Psalm 48:9, NIV).

The Hebrew word translated in this passage as "unfailing love," is (*hesed*), pronounced "kheh'-sed". The word's use describes the character of God in terms of intimacy and relationship; it denotes His infinite mercy and loving-kindness. God does not have a heavenly reservoir filled with mercy as the resource from which He draws it; this would imply the finite notion that it can be exhausted. No, He *is* mercy, and just as He cannot be exhausted, neither can His ability to redeem the hopeless, restore the wounded, and even resurrect the dead.

As a New Testament saint, you are a temple of God; "Do you not know that your body is a temple of the Holy Spirit who is in you" (1 Corinthians 6:19)? God's temple is not a mosque, a church building, a monastery, or a cathedral; His temple is your inner-man—your heart (mind, affections, and will). What dwells there?

With the above two points in place, are you meditating upon God's infinite mercy demonstrated in your life? What is the condition of your thought life? A person is only as pleasant as his or her thought life (or the pleasance is an act). Miserable people are miserable because their thoughts are fixed upon miserable things. Many believers are consumed with malcontent, bitterness, and un-forgiveness toward others who have wounded them. Because of this they meditate upon their own wounds, rather than Christ's wounds that rescued them from their life of sin. If they were consistently meditating upon Jesus, who *is* God's unfailing love (mercy), they would not be brooding in self-pity over how deeply others have wounded them or how unfairly life has treated them. Disappointed people become disappointing people because they meditate upon their own disappointments rather than the cross of Jesus Christ. To the disciples, Jesus' crucifixion was an outrageous disappointment at first. But three days later it would prove to be God's merciful disillusionment of their fear of death.

"Love never fails" (1 Corinthians 13:8). God, who *is* unfailing love, never disappoints, He only disillusions. Do not mistake His disillusioning you for His disappointing you. Meditate upon Jesus in your temple and be free from the imprisonment of your selfish thoughts.

For Thought:

Have you ever initially been "disappointed" only to realize later, in much humility, that it was the best thing that could have happened to you? What was it?

Have you ever been overwhelmed by such great darkness in your life, and when the light finally came it was so much sweeter to you because of the massive contrast?

Disillusioning Your Thoughts

"We are taking every thought captive to the obedience of Christ" (2 Corinthians 10:5b).

For Paul to use the terminology "taking every thought captive," implies his having thoughts needing to be taken captive. Paul would have only known this to be true through his own experience. This should bring great hope to both the infant and mature believer in Christ. Paul is telling us that he knows what it is like to have thoughts that need to be taken captive. It can be done, Paul assures us, and he tells us it is possible to continue victoriously in this spiritual discipline.

We do not take allies captive; we only take our enemies captive. A thought in need of captivity is any notion or ideal that is opposed to God and His holiness. Taking a thought captive in obedience to Christ is only a fancy sounding spiritual discipline if it is not understood.

Vengeful, prideful, and self-gratifying thoughts that produce full-blown sin are in view here. These fiery temptations often come out of thin air and are completely unintentional. They usually come in a friendly guise but are totally hostile to the Christian walk. They are geared only to disfigure the image of Jesus in us, render us incapacitated, and ruin our fellowship with Jesus. The Devil then utilizes that maimed state to create a pseudo-hell on earth, and if not repented of, to carry us to an eternal hell later. Keep in mind, the practical definition of hell is "the absence of God and the absence of hope." Hostile thoughts are chocolate-covered lumps of festering poison. They must be seen as what they really are; they must be disillusioned!

One way to do this is to imagine going back in time to Calvary and actualizing that foul thought into performance right in the presence of

Jesus hanging on the cross. Could you do it there? This forces you to see whether the thought is something that honors our Savior's death or mocks it. Jesus is the Living Water that washes the chocolate coating away and exposes the otherwise delicious looking sin as the lump of maggot-infested poison it is.

Evil thoughts and fiery temptations are not your friends or pals; they are your sworn mortal enemies, and they are set to kill you and take you to an eternal absence of Christ and hope. If you do not take them captive they will take you captive. If you do not take them captive you are basically aligning yourself as their ally. Two seconds are too long to dwell on a thought that dishonors Jesus. See it as His enemy first, and then you will see it as yours.

For Thought:

Once a sinful thought is deemed as good and pleasant it is nearly impossible to change your mind before you give over to it.

Day 86

The Source of Life, Not its Decoration

"And as Jesus returned, the people welcomed Him, for they had all been waiting for Him" (Luke 8:40).

Jesus had just returned from a brief tenure of ministry in the Gadarenes on the other side of the Sea of Tiberius, directly across from Galilee. While He was there He had cast out a "Legion" of demons from a man. Jesus had barely placed one step out of the boat upon the shore before the demoniac came rushing to meet Him. Similarly, upon His return back to Galilee, He was blitzed with a tide of eagerly waiting people. However, other Scriptures reveal to us that just like most of the people, they were only eager for the benefits of His miracles, not Him personally. Most of these same people would be yelling "Crucify Him" later on! They wanted what Jesus could *do for* them but not what He could *become to* them. Many waited *for* Him, but very few waited *on* Him. They wanted His benefits but not His employment, because it is a crucified life of service, persecution, suffering, and devotion.

The crowd welcomed Jesus because they were expecting Him to do something. Desiring His assistance rather than His presence, they warmly welcomed Him. People are always quite welcoming of someone they are eagerly expecting, especially when they believe there will be personal benefit from the visit. They will wait patiently and even go through grueling measures for the beneficial payoff.

Equally today, there are many who welcome Jesus because they are waiting for Him to do something for them. The problem with this is not so much the selfishness of the attitude (we all come to Jesus selfishly at first). No, the problem is they miss that He has already done everything for them through His finished work. Anything beyond that is merely a bonus. He is the Source of life, not a decoration for it!

Are you waiting for Jesus for what He can do for you, or are you "waiting on" Him (serving Him like a waiter) because of what He has already done? Do you welcome Him for fellowship and intimacy, or only for assistance and blessing? When is the last time you warmly welcomed someone who showed up when you were not expecting it or least desired it? Jesus often comes to His people in this manner, in order to distinguish His faithful ones and bring the backslidden to repentance and reformation.

For Thought:

If God were never to give you another "blessing," would you still worship Him?

God knows our prideful defenses and arranges surprise visits to catch us off our guard. Those that love to be transformed welcome these surprise visits. Those who love themselves hate them. This is why so many churches and believers are terrified of true revival; when God shows up in revival reformation, He comes to make a mess of all they love to keep so neat.

Day 87

The Agoraphobic Hoarder

"I pray that the eyes of your heart may be enlightened" (Ephesians 1:18).

The enemy of sin within us as Christians desperately demands our understanding. The problem is that sin is deceptive (Hebrews 3:13) and the heart is just as deceitful (Jeremiah 17:9); we need an outside Source to reveal to us the reality we otherwise would never see.

Here is an analogy to illustrate: There was an agoraphobic man who never left his house. He was also a hoarder that never cleaned his house, both for 20 years. He lost sense of what his house looked like on the outside as well as on the inside. As far as he knew, the outside was still as maintained as it was twenty years ago. Only an outside visitor coming in has the ability to reveal the realities of both the outside and inside of the house. Through progressive desensitization, the agoraphobic hoarder had adapted to the repulsive conditions of the interior; and because of his solitary lifestyle, lost all concept of the exterior condition as well.

Bring that man out of his house for an hour so he can see it from the outside and he will be devastated by the reality of its appearance. Simultaneously, the man will breathe in the fresh clean air for that hour, and then when he goes back inside he will be even more devastated by the stark contrast. This will reveal to him the revolting reality of its inner condition.

Your enemy's desire is to assimilate you, through repetitive exposure to sin, into his kingdom. The more you are exposed to the filth of sin without being mortified by it, the more you will adapt to it. Self-deception then develops and will require the intervention of someone from the outside.

Have you ever allowed Jesus to pull you out of yourself and reveal to you the true conditions of your life the way He sees them, both inside and out? If you have then you have truly had the eyes of your heart enlightened, thereby exposing your desperate need for Him. If ever your neediness for Him is decreasing then so is your enlightenment. The longer you walk with the Lord the more holy you see Him. The holier He becomes to you, the more you see the vast difference between Him and you. It may even seem like you are growing apart. Nevertheless, the result should be the increase of your longing for His presence. Devote yourself fully to Jesus and you will breathe in the refreshing Breath of His Holy Spirit.

For Thought:

Read Hebrews 2:1-3. The longer you walk with Jesus, the more you need Him. Why is this true?

It is quite popular and prevalent in Christian thinking today that the longer a person has been a believer the less time they need to spend in His presence. Why is this absurd, and even dangerous?

Day 88

Timely Words are Tidy Words

"The Lord GOD has given me the tongue of disciples, that I may know how to sustain the weary one with a word... He awakens my ear to listen as a disciple" (Isaiah 50:4).

Many Christians are plagued with the annoying habit of always "having a word" to give someone else, but very few have grown up into the spiritual maturity that they only speak a word "in season"—the right word at the right time in the right spirit for the right reason. In the Old Testament, wise Solomon writes, "A man has joy in an apt answer, and how delightful is a timely word" (Proverbs 15:23, NAS). In the New Testament, Paul also exhorts us, "But speaking the truth in love, we are to grow up in all aspects into Him who is the head, even Christ" (Ephesians 4:15, NIV).

Many possess the attitude in which they believe their own opinion is the best, and so they inscribe it upon their own stony heart as if it were the Gospel. If we were speaking the Truth in the maturity of Christian love we would not be espousing our own opinions, convinced ourselves of their weighty importance. Unfortunately, spiritually immature Christians are very much some of the most opinionated people on the planet, and they comprise the larger portion of Christianity.

> *"But know this first of all, no prophecy of Scripture is a matter of one's own interpretation, for no prophecy was ever made by an act of human will, but men moved by the Holy Spirit spoke from God"* (2 Peter 1:21).

You cannot disciple others unless you are a disciple! Isaiah was able to have the anointing of the disciple's tongue because he had long listened to and followed the voice of God as a disciple. His words were pure because his heart was pure. "For the mouth speaks out of that which fills the heart" (Matthew 12:34).

A great ruler of men is the one who is greatly ruled by God. The same applies to speaking—you cannot speak authoritatively into the lives of others if God's Word has not ruled authoritatively in your own life. With a voice comes the necessity of its qualification. There are those who speak out of spiritually qualified necessity, and then there are those who speak because they "feel" the necessity. It takes Christian maturity to discern between the two. We must strive for the former.

For Thought:

Some believers cannot even handle one revelation from God without broadcasting it to everyone. Consumed with pride and desire for attention, they expose everything God wanted to take root in their own lives. They become devoid of any "hidden life" with Christ.

Day 89

Don't Remember what God Forgets

"I, even I, am the one who wipes out your transgressions for My own sake, And I will not remember your sins" (Isaiah 43:25).

What love is this that blots out our sin like an absorbent sponge, taking into itself the filthy mess of our rebellion so we can have our garments made white? What fathomless mercy dwells in the fountain filled with the precious blood of Jesus? What joy floods the sinner's heart whose sin is remembered not one second past Calvary?

Who are we to remember and keep on remembering the injuries received by another person, whether small or large? "Love . . . thinks not the evil" done to it (1 Corinthians 13:5). In other words, saints possessing the love of God do not long consider the sins committed against them. The world calls that "holding a grudge," but the Lord would call it a criminal insult to Calvary. As abominable as this plague of the heart is—keeping a record of another's sins—there is another that is an even greater spiritual crime: It is one thing to internally remember the evil others commit, but quite another to remind them of it.

Satan is the accuser of the brethren (see Revelation 12:10), and since he can no longer bring our sins before God, he vigorously brings them before us. Praise the Lord that God just points to the cross and declares us righteous, speaking with silence, "Not guilty!" However, if you remind someone of their past sins, you are acting on the behalf of Satan.

If you are struggling with a critical spirit, stop calling it by its worldly euphemism. It is not "holding a grudge!" As long as it continues to be obscured by this weak and foolish language, you will never be free of it because you refuse to agree with the devilishness of it. See it for the spiritual crime that it is, confess it before God, forsake it, replace it with mercy, and enjoy the liberating fruit of true repentance.

Sin was paid in full at the cross of Christ so it could be remembered no longer. You must take every evil committed (by you or against you), drop it in the rushing river of Jesus' blood, and watch it disappear forever. All sin is ultimately against God. Therefore, if you make it only about yourself being offended, you make yourself the judge over God and belittle the cross. Only Jesus has the power and authority to forgive sin. Agree with His judgment for sin at the cross rather than your own, and you will free yourself by freeing others. Once a particular sin is washed in the blood, never again remember what God forgets.

For Thought:

Read Matthew 18:23-35. In this parable of the unmerciful servant, Jesus proclaims un-forgiveness is an un-forgivable sin. True or False?

Day 90

Give it All or Keep it All

"For they all put in out of their surplus, but she, out of her poverty, put in all she owned, all she had to live on" (Mark 12:44).

*J*esus had just watched a poor widow drop her only two mites into the Temple treasury while others were putting in large sums out of their abundance. A mite was a Flemish coin made of copper with the lowest face value (very similar to the U.S. penny). The Lord missed no opportunity to use ordinary events of life to teach His disciples, and this one would bring with it profound spiritual truth, both for them and for us.

Many preachers have used this passage (quite mistakenly) to encourage poorer members to not forsake giving their offerings due to feelings of shame or inadequacy. However, with a more spiritually in-tune analysis, we should come to find this is not the lesson Jesus wanted to teach at all.

Let us say that there are two women and both have all the money they own in their pocket—one has two million dollars, the other has two mites. Jesus gives a command to give all they have in their pocket. For which one is it most difficult to obey? The obvious answer is the one with two million dollars. Because the contents in her pocket are so extremely valuable to her, she clenches it with a mighty grip. Therefore, it possesses an equally strong grip upon her and she cannot bring herself to give it all. She even goes so far to justify herself by saying, "Well, it was easy for that other woman to obey, because all she had were those worthless two mites." Jesus would say, "Exactly!"

Somewhere else Jesus exclaimed, "Whoever wishes to save his life will lose it, but whoever loses his life for My sake and the gospel's will save it" (Mark 8:35). The Lord does not desire our money; He desires our heart. And He came to repair it with His mercy to enable us to give it back in response. The reason we hold some back from Him is because we put such great value on our offering. If we would see what Jesus was trying to teach His disciples—that our offering is just a penny in the basket—we would more easily give it all without a shred of reservation. See His devotion to you first, and you will make the all-or-nothing decision of devotion. Pray this prayer: "Lord, I am the offering You desire; I give myself to You as all I have, even though it is just a penny in the basket."

For Thought:

"Self-love makes a person so consumed with personal comfort that he is unwilling to give himself away to others." [13]—Glenn Meldrum

"Everything of yourself, of your own life, must go if you are to be an intercessor. But you cannot give your life for others if it still belongs to you."[14]—Rees Howells

Day 91

God Counts it as "Done"

"They confronted me in the day of my calamity, but the LORD was my support" (2 Samuel 22:19).

If the Bride of Christ could choose any affliction, she would select everything else before enduring the pain of being a broken-down instrument, unserviceable to God. It is this devoted servant who values her life only by the opportunities she has to glorify her master. Christ Jesus has truly become her life so she gives away the mercy she has so freely received—without condition, coercion, or anything in return.

When afflicted to the point of disability, she considers it a deep sorrow that God is no longer using her the way He once did. However, she is not sorry that God's work will go on with or without her. She knows He can perform His will without using any creature for His instrument, but deep inside her there is a struggle. The very thing she had viewed as her life's value—serving God through her anointed devotion—has become debilitated through the physical limitations of the affliction.

The heart of the Bride aches with sorrow to be taken from any work where she might glorify her Husband. Yet she has this unique and unalterable truth, which no thief could ever "break in and steal": When the saint sincerely desires to serve the Lord whole-heartedly, but is unable through the limitation of affliction, God counts it as done! Now she is free to sail the uncharted waters of new service to God. Upon these new horizons rests a sweeter communion; a new, deeper fellowship awaits her, and a new unveiling of the radiant glory of God will shine in her heart. She is free because she is assured of the pleasure of her Master. No longer is she bound by those former struggles within. Though she may be bound in body, she is free in her spirit. She comes to know that whenever God counts one thing done in her life, there is a new thing He is ready for her to do, attached with a fresh revelation of who He is. Bed-ridden-saints are in a perfect position to become sin-ridding *suppliants. They become this or else they become grief-stricken grumblers. If you are going through the desert of debilitating affliction, utilize the opportunity to draw near your Savior by imitating Him. He prayed for you while He was immobilized on the cross; you can also begin your new full-time ministry of intercessory prayer for others with joy and divine purpose. Will you? The next time you are down, remember no one or no thing can keep you from praying for others. You will be lifted up and out of yourself, and into a higher realm of purpose.

For Thought:

("Suppliant" is a person making a humble plea to God on the behalf of another.) It has been said that God uses His people on their feet, but teaches them on their back.

Day 92

Others-Supplying is Self-Denying

"If anyone wishes to come after Me, he must deny himself and take up his cross and follow Me" (Matthew 16:24).

Self-denying saints are those who supply Jesus to others. It is the lifestyle that is diametrically opposed to the old life of loving self. Paul told Timothy this old life is the cause of all the difficulties and problems in the church; "In the last days difficult times will come, for people will be lovers of themselves" (2 Timothy 3:1-2). Notice Paul named the source of all the problems first, for every evil trait that follows stems from the love of self. For instance, lovers of money love themselves; boastful, proud, arrogant people love themselves; lovers of pleasure love themselves rather than God, etc. Self-loving people are those who follow hard after self, not Jesus.

The problems teachers have with addressing self-denial are their perception and approach. They perceive that self-denial is merely abstinence from vices, pleasures, or comforts. Their approach is just saying "No" to self. This only leads to legalism and self-ascetic lifestyles. Paul rebukes these errors in Colossians; "These rules may seem wise because they require strong devotion, pious self-denial, and severe bodily discipline. But they provide no help in conquering a person's evil desires" (2:23, NLT). The delinquency with saying no to self is that it does not necessarily mean you are saying yes to Jesus or to the needs of others.

Pouring yourself out for the needs, hurts, and problems of others makes it impossible to cater to self. You cannot do both at the same time. Others-supplying is self-denying. Jesus said, "Whatever you did for one of the least of these, you did for Me" (Matthew 25:40). Five verses later He gave us the sobering reverse side, "Whatever you did not do for one of the least of these, you did not do for Me." Paraphrased, if we deny mercy to others, we not only love ourselves; we deny Jesus!

In Mark 14:31, Peter emphatically said he would never deny Jesus. But when the time came for being identified with the cross of Jesus Christ, he denied the Lord to preserve himself. Self-love and self-preservation are the same, and they will always deny the Lord. A self-denying saint takes up his or her cross by bearing the burdens of others for the sake of supplying Jesus to them. True love comes down vertically from God to us; only then can we give that love horizontally (man-to-man). If you practice love to others without first receiving it from God through Christ, you are only drawing from your own "I am a good person" reservoirs. The worst thing that could happen to you is to think you are a good person and have much to give apart from Jesus. Get it from Jesus then give it to others.

For Thought:

Read 1 Corinthians 13:1-8. How loving are you?

Day 93

I'm Still the Chief!

"Christ Jesus came into the world to save sinners, among whom I am chief of all" (1 Timothy 1:15).

Paul never lost sight of the ruinous life from which he was saved. He did not say that he "used to be" the chief of all sinners; he said, "I am chief." This resonates with David's statement in his Psalm, "For I acknowledge my transgressions: and my sin is ever before me" (51:3). Paul's remembrance of the exceeding sinfulness of his past continually brought with it abundant humility. But it was not just this fact that repeatedly humbled Paul for the rest of his days; it was the fact that these deep scarlet sins had been made white by the precious blood of Jesus—the One he had railed against with such great pride and persecution. He had received perfect love and forgiveness from the One he had persecuted and that never ceased to melt his heart. Jesus made it clear that a person who is forgiven much will love much, and a person who has been forgiven little will love little (see Luke 7:47).

A humble man never sees anything but his own pride; a proud man never says anything of his pride. A humbled man does not spotlight the weighty sins of others because the weight of his own sin is so great. His humility increases ten-fold with the revelation of his unmerited pardon and the price paid for it. In pride, a man turns the spotlight away from himself onto the "lofty" sins of others. His pride never stops increasing because he cannot see (or will not see) how much he has been forgiven.

The most loving, compassionate, and patient people on earth are those who have seen and acknowledged the enormity of their sin, its pardon, and its cost (Calvary). If you are struggling with un-forgiveness and resentment, and are lacking in godly love toward someone, drop to your knees at once, confess your pride, and plead God's mercy; you have fallen victim to one of the fiercest enemies of your soul—the sin of self-deception. The worst thing that could happen to you is to see yourself as a "pretty good person" apart from the Lord and without a devotional life to Him.

For Thought:

Write out (Psalm 32:5).

Write out (1 John 1:9).

Read 2 Peter 1:5-9. Christians can be very prone to forget their own mercies. This is one reason why partaking of the Lord's Supper is so important, and why we should do it often as Jesus said. There are some who say doing it too often makes it trite. Well then, they had better not pray too much either. Do not throw out the baby with the bathwater. The triteness is not in the ordinance, but in the heart.

Day 94

Falling is Rising

"They will say of me, 'Only in the LORD are righteousness and strength'" (Isaiah 45:24).

The biblical principle of behavior replacement is a dynamic fundamental that is scarcely taught these days. However, it is the most powerful teaching around when it comes to being set free from life-dominating sins. Replacing the old unrighteous behavior with new righteous behavior is the thrust of this victorious fundamental. The Apostle Paul called it "Put off . . . and put on" (see Ephesians 4:22-24, Colossians 3:9-10). When Christians get trapped in a cyclic sinful behavior pattern, many are too apt to believe the lie that they cannot escape from its clutches. And those that do not fall for that lie generally think the way of victory is to just stop the old unrighteous behavior.

The problem with this thinking ("putting-off" only) is that ceasing sinful behavior does not necessarily glorify the Lord. It is only godly behavior that glorifies God. Even unbelievers can stop an unrighteous behavior, but they cannot glorify the Lord because that requires believing and obeying God's Word (this is impossible for them because of their unbelief).

Just like it is impossible to breathe in and breathe out simultaneously, it is also impossible to behave righteously and sinfully at the same time. Many believers attempt to rise out of deep sin by just quitting the sin, rather than replacing the sinful behavior with godly behaviors. Since sin is a devotion to self, quitting sinful behavior does not get to the root. Only devotion to another person will kill the root of the problem. In other words, if I am truly devoted to Jesus, I will not be devoted to myself. Therefore, not only will I not be sinning, I will also be glorifying God.

Falling deeply in love with Jesus *is* rising out of deep sin. The depth of your deliverance will be equal to the depth of your devotion to Jesus. Devote yourself entirely to Him; hate what He hates and love what He loves. Daily fall before Him in worship for the life He poured out so you could rise from death. He will become the Love of your life, not just the One who decorates and blesses it. Then, like people said of Isaiah, they will also say of you: "Only in the LORD are righteousness and strength." You will know deliverance by true experience, and He will have all the glory!

For Thought:

There are many people who set out to stop unrighteous behaviors because of their troublesome effects. If they succeed without devotion to God's Word, they may be happy in this life, but quite likely miserable in the next; they would have accomplished "victory" without a relationship with Christ—a tragic victory indeed.

It has been said, "If we have Jesus, we have it all." Do you concur? Is your life proving it?

The Weight of Guilt (Part 1)

Read (Hebrews 10:22) and (Romans 5:1-2).

People who live in a state of guilt because of unrepentant sin are very vulnerable and overly sensitive. They are intensely self-conscious, for what is a person in habitual sin but conscious mainly of self? But remember, un-forgiven sin is only un-repented and un-confessed sin. Any guilt after confession and true repentance is nothing more than self-condemnation, which is just another way self-devotion is manifested.

A man once said, "I know Jesus forgives me, but I just cannot forgive myself!" The reply to him was, "We don't have the power or the authority to forgive ourselves. If we could, then Jesus' death on the cross was unnecessary. We must only receive by faith the forgiveness that His agonizing death purchased; anything else is sheer unbelief or devilish pride." Guilty people are either unrepentant, or self-condemning; both are the result of refusing to agree with God's Word. It was the pride of the Pharisees that caused them to reject Christ, and just like them, the un-forgiven man is his own judge. He does not have the humility to receive God's costly forgiveness. God hates pride and unbelief because they keep us from receiving His love. They cause us to reject the mercy that cost Him so high a price, His only Son.

The word *guilt* has been used out of context for so long that its true definition has become lost in obscurity. Guilt is not a subjective feeling; it is an objective fact—"guilty or not guilty!" If you are struggling with guilt, the question is not whether you are guilty or not; you are guilty, just like everyone else. The key is discovering why you still feel the weight of your guilt after confession and repentance. The reason? You continue to be your own judge. Your self-judged *feelings* have trumped the one Supreme Judge who declared you "Not guilty" through His death on the cross (see Romans 5:1 and Hebrews 10:22).

For the guilt-ridden believer: You have exalted your judgment above God. Your "feelings" of guilt are drowning the faith that would give you instant relief—the faith that Jesus Christ paid in full the wages of your sin to declare you "Not guilty." Therefore, continued guilt is faithlessness (unbelief). Realize that since birth our behavior has been dictated by our feelings, and that guilt is just another way our feelings-dictated living robs us of our promised joy in the Lord. Put off your feelings of guilt and put on faith in the finished work of Christ. Your heart will then be lifted, resulting in wonderful feelings of weightlessness and overwhelming joy. Godly behavior (faith in Jesus' finished work) produces godly feelings. Be free!

For Thought:

In light of the cross, continued un-forgiveness and guilt are only unbelief and selfish pride.

Day 96

The Weight of Guilt (Part 2)

Read (Hebrews 10:22) and (Romans 5:1-2).

Try this experiment: Hold your arms straight down at your sides like a soldier. Have someone come behind you and pin your arms to your sides as hard as they can, while you try hard to raise them outward. Do this for thirty seconds to a minute. Then have the person let go. You should notice that your arms go flying uncontrollably outward like they are floating.

Like the experiment above, once the weighty pressure of guilt is removed through faith in Christ's finished work on the cross, the Christian should feel a sense of weightlessness (freedom). I like to define grace as such: "Freed from the law, yet bound in awe." The freed Christian lives a life bound in awe-inspired worship of the Lord that rescued him. Guilt in any sense is a heavy load to carry, and the more sinful behavior a man continues to practice, the heavier his burden is. The weight presses down (depression) upon his conscience incessantly. Below is an illustration:

There was a lady who accidentally stumbled upon a magical can of invisible spray. She conspires within herself to take her new discovery and go to the local Mall. Then, when no one is watching, she begins to spray whatever she likes. She cannot load the invisible items into a cart because she wants absolutely no suspicious behavior (imagine someone struggling to push an empty cart out of the Mall). So she decides she must carry by hand whatever she sprays if the plan is to succeed.

Her greed quickly progressed from tamed to unrestrained as she began to spray her desired items. Though invisible, the weight of each sprayed item was real. With each additional item came its additional burden while she loaded herself down to full capacity. Satisfied, she confidently, yet with great difficulty, proceeded toward the exit. Seemingly home free, she approached the doors, only to be stopped by a security guard, one with the gift of an acutely discerning eye. "What are you carrying?" he demanded. She replied, "Nothing! As you can see, sir!" The guard retorted, "Miss, you can make fun of my uniform, and even belittle my job, but you may *never* insult my discernment. For though you are right that I cannot see what you are carrying, I can certainly see its weight upon your back, and the sweat upon your face."

For Thought:

God could tell that Cain was carrying the weight of guilt. Are you carrying anything that although people cannot see it they can see its weight upon your conscience? Jesus paid too high a price for you to suffer under its heaviness one moment longer. Lighten up today at the feet of Jesus.

Day 97

The Weight of Guilt (Part 3)

Read (Hebrews 10:22) and (Romans 5:1-2).

Guilt of any form may itself remain unseen, but the effects of its weight will always give it away. Un-forgiven sins, whether they are because of un-repentance or self-condemnation are indeed the invisible items in yesterday's (Day 96) illustration. What if the lady had sprayed a grand piano and was carrying that upon her back? We might not be able to guess for certain it is a piano, but we would definitely know she's carrying something heavy. Every unresolved issue of the heart will eventually become visible by the outward behaviors.

Much like the security guard, the Holy Spirit says, "Stop! Put down what you are carrying!" If you say to Him and the world, "I'm not carrying anything," you are not in "denial;" you are in rebellion. You know the things you are carrying, and only want to get away with them unseen and uncontested. Whether you love them or hate them is irrelevant. More often than not, there is usually one sin with which the Christian is infatuated, but the weight of its guilt has not grown heavy enough to crush his or her lust affair with it. Apart from true repentance, sin issues are never dead, and what is not dead grows. Inevitably the believer will either be crushed by the weight of guilt or must drop the entire load—every last invisible item!

As we have seen, a man carrying guilt remains guilty because of unbelief and the pride of his own self-judgment. Being his own judge, he sentences himself to a life of standing guilty in the courtroom after the true Judge pardoned his sentence. Not until he agrees with God's Word will he receive his relief. He must agree that because of Christ's atoning death he has "been declared righteous by faith," and "therefore has peace with God" (Romans 5:1). Then and only then is his "heart sprinkled clean from an evil conscience" (see Hebrews 10:22). The same way we confess our guilt before God is the same way we confess our innocence—by the Standard of God's Word.

For Thought:

Music is constantly being transmitted through radio waves; it is up to you to raise your antenna and tune-in if you want the pleasure of listening. Forgiveness is Christ's transmission; faith is tuning in to receive.

What would happen if you began the first minutes of each day thanking God for declaring you "not guilty" by the precious blood of His Son Jesus? Could you worship Him because of it for the rest of the day?

Day 98

The Weight of Guilt (Part 4)

Read (Hebrews 10:22) and (Romans 5:1-2).

We are declared righteous when we agree with God's Word through faith. We must approach it this way: "You said so Lord, therefore it is true." In other words, whether the Holy Spirit tells us that we are unrighteous and in need of repentance, or declared righteous by faith, we must simply agree (homologéō). This is the form of the word *confess* in (1 John 1:9)—it means "to voice the same conclusion because in full agreement." We see a slightly different form of the word in (James 5:16): "*Confess* (exomologéō) your sins one to another." It basically means the same thing: "To fully agree," but with an added "publicly, without reservation." This is where we get the phrase, "Making the great confession." *Confess* means either agreeing with what God says about you, or agreeing with what God says about Himself, as revealed by His Word.

The reason people cannot or will not agree with God is because they are in agreement with themselves. Lust, greed, anger, slander, gossip, profanity, revelry, hate, bitterness, resentment, malice, etc.—all these are merely exhibitions of self-agreement. Since they have created their own standard apart from God, they continue to live by that self-made standard.

Here are some fundamental ways a guilty man will act out: He will have repetitive outbursts of anger. He will tend to wallow in self-pity. He will be chronically depressed. He will take otherwise harmless intentions as personal attacks. He will believe and even say that a sermon was personally designed and catered to assault him. He will object to some incidental feature of a sermon or take offense to its deemed harshness. He will become overly critical and look for any blunder in every message or messenger just to justify his unwillingness to concede to its truth.

On the other hand, if you have put your heart in agreement with God's Word, you are at peace with God. You walk uprightly and not slumped over by the invisible load of guilt. You are weightless and free, and the joy that these godly feelings bring you drives you to honor and love the One who accomplished it. You are therefore filled with love that "seeks not its own," and "does not get offended" (see 1 Corinthians 13). You realize that in comparison, the weight of your own guilt outweighed the guilt of the entire world. You are now not only able to carry others' burdens; you are joyful and willing to do so. The cumbersome weight of guilt has truly been lifted and you are free! "Thus says the LORD of Hosts!"

For Thought:

Is it possible that the weight of guilt caused by unbelief, pride, and unrepentant sin is keeping the hands and feet of much of the church shackled?

Day 99

Compassion Versus Pity

"Moved with compassion, Jesus touched their eyes; and immediately they regained their sight and followed Him" (Matthew 20:34).

One day I saw a man struggling to get into his wheelchair. I approached him to see if I could help. I saw his plight and felt pity for him and asked if I could assist. He responded quite sharply, "Don't need it!" I then asked him if I could pray for him, to which he replied even more heatedly, "No! I've been doing this just fine on my own for nine years and I am sick of people looking down upon me with their pity! They see me, feel sorry for me, and then want to help me just so they can walk away feeling good about themselves for fulfilling their obligation to the less fortunate!" He continued, "I've found they really are not concerned about me at all; 'helping me' is just their drug. And the last thing I want is for someone to pray *for* me."

I realized he had a point. I wondered how many people would ask if they could help him or pray for him if he were never in that wheelchair. Then I thought about how insignificant he must feel with me (and the rest of the world) towering over him. And then I understood. There is a vast difference between pity and compassion. Pity sorrowfully looks down upon another to pull them up to itself; compassion joyfully gets beneath another to lift them up above itself.

I then slowly got down upon my knees in front of his wheelchair—to get lower than him so *he* could look down upon *me*—and asked if I could pray *with* Him. With tears welling up in his eyes he asked, "Do you know how long it's been since someone asked if they could pray *with* me?" Before I could answer he answered for me, "Never!" He then apologized for his attitude and said with a fresh gentle kindness in his voice, "Pray on, brother!"

Jesus was not given over to the worldly counterfeit of pity; He was pure compassion, and He knew how to minister to afflicted and hurting people—on His knees to wash their feet. He humbled Himself to the lowest point of death on a cross so we could be lifted up and healed of our sinful blindness. This is what moved us to follow Him and He said for us to do the same (Philippians 2:5). Pity is prideful but compassion is costly; choose. Pity stultifies (belittles); compassion identifies.

For Thought:

Read Luke 19:9-14. I saw a man bitterly weeping under great conviction at the altar. Suddenly a woman approached and chided the man saying, "Oh brother, I hate to see you like that, you need to get up here with me and put a smile on your face." She could have prayed *for* him, but could never have prayed *with* him. She'd never been where he was (broken over sin) and therefore could not identify herself with him.

Day 100

Lifted by Love into Holiness

"Can't you see that his kindness is intended to turn you from your sin?" (Romans 2:4, NLT).

The fear of missing heaven is not strong enough to keep a man from returning to his sin; only the joy of already possessing heaven through Jesus' lifting love has the power to do that. Many Christians set out through improper motivations to live holy lives and fail because they are typically fear-based or performance-based. Andrew Murray writes,

> "Many set upon the practice of holiness with a fervent zeal, and run very fast, but tread not a step in the right way; and finding themselves frequently disappointed and overcome by their lusts, they at last give over the work." [15]—Andrew Murray

We must be persuaded of our peace with God (Romans 5:1), persuaded of the promised enjoyment of our heavenly inheritance (Romans 8:17), and persuaded of God's provided strength, "both to will and to work for His good pleasure" (Philippians 2:13). In his first Epistle, John informs us of a powerful truth: That we *are* strong because the word of God lives in us, and we *have* overcome the evil one. Therefore, we are empowered to refrain from loving the world and all its vanities (2:14-15). We should not want to resist unrighteousness merely because it is wrong, we should want to resist it because resisting it is right.

Mortifying sin means putting to death sinful behaviors and attitudes (Romans 8:14). Mortifying sin just because it is wearisome to us is futile and unsuccessful because there is no love in it. We must hate sin 1) because it cost the excruciating death of Jesus who first loved us, and 2) because it separates us from intimacy with Him. This is the correct entrance into holy living. We mortify sin by loving our Lord just like we mortify Jesus by loving sin. It is godly love that lifts us into the action of holiness and the mortification of our sins.

"I was sinking deep in sin far from the peaceful shore. Very deeply stained within, sinking to rise no more. But the Master of the sea heard my despairing cry. From the waters lifted me, now safe am I. Love lifted me." [16]—James Rowe

For Thought:

Have you been lifted by love into holiness, or motivated by fear?

Read Luke 7: 36-48. When the prostitute came to Jesus she needed the one thing that could liberate her from her sinful lifestyle—forgiveness of sins. Caring not about what anyone thought of her, she radically came to Jesus, disrupting the whole event. The three Jewish customs for welcoming someone into your house, those that Simon purposely neglected to do for Jesus, she did. Jesus did not tell her to go mortify her sins, quit being a prostitute, or go make sacrifices. He forgave her sins. And because she had been forgiven much, she loved much, without needing to be coerced.

Day 101

The Dirtiest Becomes the Cleanest

"These are the ones who come out of the great tribulation, and they have washed their robes and made them white in the blood of the Lamb" (Revelation 7:14).

Knowing that I enjoy fresh cherries, my wife had purchased some for me and I was down to the last few. While cleaning the kitchen, I had just swept the floor into a dirt pile that had not yet been gathered into the dustpan. Looking at those last few cherries, I decided to eat them while cleaning but I dropped one of them right into that filthy dirt pile on the floor. Not willing to waste that dirty cherry, I took it over to the sink, ran it under the water, and spent some time scrubbing it clean. As I brought it back over to rejoin the others I noticed that because of the special attention and care I rendered that formerly dirty cherry, it made the rest look dirty. They all looked acceptable before, but now that was not the case.

I thought about the possibility of all the other cherries condemning, mocking, and scoffing that cherry because it fell into the dirt and became filthy. But now this cherry had become the cleanest of the bunch. I then hoped that this cherry would be like Joseph in the Old Testament, and not use its exaltation as means to look down upon the others and retaliate. Because the truth is, many times the dirtiest cherry becomes the cleanest cherry in the end.

There are many Christians who fall into the foul cesspools of filth and sin and experience the greatness of the tribulation it brings. Sadly, there are even more "Christians" that are ready to condemn them as filthy, and like the Jews of the New Testament, see the leper and cry, "Unclean!" Like the cherries that never fell into the filthy pile, we can easily look around and deem ourselves acceptable, and by doing so become blind to our own need for being cleansed "by the washing with water through the word" (Ephesians 5:25).

The next time you see a Christian fall into the filthy pile of sin, be careful. It is very likely they will spend much time underneath the Living Water of Jesus being fervently scrubbed by Him. Then when they return in all their Christ-made whiteness, they will be a reproach to you and your status quo.

For Thought:

For decades a lady prayed for her husband's salvation. One Sunday morning the man was powerfully moved to repentance and gave his life to the Lord. God moved on his heart to leave everything and go to Seminary to become a preacher. His wife divorced him. Her reasoning was, "I wanted him saved, but not *that* saved!"

Day 102

Two Steps Too Far!

"The fear of the LORD is clean, enduring forever" (Psalm 19:9).

Considering a list of biblical principles that have been botched to the point of effecting damage upon the believer's view of God, among the top five would be "Fear of the Lord." Particularly, when only continuously preached in the context of wrath and judgment, this topic does great damage to the hearer. The fear of the Lord is a wonderful thing, not a wrathful thing.

There was a father who took his young son out to the fair. To the boy, it was loud, unfamiliar, and foreboding. At the fair, the father ran into a preacher friend of his, who asked to be introduced to his little son. The preacher noticed how sheepishly the boy was hiding behind and tightly clinging to his father's leg. The preacher had a spiritual epiphany right there. He understood something about the fear of the Lord that he had never seen. To the little child, the fair was the entire world in all its unfamiliarity, boisterousness, and dangers. The little boy knew the possibility that any space between him and his father would be space for someone or something to wedge them apart. He *lived* his belief that "two steps from my father are too far." Therefore, he clung to his father as if there was no tomorrow. Attached to his father he was protected, provided for, and at peace. The boy was surely apprehensive of his father's discipline, but it was his father's love that motivated him to good behavior, not his wrath. The boy was not fearful *of* his father; he was fearful of being *apart from* him. The child feared separation from his father, not condemnation.

The above illustration should prove helpful toward understanding the fear of the Lord in the proper way. This is why Jesus exhorted us to remain attached to Him (John 15:1-8). The following is a miniature systematic theology based on the Proverb, "The fear of the Lord is the beginning of wisdom" (9:10):

Fear of destruction leads to fear of disobedience; Fear of disobedience leads to delight of obedience; Delight of obedience leads to fear of separation; Fear of separation leads to oneness in relation; Oneness in relation leads to the joy of perfect love; Perfect love casts out all fear which leads to pure worship. This is the fear of the Lord in maturity.

For Thought:

Those who rightly fear God cling to Him joyfully with all their might. This baffles the humanistic mindset that says to flee from things you fear.

Read 1 Corinthians 3:19. Do you understand more about the foolishness of the world or the wisdom of God?

Day 103

Just Keep Walking!

"Even though I walk through the valley of the shadow of death, I fear no evil, for You are with me" (Psalm 23:4).

Take a walk outside on a sunny afternoon and you will see your own shadow attached to your feet. Your first thought may be that you are the cause of the silhouetted darkness you see. Now, if I happened to say, "I'm weary of standing in that person's shadow," most would take that to mean that I am weary of not being seen or noticed for my accomplishments. Rational people are not fearful of their own shadow because they are casting it, but what about the large ones that do not belong to them? What about walking in the shadow of a mountainous trial? The truth is that people are not really weary of walking in a shadow because they cannot be seen, but rather because they cannot see. Shadow is darkness, which requires the spiritual discipline of walking by faith, not by sight (2 Corinthians 5:7).

When walking in the shadow of mountainous trials, we are inclined to notice the fearful darkness and its enormous cause. Everything is a black shadow on this side of the menacing mountain. Though the mountain may be a big culprit for the shadow you see, it is not the *only* source of it. There can be no shadow without light! Therefore, the shadow proves there is light on the other side. Although you may not be able to see the light because of the shadow that your monstrous trial is casting, you know there is light on the other side. Therefore you, like David in this Psalm, must keep walking.

Death casts the blackest shadow on earth, but it cannot do so without light. In the book of Revelation, Death comes riding on his pale horse with Hades following close behind. However, both were *given* limited power (6:8). Jesus is greater than the shadow of death, and He is the

Light of the world. Trials or death may be mountains casting long shadows, but for the blood-purchased saint, there is Light on the other side. The same Jesus that bought you is forever with you (Hebrews 7:25). Just keep walking, and one day you will also echo the words of the Prophet Hosea and the Apostle Paul, "O death, where is your victory? O death, where is your sting?"—(see Hosea 13:14 and 1 Corinthians 15:5)

For Thought:

Read 1 Peter 5:8. To what does it liken our adversary the devil?

Did you know that one reason a lion roars is to get all possible prey within earshot to stop in their tracks? They hunker down in fear because they cannot tell from what direction the lion's roar is coming. The lion now has near perfect opportunity to catch, pounce, and devour its victim. Keep walking!

Day 104

Our "Dash in the Middle" (Part 1)

"And those He justified, He also glorified" (Romans 8:30, HCS).

If you have ever seen a gravestone, you know that upon it are two dates, a birthdate and a death date. More significantly you will have noticed the dash that is in between. You may have heard the cliché, "It's all about the dash in the middle." This expresses the greater importance of the life lived, which brings any meaningful substance to its beginning and end. In other words, the dash in the middle is what gives meaning and purpose to the two dates. This is a trustworthy saying. However, we err when we try to apply the same concept to the sanctified life. In fact, it is the other way around.

It can be said that our birthdate is justification by faith, and our death date is justification's outcome—complete glorification in heaven. We already have a Beginning and an End and His name is Jesus (Revelation 21:6). He is the Author *and* the Finisher of our faith (Hebrews 12:2). Therefore, we do not seek to live sanctified lives in order to bring meaning and purpose to our birth and death dates. No! On the contrary, it is because we *already are* saved; and because we *already possess* our heavenly inheritance that we purpose to live a meaningful life—one that is overflowing with gratitude in worship-filled response to these Gospel Truths. The sanctified life is our *dash in the middle*. It is the Christian thankfully honoring what he or she already possesses (justification and eternal life) by living in obedience to God's Word. Jesus said, "If you love Me, you will keep My commandments" (John 14:15). Paul wrote that God "will give eternal life to those who keep on doing good, seeking after the glory and honor and immortality that God offers" (Romans 2:7, NLT).

Heaven represents justification's end. This consists of our ultimate salvation as well as our full glorification (our perfection of holiness for eternity). If believers despise becoming like Jesus, dislike worshiping Him, and avoid daily fellowship with Him here on earth, they will loathe heaven. "We know that when He appears, we will be like Him, because we will see Him just as He is" (1 John 3:2). Logically, the gaining of heaven is merely the completion of living a heavenly life on earth. Theologically, the gaining of heaven is produced through repentance and faith in the finished work of Christ (Ephesians 2:8-9). His finished work obtained for us the beginning (justification) *and* the end (glorification) of our Christian journey. By faith, we enter into this Truth; through obedient love we honor and keep it, showing that we have gratefully received it.

For Thought:

Prayerfully consider and answer these questions: What will your "dash-in-the-middle" declare? Will it glorify Jesus or will it glorify someone else? What is it proclaiming right now?

Day 105

Our "Dash in the Middle" (Part 2)

"And those He justified, He also glorified" (Romans 8:30, HCS).

When we were baptized into Christ's death and raised with Him to the newness of life (Romans 6:4-7), not only were we justified; we actually began our eternity in heaven. Consider the following verses: "For we know that our old self was crucified with him . . . anyone who has died has been set free from sin" (Romans 6:6-7); "It is appointed for men to die once and after this comes the judgment" (Hebrews 9:27). If there is only one death, and we truly died with Christ, then our eternal judgment is fixed and we only wait for its arrival. Did you ever think that when you were saved you began your eternal "fellowship" with Jesus?

"I never knew you! Depart from Me" (Matthew 7:23). Whoa! Coming from the mouth of the Creator of the universe, these would be thunderously frightening words. Imagine living your entire life thinking your eternity was secure because of a mere "ticket in the pocket" belief in God. Then in the next world, as you are standing before the Almighty Judge, you hear Him say, "Depart from Me, I never knew you!" If you think He is referring to unbelievers, think again; Jesus is speaking about believers, because only believers do things *in His name* (see Matthew 7:22).

It is well proven that people who are truly in love devote their lives to one another. When Jesus says "Depart" to a soul that has passed into the next world, He is not telling that person to do anything new; that person has lived their whole earthly life departing from Jesus, and He basically just dispatches them to an eternity of doing what they have always done. Put another way, since there was never a fellowship of intimacy and devotion on earth, why would Jesus give them an eternity of what their life has proven they despise? Countless people call themselves Christians, but few live their lives in intimacy and devotion to Him. Doing duties "in His name" is one thing; devoting ourselves to Him is quite another.

Therefore, we as saints live with a desire for a sanctified life and strive toward our own progressive Christ-like transformation, not so we *will be* justified and glorified, but because we *already are*. We have heaven now and once we embrace this Gospel Truth we will certainly begin to live like it. It was a common style in Scripture for God to decree something as already accomplished that was yet to be. Such is the glorification of all His adopted sons and daughters.

For Thought:

Not one soul can live a worldly life in heaven. Living a heavenly life in this world proves you have been fit and prepared for that eternal destination.

Day 106

Expense is Immaterial

"There came a woman with an alabaster vial of very costly perfume of pure nard; and she broke the vial and poured it over His head" (Mark 14:3).

We learn later in this passage that this perfume "could have been sold for over three hundred denarius." In Emperor Nero's time one denarius was equal to roughly 53 grams of silver. At today's (2013) standard, this amount of silver would value $38. Multiply this by one Jewish year (300) and it totals $11,400. This is a lot of money today, and in that day would have been an amazing amount. If you make that much a year, how long would it take you to save that amount? Where did this woman get that kind of money, and why did she spend it on perfume only to pour it out upon Jesus?

Some subjectively believe she spent her Dowry, meaning she would never get married, thus declaring her dependence and devotion to Jesus. This was an exorbitant offering, and it seemed as nothing to her. It was not because she was wealthy; it was because she greatly loved the Lord. When you are in love, sacrifices and their expense become immaterial. Some say she was the same "sinner woman" of Luke 7 that was *forgiven much*, who was Mary of Bethany. Nevertheless, she longed to cascade her love upon Jesus, publicly, passionately, and personally, demonstrating her unrestrained adoration and worship to Him. She expected nothing in return because she had already been given everything. She desired no reward because Jesus was her reward, and His response to her was an exclusive and unique exaltation: The precise Greek translation is, "What she could do, she did" (14:8). In other words, she did all she could do, and would have done more, if able.

Her devotion was a walking reproach to the others' pitiable religion, and all that reproached religious people can do is scoff in order to feel better about themselves. Nonetheless, Jesus memorialized this woman's beautiful devotion in the presence of all her scoffers—"Wherever the gospel is preached throughout the world, what she has done will also be told" (14:9).

Whatever of ourselves we give, and to the degree we give it, it is indicative of our dependence upon God and our devotion to Him. To those who long to shower Jesus with love, expense is immaterial. Like the alabaster jar, the offering must first be broken, and then poured out entirely. Are you a broken vessel pouring out all you can to Jesus?

For Thought:

This woman poured out all she had. Why? Did someone have to coerce her into this act of immaculate love?

This was her first love. Can you remember your first love for Jesus? Where is it now?

Day 107

The Goodness of Loneliness

"God in His holy dwelling is a father of the fatherless and a champion of widows. God makes a home for the lonely" (Psalm 68:5-6).

You may be struggling with loneliness. You may see your lonely condition and mourn, wish you were married, give over to sin as an escape, or despair even of life itself.

In 1 Kings 17-19, Elijah had called down fire from heaven and worked many astounding miracles. But once Queen Jezebel promised that she would kill him or else suffer death herself, Elijah ran in fear. And because of his faithless failure, he fell into self-pity, despaired of his life, and went to go die alone in the desert. Then the Lord came and strengthened him for a forty-day journey to the highest place of privilege given only to one other man (Moses). God took him to the top of Mt. Horeb (Sinai), the most holy place in existence—a place where no man could tread and live. Elijah was thoroughly alone, but not lonely. The Lord ministered to him there in such a way, that Elijah's ministry after being alone with God made his ministry before seem little. I don't think Elijah ever looked back at his aloneness with regret.

In Genesis 32:22-28, God had Jacob send away his entire family and all he owned where "Jacob was left all alone" (vs. 24). God wanted him alone to wrestle Jacob's transformation into Israel. Regardless of his limp, I don't think Jacob ever looked back at his aloneness with regret.

In Revelation 1:9, John was alone on the Isle of Patmos. He was cut-off from all the churches he had labored to build. There is no mention of any other saint or friend with him. He was old, tired, likely treated as a criminal slave, and could have drowned in the despair of loneliness. What was he doing? He was worshiping the Lord "caught up in the Spirit." The Lord lifted John into the realm of heaven where he saw what few saints would ever see and live to tell—Jesus fully glorified. As a result, he wrote the most heavenly book of the New Testament, the Revelation of Jesus Christ. I don't think John ever looked back at his aloneness with regret.

Jesus was fully God but also fully man, and He certainly felt aloneness at times. This is one reason He was constantly praying to His Father. As God Incarnate, there was not a person on earth to whom Jesus could relate. Did Jesus say, "I feel so alone; no one can relate to me?" No. He humbled Himself to take upon our sufferings so He could relate to us (Philippians 2:6-8; Hebrews 4:15). Only pride chooses to be lonely. Lonely feelings are not bad; staying lonely is. Jesus loves to get His children alone, because through it He can work something profoundly transformational. God speaks to His lonely child, "Dear one, you are not all alone; you and I are finally alone together. That's what I've been waiting for!" Turn your loneliness into alone time behind the curtain with Jesus. You will come to know Him in a deep, more intimate way, and your heart will be profoundly transformed.

Day 108

When Our Answer is "No!"

"For as many as are the promises of God, in Him they are yes" (2 Corinthians 1:20a).

How many times have we greatly desired something we needed to ask someone for, but never asked because we knew the answer would be "No"? If we are certain the answer is "No," we usually never even ask, because we figure, "What's the point?" How many people have we never spoken to because we knew they would never listen? Some people never hear from us because of this. Perhaps, when we wonder why we haven't heard from so-and-so in a long time, it's for the same reason. Maybe they became weary of talking to us because we never listened; all we did was talk. It is near impossible to talk and listen at the same time.

There are many believers today, even preachers, who claim we cannot hear from God and that He never speaks outside the Bible. Are they talking too much? When God speaks to us through His Spirit and through His Word, it is to reprove, correct, or teach us righteousness (2 Timothy 3:16). However, His voice always comes laced with a request or command. Perhaps another reason that these naysayers never hear God speak is because their answer is always "No" to the things God says that they fail to agree with. Let's discuss this.

Why do things seem dead, dry, or uneventful? Why is our church empty? Why does heaven seem silent? Has God ceased speaking because we talk too much, and our answer is often, "No?" He is not interested in asking us to do what we already like; He wants His desire done, and His desire will often collide with ours. "For as the heavens are higher than the earth, so are My ways higher than your ways and My thoughts than your thoughts" (Isaiah 55:9). Preachers and elders would hear, "Repent and pray, or move out of the way so My Holy

Spirit can fall on your assembly and shake it from its status quo." But they are talking, "Let's build more gyms, programs, buildings, and committees. The Lord says, "Love, forgive, and bless that person who mortally wounded you." Dare we say no? If you groan, "It doesn't seem like God hears me," find out if you are hearing Him.

In Mark 9:5-7, Peter was talking too much, so God thundered from the cloud, "This is My Son whom I love. Listen to Him!" How often has God spoken but you couldn't hear over your endless chatter? How often have you said no because He didn't with agree your theology or traditions? Mercifully, God has not figured, "What's the point?" and then left us alone to build like we wanted—our way! If you will humbly listen, His promises are "Yes and Amen." Even when He says, "No," it is "Yes" to something eternally better for you. Listen to Him; He always listens to you.

For Thought:

Have you recently noticed an awkward silence from God?

Day 109

Branches are Not Fruit

"You are the branches" (John 15:5).

Jesus said, "I am the Vine; you are the branches" (John 15:5). What do branches do but bare fruit? Branches are not fruit, nor are they attractive to look at without fruit. Many problems for believers arise when branches desire to be fruit out of pride and self-ambition. Branches are rarely the conversation among man-worshiping circles. If, through pride-jaded eyes, the branch sees those circles as desirable, being overlooked will be seen as unfavorable. On the other hand, through humble eyes fixed on devotion to Jesus, the branch will see being overlooked as wonderful. The sincere branch seeks nothing other than being hidden by fruit in season and hidden in Christ out of season. Out of season the sincere branch looks only to the Vine's nourishment for the next harvest of fruit.

Spiritual fruit is meant to nourish others, not to be marveled over by its sumptuous appearance. Whenever the fruit is plucked, squeezed, and enjoyed, the branch should rejoice. When the branch is pruned it will certainly feel the sting and the pressure, but will never become destroyed as long as it is rightfully attached to the Vine.

People do not generally invite their friends to come and see their rose bushes right after they have been pruned. Being mostly branches, they are certainly not as attractive, so some people refuse to prune them. For the sake of short-term vanity, they put off what is best for the bush in the long run. The un-pruned rose bush might look prettier for longer this year, but next year, those who pruned their bushes will have the best looking roses.

Because of the contagious mindset of the world that is so accustomed to looking at the outward appearances, many believers are tempted to do the same. Equally, you may be so infatuated with visible growth that when you do not see it you become greatly discouraged. Never fall for that! What you may not know is that because of your daily intimate abiding in Jesus, He has been developing much invisible growth underneath the surface, way down deep in your hidden inward life. The downward growth is more important than the above ground growth; the former determines the health of the latter ("deep healthy roots reap healthy fruits"). Furthermore, if you are top heavy with fruit without much downward growth, you will likely topple over at the first gust of a stormy trial.

We as saints should deliberately crucify our propensity to be praised for our appearances or look to our outward fruit for approval. We must fix our eyes upon Jesus the True Vine—from which flows our life—abiding in Him and producing fruit. This will produce the steadfast life He so desires. Be joyful just being a branch that abides.

For Thought:

Read 1 Samuel 16:7. How is your heart?

Day 110

Nothing but the Present (Part 1)

"You shall set the bread of the Presence on the table before Me at all times" (Exodus 25:30).

"I Am the Bread of Life" (John 6:48).

When we see the unbroken constancy of this "bread of the Presence" in the Old Testament, and it being perpetually before God on the table, we should not have to guess that this is a typology of Jesus Christ the Bread of Life. As we meditate more on this heavenly truth, we will also see many other spiritually significant parallels in why God said to keep it before Him "at all times."

We see more clearly the loftiness of God's vehement hatred to have any other gods "before Him," as that is the exclusive position of His only begotten Son, Jesus Christ.

We see that when God looks down from heaven upon His creation, He fixes His eyes only upon Jesus and His finished work, "When I see the blood . . ." Since we are in Christ, having been baptized into His death, God fixes His gaze not on our feeble walks, spotty prayer lives, broken vows, corrupt natures, or vain attempts to be holy; He sees His Son Jesus and the perfected work of Calvary's tree. Andrew Murray writes from man's perspective, "It is the faith that continually closes its eyes to the weakness of the creature, and finds its joy in the sufficiency of an Almighty Savior." [17]

Moreover, we see that God will only fix His eyes upon that which He can see the reflection of Himself. "But we all, with unveiled face, beholding as in a mirror the glory of the Lord" (2 Corinthians 3:18a).

We see that God prepares this table before us, upon which the Presence of our Lord Jesus is set as the "true drink" and "true food" that He alone is (John 6:55). He prepares this table in the presence of our enemies (see Psalm 23) so that we never forget that our Lord's Presence alone conquers the presence of our adversary. We should keep Him "before us at all times."

For Thought:

Read John 15:1-5. What does it mean to abide in Christ?

However real the death of Jesus is to you; that is the measure of the effect this truth will have upon the world through you.

A floor lamp abides. A rechargeable flashlight still has self in the mix. Ponder and discuss this.

Day 111

Nothing but the Present (Part 2)

"You shall set the bread of the Presence on the table before Me at all times" (Exodus 25:30).

"I Am the Bread of Life" (John 6:48).

We can see the meaning of "at all times" as the portrayal of His infinite nearness: 1) As our infinite Immanuel ("God eternally with us"); and 2) As our ever present help in time of need (Psalm 46:1). He is the "I Am" (present tense) God. His Presence is always with us as we walk through our own valleys of death's shadow. He will never leave or forsake us. He is the relentless pursuer of our souls; praise His holy Name!

We should see that He alone is our eternal Author of life; the Finisher of our eternal life; our life's eternal Sustainer, and the eternal Provider of all of life's needs. We should also recognize the striking congruence between heavenly eternity and the present on earth. The present never ends, as it is always right now. God also never ends, as He is always right now—"I Am." Bound by time, we are linear minded people and it is quite difficult for us to grasp the eternal concept of always and forever now.

Consider the following illustration: The goldfish is content to swim in what seems to us as maddening circles, because it does not store up memories. Every circle to the fish is always a new one and therefore each maintains the element of freshness. In contrast, we do store up memories, so we can see how our past can rob us of the fresh joy of the present. In a lavish, self-indulgent lifestyle, things get worn-out through repetition. And finding nothing on earth that can continuously provide newness, the future outlook is rendered bleak or trite. Lust and coveting are a hopeless prison!

Past miseries also have the tendency to train our minds to detest the present and fear the future. As a result, we disallow the blessings of present joy and peace that are in Christ Jesus; we regret backward and fret forward. However, once we simply turn to the Bread of the Presence and drink in His fresh living water, we begin to be filled with overflowing contentment. We learn the wondrous truth that He is the only One in existence that is inexhaustible in all things; He alone brings newness to even the most monotonous tasks. He is always there, always able, and His mercies are always new. The present becomes what the Lord initially designed it to be, and what eternity is—filled with life, light, and love. What is the spiritual condition of your heart and how is your relationship with Jesus right now? Cultivating a "right now" mindset through intimacy with Jesus cures depression and fills the heart with gratitude (see Colossians 2:6-7).

Pray rather than think, and pray only for others.Do not give up—the present is extremely precious; Do not look back—the dark past is a thief to your present; Do not look to the future—it is a bully to your peace. The present-minded saint presses onward with boldness because the present is the earthly version of eternity (perpetually and forever now). If you have peace with God right now because 1) you have been declared righteous by faith in Christ's forgiveness, and 2) you remain in that abiding faith, what can yesterday and tomorrow do? Why do you think our enemy is so busy trying to distract and discourage us with yesterdays and tomorrows? Never give up. Don't regret backward or fret forward. Just trust and obey "right now" while you hold onto hope. Jesus promises us His presence in our present, and promises us that continuously without fail. We just need to abide.

For Thought:

Hope is not a subjective feeling; hope is an objective fact. It is a Person not an emotion.

Write out Hebrews 6:17-20. Note: See how the author uses hope and Jesus interchangeably.

Once you discover that Satan's counterfeit of hope is wishful thinking, and that real hope is an eternal Person whose name is Jesus, you are on your way to understanding why so many are so hopeless in a world that claims to offer so much. The world is always striving for better—a better day, a better job, a better house, a better life, etc. Children of God already have the best—Jesus—and strive to better the world by giving the best they have.

Day 112

Who's Touching My Bride?

> *"Were not our hearts burning within us while He was speaking to us on the road, while He was explaining the Scriptures to us?"* (Luke 24:32)

The word for "burning" in Luke 24:32 is *kaio*, which means, "to set ablaze." However, there is also another Greek word meaning "to set ablaze" found in 1 Corinthians 7:1, where Paul is speaking to single men: "It is not good for a man to touch a woman." The word for "touch" is *haptesthai*, having its root in the word *hapto*, which means, "to touch in such a way to set ablaze or stoke passion."

What is the difference? One comes by God's presence and the other by human touch. *Kaio* comes by the Lord's presence causing the heart to burn; *hapto* comes by human touch or effort, causing the heart to burn for the one doing the touching. The hearts of the two men walking with Jesus to Emmaus burned because they were in the presence of God. Paul said it was not good for a man to touch a woman other than his own wife in such a way to stir her passions into fire. *Kaio* comes by the fiery presence of God, and *hapto* comes by selfish lust.

Throughout the Bible (especially in Revelation), the Bride of Christ is referred to as "the woman." Therefore, when we apply the above knowledge, *kaio* would be when God's presence alone kindles the heart of His Bride into fire for Him. On the other hand, *hapto* is when people, through selfish lust, touch His Bride to stir her heart into passion for themselves. This is a twisted yet pandemic reality in many churches. People (from pastor to lay member) filled with selfish ambition, slither into the fold to hypnotize Christ's Bride with their cunning charms and dynamic charisma, thereby touching her in such a way to get her to fall in lust with them.

What is God saying to this? "If you're trying to start a fire in My Bride with your own hands and without My presence; if you're wooing My Bride to yourself, trying to get her all fired up and passionate about you . . . First of all, you are committing spiritual incest; secondly, get your hands off My Bride!"

God shares everything He has with mankind. I have heard preachers say that He will not share His glory, but that is not biblically or theologically correct. He loves to share His glory with us as long as we do not lay claim to it and use it for selfish gain. However, there is one thing He certainly will not share, and that is His beloved Bride.

For Thought:

Selfish ambition has wrecked more churches, ruined more souls, and thoroughly pleased the Devil more than we could ever know. If there is selfish ambition in your heart and you have ministry intentions, get it out before you "touch" His Bride.

Day 113

The Authority of a "Never" Promise

"The crowds were astonished at His teaching, because He was teaching them like One who had authority" (Matthew 7:28-29, NLT).

We could talk at length about how God's people persistently err by endeavoring to keep God's commandment before receiving His Promise; they put holy practices before comforting promises. Jesus was speaking to such people in the above passage. All they had endlessly heard from the self-righteous teachers was "keep the commandment, perform, do it, and do it more!" Their astonishment at Jesus' unprecedented teaching was not necessarily because of the wisdom or eloquence of His parabolic illustrations, as wonderful as they were and are; they were astonished at the exclusive promise-making authority with which He preached.

His was not the sense of "authority" with which we have familiarized ourselves (power, position, prestige, and wealth). Jesus' authority came from His divinity; only God possesses the authority to truly make a Promise—especially a "never" promise like the one Jesus had just given in His parable of the house built upon the Rock. He promised that His disciples would become resolute, immovable, and steadfast buildings *never to collapse*. No man—scribe, law-keeping Pharisee, priest, or earthly king—could ever make that kind of statement, let alone guarantee it with a promise. It was the comfort of that unearthly "never" promise that would move them to keep His commandments.

They did not keep His commandments in order to be righteous; they kept them because they believed that no mere man could make such promises. They would embrace who Jesus really is (God Incarnate) only after He was crucified, resurrected, and ascended to the Father.

This would open the eyes of their blinded hearts to see His exclusive divinity. They would then understand that His death, burial, and resurrection were the oath's guarantee, and their initial belief would turn into steadfast obedience out of love.

Obedience must be built upon the foundation of His blood-purchased promise (see Hebrews 6:17-20). We do not keep His commandments in order to secure His promise; we already have it. Therefore, since His promise is steadfast so should our obedience be. If you are living for the glories of your heavenly promise, you cannot be threatened by death, and will not be given over to sin. Because of the foundation of Christ's eternal Promise, our house will stand, even through the storms of death. Are you honoring that promise with your lifestyle?

For Thought:

A strong man would be expected to work first and then receive his wages; but one who is weak and starving needs food first before he can work. Our obedience should always be built upon God's promises, never the other way around!

Day 114

He Reigns! (Part 1)

"Don't be afraid. Stand firm and see the LORD's salvation He will accomplish for you today . . ."
(Exodus 14:13a, HCS).

Moses was speaking as an oracle of God to a nation riddled with fear, doubt, and unbelief. From their perspective the situation was terrifying and inescapably hopeless. From God's perspective it was a perfect situation, one in which He could reveal Himself to them in an unprecedented way. Let us examine the verb phrases of this passage.

Don't be afraid. The words "Fear not" were unique to a messenger/angel of God. Have you noticed each time an angel of the Lord appeared to man, "Fear not" was almost always spoken first? This gives great confidence to the fact that God authoritatively spoke to His people through Moses.

Stand firm. In the midst of trial, calamity, and opposition, God encourages us to stand firm. "Take up the whole armor of God, that you may be able to withstand in the evil day, and having done all, to stand firm" (Ephesians 6:13, ESV). Jesus affirms He is the rock upon which our house will forever stand. Therefore, we can labor for Him "steadfast, immovable, always abounding in the work of the Lord, knowing that [our] toil is not in vain in the Lord" (1 Corinthians 15:58).

See the LORD'S salvation. God eradicated our enemy, not with manmade weapons but with His Sovereign power over His creation. David said, "All this assembly may know that the LORD does not deliver by sword or by spear; for the battle is the LORD'S and He will give you into our hands" (1 Samuel 17:47). Jesus said from His throne, "Behold, I make all things new" (Revelation 21:5).

He will accomplish for you today. "Today" means the present, which implies any moment we cry out for mercy. Moses' final words to God's people were, "The LORD your God is the one who goes with you. He will not fail you or forsake you" (Deuteronomy 31:6). David said, "Surely He will save you from the fowler's snare and from the deadly pestilence" (Psalm 91:3, NIV). When you are in the midst of a tempest of a trial or an insurmountable problem, can you agree with God to fear not, hold fast, and behold the salvation He has provided for you at Calvary? Jesus' last declaration from the cross was, "It is accomplished!" He has defeated the enemies of sin, death, and Satan. He will also take the antagonistic trial you are currently facing and turn it into a victory, because He always has the last Word.

For Thought:

Read Hebrews 6:13-20.

God's ultimate oracle is His Word, which is inerrant and eternal. When a messenger corrupts, people tend to disqualify the message. Who does this reveal is their focus?

Day 115

He Reigns! (Part 2)

"For the Egyptians you see today, you will never see again. The LORD will fight for you; you must be quiet" (Exodus 14:13b, HCS).

The Egyptians will never again be seen. Egypt symbolizes all that is opposed to God and all that would attempt to ensnare His people in bondage. By God's mighty hand, Egypt would be defeated, demobilized, and rendered utterly powerless. "Our soul has escaped as a bird out of the snare of the trapper; the snare is broken and we have escaped" (Psalm 124:7). "As far as the east is from the west, so far He has removed our transgressions from us" (Psalm 103:12). "I will also deliver My people from your hands . . . and you will know that I am the LORD" (Ezekiel 13:21). And finally, sin "shall no longer be your master, because you are not under the law, but under grace" (Romans 6:14).

The LORD will fight for you. Nehemiah beckoned, "At whatever place you hear the sound of the trumpet, rally to us there. Our God will fight for us" (4:20). Paul triumphantly tells us at the last trumpet "the dead will be raised incorruptible, and we will be changed" forever (1 Corinthians 15:52). The voices of heaven declare that upon the seventh angel's breath the final trumpet will sound, and "The kingdom of the world has become the kingdom of our Lord and of His Christ; and He will reign forever and ever" (Revelation 11:15). Paul writes in Romans, "What then shall we say to these things? If God is for us, who is against us?" (8:31). Jesus is completely able to save those "who draw near to God through Him, since He always lives to make intercession" for us (Hebrews 7:25).

You must be quiet. The Lord promised Joshua that He would victoriously fight for His people to bring down the stronghold of their enemy (Jericho). But before Jericho was brought to rubble, Joshua commanded, "You shall not let a word proceed out of your mouth, until the day I tell you" (Joshua 6:10). God's people were commanded to be silent just before the victorious blast of the trumpet when God revealed His conquering might. In the book of Revelation there is also silence in heaven directly before the fearsome blasts of the trumpet, where "there followed peals of thunder and sounds and flashes of lightning and an earthquake" (8:5). Therefore, you must "be still and know" that He is the God who will ultimately reign over all that would oppose Him, afflict you, or ensnare you in bondage.

For Thought:

Read Psalm 46 and Romans 8. Are you persuaded that God is inseparably in your midst?

When you may not *feel* victorious, are feelings Truth? Will you put-off feelings and put-on faith?

Day 116

Do You Really Know Him?

"Draw near to God, and He will draw near to you" (James 4:8).

There are two reasons why anyone refuses to draw near to God: 1) They are angry with God, and 2) they believe God is angry with them. It would be beyond the scope of this devotion to discuss all the details of both reasons. One may dispute that those who do not know God, or those who do not believe in God will not draw near to Him.

To the former, Paul argues, "What may be known about God is plain to them, because God has made it plain to them. For since the creation of the world God's invisible qualities—his eternal power and divine nature—have been clearly seen, being understood from what has been made, so that people are without excuse" (Romans 1:19-20, NIV). To the latter, it is impossible for anyone to disbelieve in God without first acknowledging the possibility that there is a God. If I said, "I don't believe in love," the statement defeats itself, because I had to state the possible existence of the love I have chosen not to believe in. Besides, Paul writes that although "they knew God, they did not glorify Him as God or show gratitude" (Romans 1:21, HCS).

For those who are angry with God, they are not really angry with God at all; they are only angry at their ignorance of Him (they're angry at a being they have created, not the God of the Bible). God is absolute good! It is proven that rational people are not angry at goodness but only evil. If people are angry with God, and He is absolute good, then they are either irrational, or do not know Him. It is from an irrational judgment reasoned from the fallen nature that they make their claim. They either cannot or will not see the goodness of God in the circumstances that bred their displeasure.

If you think God is angry with you, you are either living in rebellion, unbelief, or being lied to. God says if we repent and confess our sin, He is faithful to forgive, cleanse, and restore us to right fellowship with Him. And if you are repentant, the most toxic thing about continuing to believe that God is angry with you is this: You will eventually do something to prove it! "For as a man thinks within himself, so he is" (Proverbs 23:7). Sinners will draw near to a God of mercy but flee from one of wrath. No wonder Satan paints God so terribly. There is no condemnation in Jesus (Romans 8:1).

For Thought:

Very often unbelief gets misdiagnosed as "just feeling unworthy." All of us are unworthy and should be in perpetual awe that Jesus suffered for that very reason.

Grief from sinning against God will not likely come if you continue to view Him as an enemy waiting to satisfy His wrathful destruction upon you.

A promise of pardon produces repentance more readily than fear of wrath. Do you know Him?

Day 117

The Spring in the Desert

"They journeyed for three days in the wilderness without finding water . . . the people grumbled to Moses, 'What are we going to drink?'" (Exodus 15:22-24).

Just before they grumbled about having no water in the dry desert, Miriam had led Israel in a hymn to the Lord for His miraculous deliverance. The song was, "Sing to the Lord for He is highly exalted; He has thrown the horse and its rider into the Sea" (15:21). This was the Red Sea the LORD had just divided, made dry land to appear in its midst, and used to swallow up every pursuing foe. If God can make dry land to appear in the midst of the water, could He not also make water appear in the midst of dry land? They eventually did come to water at Marah, but it was undrinkable.

No sooner had they lifted their songs of praise to God, did their tune dramatically change. A new enemy—the enemy of thirst—was now drowning the miracle that had drowned their former enemy. After three days of fighting this foe of thirst, their exalted praises turned to excited petulance, and God's unparalleled miracle faded into the rearview mirror of their current struggle. However, directed by God, Moses threw a tree into the bitter waters at Marah and it became potable. This may remind us of another "tree" that turned the bitter wastelands of sin into springs of Living Water.

What the Israelites did not know is that God's super-abundant provision was only five miles away at Elim (less than two walking hours). There they would enjoy twelve springs and seventy date palms. So great was the provision that they were able to dwell at that place. If they had trusted God's shepherd for just another couple of hours, and walked a little further in faith, they never would have grieved God with their grumbling unbelief.

The above should also remind us of another three-day thirst—when Christ the Living Water was brutally removed from His disciples. Between Jesus' death and resurrection, His disciples were moved to drink the bitterness of fears and sorrow. They did not know that God's super-abundant promise was only one miracle away, when God's mighty power would raise Christ from the dead. Calvary's tree turned bitter waters into thirst-quenching springs of eternal life for us. On the cross, He hung and cried out. Now at God's right hand He sits and reaches out, saying, "If anyone is thirsty, let him come to Me and drink" (John 7:37). He is the Spring in the desert, and so great is His provision that we are able to dwell there eternally. If you are struggling in a baron wilderness and feel like quitting, keep going; abundant relief is not much further away.

For Thought:

If you die of thirst with an endless spring of water at your disposal, it is your own fault.

Day 118

Becoming the Message

"For if I do wish to boast I will not be foolish, for I will be speaking the truth; but I refrain from this, so that no one will credit me with more than he sees in me or hears from me" (2 Corinthians 12:6).

Paul's desire was that people see Christ Jesus in him as a result of his inner-man being governed by the Holy Spirit, not just for people to hear about it. When he said, "forbid that I should glory in anything" other than Jesus (Galatians 6:14), he meant it. His concern was that all glory should go to the One that rescued him and dwelt in him, and to take none for himself from people. His ambition was to be united with Him in the likeness of His sufferings and resurrected with Him in His glory.

Are you learning that it is all about the finished work of Jesus, and His Promised Holy Spirit that comes to build upon that foundation? Have you come to see that the one true and noble ambition is to devote your life to Jesus because of His Gospel that rescued you? This ambition will never fail you because it is one of love, and "love never fails" (1 Corinthians 13:8). Are you realizing that all those other selfish ambitions produce nothing but torment, despair, and anger? We set them up as pseudo-promises that will satisfy us and bring us great fulfillment in life. And then when we fail to meet them we acutely fall, or when they are removed we aggressively react. No wonder James said that with selfish ambition also comes every evil thing and disorder (James 3:16).

Countless people ambitiously say, "I want to become the next so-and-so," or "I want to be in that great position." And when God molds them and puts them in the place that He wants, they get depressed. Tormented by their deemed failure, they become angry at the world, with God, or both. However, if your ambition is to die to self and live for Jesus, you will never be disappointed when things do not go your way. "Ministry" is secondary when devotion to Jesus is primary (see Luke 12:11).

Paul was meticulously careful that people would see in his life the same Truth they heard from his lips. He longed to be conformed to the likeness of His Savior—to become the message, not just proclaim it. He was a living epistle. There is a major difference between being a gramophone of the Gospel and a living oracle of it. What do you want to become when you grow up?

For Thought:

There is a foolish and increasingly popular cult growing today that claims to be a "training school for prophets." They practice rituals that are the residue of pagan mystery religions brought into early Christianity. One in particular passes a stone around where the one who receives it must instantaneously "prophesy." This caters to the fleshly lust of "experience seeking," offering only an intoxicating high, and resembling nothing of a true prophet of the Bible.

Day 119

Obeying the Message

"We have received grace and apostleship to bring about the obedience of faith among all the Gentiles for His name's sake" (Romans 1:5).

A leader of an expedition came to the edge of a cliff. Its wall was three hundred feet straight downward. On the other side of the chasm was their final destination. An angel of the Lord appeared to the leader and told him that if he and his men jumped, the Lord would carry them across the chasm. Because God spoke it through his messenger, the man believed it. He told all his men what the Lord had promised, and they too believed, so they decided to camp there. Days turned to months, to years, to decades, and long after their passing, an entire town had now been established. They had built a bridge across that daunting chasm. Next to that bridge at the cliff's edge was a monument for those early founders with the inscribed words, "The men that believed they could fly!"

The true story had ascended to legend that said those men actually did fly. But now jumping across by faith would be absurd because of the bridge built by the tenacious efforts of the current town. However, one day a peculiar child was born in that town whose mother would tell him the legend over and over. When the child became a boy, he coaxed his mother into taking him to the cliff's edge, and there he read those words, "The men that believed they could fly!" The boy thought to himself, "If they could fly so can I," and when his mother was unaware he jumped. She heard the sound and turned around and to her sinking terror she screamed, "NO!" But suddenly her plight transformed to delight and what she saw she could not believe. With thunder and light her son just took flight and was miraculously carried across the chasm. The power was so unearthly that the bridge crumbled down. The promise still stood, so nothing else could, while a voice roared from the heavens. "This is My child in whom I'm well pleased, because today faith has been perfected. This town was built upon unbelief, and on the wrong side of the chasm erected!"

Where they could have had faith and its promised reward, they had settled for mere belief. There are many who hear God's Word and believe it. And though they may never contest it, they never act upon it in faith. Man-made bridges have largely replaced taking God at His Word against all humanistic reasoning. Faith is only faith when it is put into obedient action. Therefore it requires the releasing of man's reasoning and the forsaking of trusting only in human efforts. There must be an abandoning of the self-life to the hand of God. Human efforts to cross the abyss will come to nothing and all that will be left is perfected faith, all devoted to God by acting upon His Word.

Human bridges—like "Say a sinner's prayer and attend church," or "Be a good law abiding person"—are an affront to God who has given us His Son. Only obedient faith and dependence upon Jesus will carry us across. He is the Bridge not built by human hands, and walking in Him requires intimate devotion.

Like the leader of the expedition, you may tell everyone that you believe. But even the "demons believe and shudder" (James 2:19). God knows those who are truly His. Their lives are a reproach to the demonic folly of dead belief because they are radically devoted to His will. They are the ones (like the little boy) who are carried across by God's promise because they jumped. All else are like the town that was built upon unbelief and only try to cross with their own self-made standards. They will always remain on the wrong side. What side are you on? Let devotion tell the truth rather than words.

For Study:

There is a big difference between dead belief and lively faith. Read and the study the following:

Genesis 6:5-22	Hebrews 5:9
Genesis 12:1-4	James 2:14-24
Exodus 3:11-4:13	Luke 13:3
2 Kings 5:9-14	1 Peter 3:21
Romans 3:28	Acts 2:38-41
Ephesians 2:8	Matthew 7:21-23
John 14:15	Romans 10:17
Philippians 2:12-13	James 1:22

Day 120

Hating or Loving the Message

"But as it is, you are seeking to kill Me . . . If God were your Father, you would love Me" (John 8:40; 42).

A man had two children he loved more than his own life. One night a perpetrator broke in the house and kidnapped them. Desperately frantic, he called the police who immediately began the search. Three days pass with no sign of them. No time to sleep, no appetite to eat, and soon seven days had passed. Could you imagine? Time had come to a halt, life had become a nightmare, and his entire world had been turned upside down and emptied. He looked at the dead toys on the floor that once were animated with the life of his dear children. The bedrooms once filled with laughter are now filled with only disturbing silence. Two weeks go by and his arms are covered with the whelps of pinches to "wake up!" His thoughts become his mortal foes as they continue to guess, project, and ponder what horrible things may be happening to his children. All he can hear are the imaginary cries of their voices, "Daddy! Where are you?" Could you imagine?

Sorrow becomes mixed with anger because of the unbearable separation from his precious ones. He is at his breaking point now, and his feelings escalate into desires for the death of that kidnapper. Wouldn't you? A father without these thoughts would be questionable. Put yourself in his shoes now.

Suddenly the phone rings. "It's the FBI and we're here with the local police. We have found where your children are, and they're . . . alive! We'll be there in 5 minutes to pick you up. Be ready because you are coming with us to go get him so your children will have you there."

One shoe is on the wrong foot and your jacket is on inside out; you cannot even get ready properly.

Miserable roads wind through eerie stretches of woods you would never attempt driving through alone. You would rather suffer standing on hot coals for three hours than suffer this twenty-minute anticipation. Your vehicle is up front with a black FBI van behind. Arriving, you see a most appalling structure and your heart sinks in terror filled waves, thinking of your children being in such a condemned place. The FBI enters and all you can fathom is seeing your children's faces and them running into your loving embrace. It is why you came.

There is a commotion of struggle and the FBI emerges shoving a man from behind with his hands cuffed above his head. They open the back doors of the van and force him to sit on rear bumper. His face is filled with the blackest evil and you think to charge over and destroy him. But there is a higher agenda outweighing this feeling and your eyes turn back to the doorway. First there is hazy movement, and then clearly you see faces. Battered and bruised, your children exit, which causes you to momentarily glance back at the kidnapper and make aggressive eye contact with him. But here come your precious ones, and it seems like they have been separated from you for an eternity. They see you. Can you imagine?

With the little energy they have left in their feeble condition, they start running. Your heart is racing with joyful anticipation as you open your arms to receive them home. "I will never let go of them," you say with silent assurance, but suddenly there is a turn of events. They unexpectedly shift their direction and instead of running to you, they run straight to the kidnapper and jump into his lap. "We want to be with him, not you daddy!" Can you imagine?

Crushed, perplexed, and horrified, you see your own children long for the evil kidnapper that separated you from them. The one responsible for all your anguish is the one that makes them happiest. The thing you hate most, they have chosen to love.

This is how God our Father sees sin from His perspective every time His children give over to it. He wanted to destroy the kidnapper too, and He accomplished it by the crushing of His own Son. Sin unbearably separated us from Him but He chose to bear it to Calvary, and He gave us this Message to proclaim how He feels about it. Hating the Message or loving the Message depends on how you view sin. Dear reader, your Father came a long way to rescue you. Whatever you do, never jump into the kidnapper's lap; your Father cannot stand it.

Day 121

It's a Worship Problem

"Therefore, put to death what belongs to your worldly nature: sexual immorality, impurity, lust, evil desire, and greed, which is idolatry" (Colossians 3:5).

If you were to scour every inch of this planet, no matter where you go you would find worship. There is no such thing as a worship-less person. If man is not worshiping God he is worshiping himself. You may ask, "What about idols or false gods?" The answer is that it still amounts to man worshiping himself. Pagans worship idols because they believe they will receive a temporal reward of some kind. It is purely selfish. The idols are not really being worshiped, because the ideal is mere flattery. People serve idols so the idols will ultimately serve and benefit them. Idols are certainly not worshiped because they are infinitely holy and good. Therefore, man either worships God or man worships himself. The moment he turns from a vertical worship of God, he immediately turns to a horizontal worship what is created (Romans 1:25).

Paul is not saying to just cease sexual sin, lust, and greed (these things are not the root problem). For instance, take a wicked, arrogant, wealthy man. If he gives all he has to the poor, he is now just a wicked, arrogant, poor man. His self-idolatry has not been dealt with. Therefore, the surface problems that Paul lists in our devotion passage are only branches stemming from the real problem. Sexually immoral, covetous, impure, and greedy people have a worship problem. This also implies that there is a real solution available. They must learn how to redirect their God-given desire to worship to its proper Source. They must realign and retrain their thinking. Their self-worship must be replaced with the worship of God.

Believers who practice these sinful behaviors often look to God and even give Him thanks for His daily provisions and blessings. However, somehow they have adopted the pagan ritual that they need to go someplace else for pleasure. In other words, God provides food, water, clothing, and shelter, but man provides his own pleasure. He is blind to the fact that only God knows how to properly fill his void of pleasure. To this person, the pleasures from God have little appeal because they have been replaced by a satanic counterfeit. It is not a behavior problem; it is a worship problem. However, continue your journey in devotion to Jesus and you will be able to say like David, "In Your presence is abundant joy; in Your right hand are eternal pleasures" (Psalm 16:11).

For Thought:

Read Acts 20:35. Medical science has recently discovered that the spikes in the pleasure centers of the brain were higher when giving than receiving. Interesting!

Day 122

The Standard Transcendent

"But I say to you who hear, love your enemies, do good to those who hate you, bless those who curse you, pray for those who mistreat you" (Luke 6:27-28).

When there has been a custom or standard steadily maintained for a long period of time, we know how difficult it is to bring change, even though that old standard is no longer be effective. However, what is more difficult is the conception of an unforseen better standard. It certainly will not be welcomed until it has been tested and proven to be more efficient and capable; and we know this usually takes much time. People are often praised for their superior intellect when able to conceive of a new method that transcends the current tradition. Generally, only a person of high authority can instill a new superior standard and its fundamentals to replace the old.

The standard of the religious leaders in Jerusalem had nearly come to the place of corrupting absolutely. Heartless formalism, and law keeping were continuously performed to monotony. Jesus' words, "You have heard it said . . . but I say to you," are more than just bossy ideals or instructive suggestions; they were pure love, authoritative, and divine! These words were not just an improvement of the old standard; they were completely new and unprecedented, spoken with unearthly superiority, wisdom, and authority.

A superior intellect is normally in operation when a "raising of the standard" produces something of a higher quality than the previous. Even greater is if someone could foresee the supernormal outcome of a new spiritual standard even though he or she has never seen it demonstrated. Jesus still stands alone here. Jesus spoke from the position of highest authority to instill such a new standard in His

Sermon on the Mount. Only God has the superiority, wisdom, and authority to declare the old standard no longer effectual, and at the same time indoctrinate a new one. This unprecedented standard was one of selfless sacrifice, love, and unlimited mercy in response to being sinned against. No man could comprehend such a standard, nor would he implement such a standard upon himself. From man's perspective, religion was reasonable, but this new standard of dying to self to be merciful to sinners was preposterous. Jesus conceived it, demonstrated it, standardized it, and commanded it. He then gave us the Holy Spirit to empower us to accomplish it. There is no God like our God. Are you ditching your worldly standards and striving toward His unearthly standard?

For Thought:

Apart from God, it is impossible to obey Luke 6:27-28, but as blood-purchased saints we have the Holy Spirit dwelling within us. Yielding to His voice produces life and change. Telling Him to hush produces death. The outcome is your choice.

Day 123

The Standard Despised

"Woe to you when all men speak well of you, for their fathers used to treat the false prophets in the same way" (Luke 6:26).

Jesus did not bring revival, He is revival, and revival always produces dramatic change. Either people repent and draw closer to God and fall more in love with Him, or they are repulsed and flee from Him. Jesus is the absolute Truth of God, which exposes sin, error, deception, selfish ambition, evil lusts, greed, and darkness. Therefore, when Jesus shows up things will usually get worse before they improve. Revival is like a sledgehammer that shatters long hardened ideals and pet theologies, especially hearts hardened by sin and pride. In our heading passage Jesus is speaking about such people, and His mention of their forefathers was a stiff rebuke to say the least. The gist is that false prophets are highly spoken of (even applauded), but true prophets are despised, rejected, and condemned to death. Jesus never told people what they wanted to hear; He told them what they needed for life.

All Christians (pastors, elders, deacons, and members) who fall in the snare of trying to please people will ultimately come to ruin. This is because people will dictate their decisions, sermons, and lifestyles rather than God. Traditionalized by man-made standards, they will continue to be dominated by a spirit of timidity. People-pleasing believers who give themselves over to worldly compromise, quite likely would never have faced the mouth of a lion for their beliefs; they would have been the first to say, "Okay! I renounce my faith in Jesus!"

The reality is that most people really want to be left unchanged, undisturbed, and comfortable in this world; they desire unrighteous living with a righteous eternity, all at Jesus' expense. Anything that exposes their religious fraud and demands repentance from selfish living will not just be unfavorably spoken of; it will be feverishly fought against and despised to death.

Dear devoted saint, if people are speaking evil of you because of your godly standard, never let it cause you woe. Jesus said woe is when they are "not" doing that. Never despise what pleases the Lord, and do not be pleased with what He despises. His standard is narrow, offensive to the selfish, despised by the self-righteous, and loved by few. Love it by your choices and with your life.

For Thought:

Read Galatians 1:10. Pleasing God demands change. People who love to fellowship with Jesus generally welcome change. People who despise Jesus despise change. His standard demands change, and is altogether "other" than any standard of man. There is no such thing as a stagnant walk with the Lord. Stagnancy is rebellion disguised.

Day 124

Not Boxing the Air

"Therefore I run in such a way, as not without aim; I box in such a way, as not beating the air" (1 Corinthians 9:26).

Doing righteous behaviors only when the enemy is not attacking, when the sinful flesh is not craving, and when the lure of the world is absent is not victorious living. That is no more victory than entering a boxing ring with an imaginary opponent and boxing the air for ten rounds makes you a heavyweight champion. No. Loving when the flesh wants to lust; giving despite the feeling to take; speaking truth when the temptation to exaggerate or lie is immense; forgiving when the desire to retaliate is strong or even seems reasonable; doing God's will when your will would be more self-gratifying; this is victorious living.

It is doing the right thing when the right thing feels wrong, rather than doing the wrong thing because the wrong thing feels right. In other words, victorious living is doing the righteous behavior in spite of the overwhelming desire to do what is unrighteous. It is quite easy to do the right things when there is no opposition or temptation. However, many Christians err when they justify their current unrighteous behaviors by all the right things they were doing when there was no battle. Ezekiel writes, "But if a righteous person turns from their righteousness and commits sin and does the same detestable things the wicked person does, will they live? None of the righteous things that person has done will be remembered" (18:24).

When there is no wind, flying a kite is impossible. Equally, a trial and temptation-free life does not work and would only produce a spiritually anemic Christian. We have a real enemy to fight, and Paul tells us it is our flesh. This enemy is not defeated through self-ascetic practices (see Colossians 2:20-23). It is only through submitting to the Word of God, as prompted by the Holy Spirit, that the corruptions of the old nature are subdued. When the flesh barks for its indulgence, remember God's love toward you and how much it cost Him at Calvary. Then, stirred by the confidence of who you are in Him, do the God-glorifying action instead.

Praying for God to remove temptation is equal to asking Him to leave you as an untrained soldier, completely unprepared for spiritual warfare. All you would continue doing is boxing the air and call that "training," yet never experiencing what true victorious living really is. The next time you are facing trials or temptations try changing your perspective. Thank God for the opportunity to practice your training in righteousness.

For Thought:

Read Hebrews 12:11. What does discipline produce? How do we feel about it at first?

Read 1 Timothy 4:6-8. With love for the Lord as the fuel and godliness as the objective, disciplined training is a joy.

Day 125

Minor Corrections

"For this command is a lamp, this teaching is a light, and correction and instruction are the way to life" (Proverbs 6:23, NIV).

Imagine an honorable captain of a large ship on the high seas. The people aboard are the cargo. He has a straight heading plotted and a three-month mission to get his cargo safely to their destination. How successfully will he arrive if he only glances at his compass twice a week?

We read in the book of Proverbs, "Stern discipline awaits anyone who leaves the path; the one who hates correction will die" (15:10). Knowing the dangerous results of neglecting his compass, an honorable captain takes great care in his mission and its duties. His own life is not his chief concern; the safe arrival of his cargo is. If he hated correction, the journey would likely end with starvation and death for all those aboard. He would then be a wicked captain and an unrighteous guide. "The righteous is a guide to his neighbor, but the way of the wicked leads them astray" (Proverbs 12:26).

Even though the heading is straight, the honorable captain knows that it is impossible to sail a perfectly straight line. He therefore is constantly studying his navigation instruments. But how successfully do you think he would arrive if he only studied his instruments? A good captain not only repetitively studies his compass; he also adheres to it by continuously making the necessary minor corrections. Many times his navigation instruments show him where he is a bit off course and he then responsibly grabs the helm and makes the slight correction. Carelessness produces large corrections.

God has also given us navigational instruments; The Holy Spirit is our Guide and His Word is our compass. How often are you paying attention to them? Are you a spiritual leader of your home or church? If you fall asleep at the helm, you not only could miss your destination, but also take an entire cargo of others with you. Remember that your navigation instruments are not just to show where you are off course; they are there to be followed and obeyed. The Way is made straight before you (Psalm 5:8), so "Let your eyes look directly ahead and let your gaze be fixed straight in front of you" (Proverbs 4:25). There is only one Person who walked a perfectly straight line on the perfectly straight path and that was Jesus. Nevertheless, you must continuously pay attention to His provided navigational instruments and make the necessary minor corrections. You will then arrive safely at your destination.

For Thought:

Compare this devotion with James 1:22. Are those who are only hearers of the Word honorable captains? Doers of the Word love correction because it leads them home.

Day 126

Humbled or Stumbled?

"For judgment I came into this world, so that those who do not see might see, and that those who see might become blind" (John 9:39).

The two words of importance in this passage are "judgment" (*krima*), and "see" (*blépō*). The Greek root word for judgment is *krino*, which means separating between what is good and evil. The word Jesus uses in our devotion passage is *krima*. It contains the suffix "ma" that stresses result. In other words, *krino* is the act of distinguishing and separating, and *krima* is the end result of both separated parties arriving at their proper eternal destination.

The word Jesus uses for "see" is *blépō*. It means to physically see something leading to the results of spiritual perception. Jesus' response to the perturbed Pharisees (vs.41) is key. Jesus said, "If you were blind, you would have no sin; but since you say, 'We see,' your sin remains." The "sight" that the Pharisees insisted they had was: Only the law, its strict keeping, their own righteousness, and the confidence they put in their Abrahamic ancestry. This is what they trusted in for their salvation. This was "the sin" that Jesus referred to that they would be without if they were "blind" instead, namely "blind" to all they refused to renounce. They would continue to have "the sin" because they would never acknowledge they had it. Their pride, prestige, positions, and pedigrees were all they could see. Those who were blind to all of that were those who would be without "the sin." To "see" meant, seeing righteousness apart from Jesus. "Blind" meant not seeing righteousness as possible apart from Jesus.

What is "the sin"? It is the sin of self-deception, the most threatening sin of all. It is most deadly because those who have it usually never see it! The law's design, as the tutor to lead them to see their desperate need for a Savior, fails.

Because all the Pharisees could see was their own righteousness, all they could see in Jesus was His humanity. Jesus was saying those who cannot see any good in themselves would be able to see His divinity— that He was indeed God incarnate sent to save all who would see their need for Him. Those who see only their human righteousness cannot obtain the spiritual perception of seeing the righteousness that is in Christ Jesus alone; those who are *blind* to their own righteousness can. That is what Jesus means here.

More powerfully stated, Jesus is Judgment. He is the line of demarcation. He is the winnowing Truth. He is the block over which people stumble. Anyone who holds fast to "I'm a good person," is the proud Pharisee that says, "I can see!" All who do not see any goodness in themselves apart from Christ are those who are humbled by Jesus, not stumbled by Him. Are you humbled or stumbled?

Day 127

Thief or Sheep?

"He who does not enter by the door into the fold of the sheep, but climbs up some other way, he is a thief and a robber" (John 10:1).

Jesus is the dividing door between the true flock of God and those who are outside. The Pharisees could not see their need for Him and had usurped His authority by commandeering the position of spiritual guidance of God's people without a spiritual commission. They were truly blind but refused to acknowledge this truth insisting that they could "see." Since all they chose to see was their own self-righteousness, they had by effect eliminated their need for repentance. Therefore, in simplicity of terms, the door to the sheepfold is repentance. Yes, Jesus is the Gate, but those who enter by this door are only those who see their need for Him, which demands repentance.

Many people want to enjoy the eternal (as well as earthly) benefits of being in the sheepfold of God without entering through the true gate of repentance, so they purpose to climb over the fence when the Shepherd is not looking. The absurdity here is that they actually think He does not see. They have blotted Him out of their lives for so long and suppressed the truth of His all-seeing ability so they could comfortably give over to their sin, that they have become fully deceived themselves. Thus they are deceiving thieves and robbers.

They climb over the fence into the sheepfold bypassing true repentance (only possible through brokenness). They put on the best sheep outfits, learn how to talk like, act like, eat like, and move like sheep. They say, "Hey, we're one of you!" However, they will never truly enjoy or appreciate the beauty, wonders, and blessings that the true sheep do inside the fold. They can never sincerely worship Jesus like the rest of the true sheep. They can never love Jesus with hearts overflowing with gratitude, all because they bypassed repentance. Only broken people will worship the Christ (Shepherd) that mended them.

Repentance is a complete turning away from the old lifestyle. No one can love the new life that Jesus provides unless they see the old life as wretched. The power and help that Jesus gives is only beautiful to those who were utterly powerless and helpless in their old life, and become fully convinced of its ugliness. You may climb into the church and adapt, but one day the fraud will be exposed, and it will be the empty worship, ritualistic religion, and lack of true joy that gives you away. Come broken, empty, and poor in spirit, and the Door is always open. Jesus the Shepherd knows those who are His true sheep. Climb over the fence and the door will be forever shut.

For Thought:

God's entry way is absolute or it is obsolete.

Day 128

Don't Be a Right-Fighter!

"Therefore, confess your sins to one another, and pray for one another so that you may be healed" (James 5:16).

People indifferent to the Spirit of God carry with them such a desperate desire to be right all the time, that they loathe biblical correction. The last thing they want is for someone to speak truth into their lives. Just look at the divorce rate in the church as proof. We see spouses wanting to win an argument so badly that they pull out every weapon in order to do so. What he or she fails to learn is there really is no winner in this. For instance if the husband fights to win, his wife loses; therefore he loses also, because they are one flesh. They are not "sexually legal" roommates living parallel lives under one roof! What affects her affects him; what wounds her wounds him. Name-calling, shouting, threatening divorce, using the kids as leverage for their selfish agenda, all this is devilishly executed just for the sake of being right. Of course all the above is performed under the title "Christian," which declares to the world that this is acceptable behavior for people who "love Jesus."

Those who confess their sins one to another see their desperate need for repentance and prayer. Self-righteous people are repulsed by anyone who would confront their sin and rebellion, even the pastor or preacher. Then there are those who have become extremely fearful to confront anyone at all. Filled with people pleasing fear of man, they submit to a spirit of timidity and allow their sheep to wander off dangerous cliffs.

The broken-down result is a collection of members who only need each other if they are sick or financially broke, but rarely because they are wrong and off the straight path. They cease needing anyone who can see unnoticed errors in their life from the outside and give the necessary biblical direction. They are "right," and desire to remain that way, usually at the cost of their marriages, churches, and relationship with God. They are called "right-fighters." They do not fight for righteousness, but only for what they are convinced is right. "There is a way which seems right to a man, but its end is the way of death" (Proverbs 16:25). We know answered prayer brings healing, but the act of praying also brings healing to the selfish heart. The ultimate healing is the removal of sin. Confessing sin allows those who love to pray the opportunity to do what they love, which becomes healing ointment to their souls. When they pray for you, your heart also gets healing. The sin is brought into the light and dealt with, which strengthens fellowship among the church. It is mercy all around.

For Thought:

Read 1 John 1:7. Tragically, biblical illiteracy and spiritual immaturity prevail, to such an extent that discipleship and biblical counseling are either unavailable or unappreciated.

Killed with Kindness

> "Uriah did not go home. In the morning David wrote a letter, 'Put Uriah out in front where the fighting is fiercest. Then withdraw from him so he will be struck down and die.'" (2 Samuel 11:13-14).

Just like Adam and Eve and the sons of God in Genesis 6:2, David saw the forbidden fruit as delightful to the eye and desirable. He inquired of it, took it, and then partook of it. James wrote in his Epistle, "When lust has conceived, it gives birth to sin; and when sin is accomplished, it brings forth death" (1:15). Sin's wages of death were menacing over David putting him in a serious quandary. He became filled with irrational desperation to cover his sin (Adam and Eve used fig leaves). Therefore, to cover his adulterous treachery against Uriah, David tried to manipulate him, and then covered that with false kindness.

Uriah was a man of honor and his loyalty was commendable. He would not receive what his brothers in arms could not. However, as honorable and loyal as he was, Uriah was now an obstacle in the way of David's lust needing to be permanently removed. Treachery and lust cannot see loyalty and honor; in fact, they are a loathsome reproach.

Treachery and conspiring lust often hide behind false faces of kindness. "No wonder, for even Satan disguises himself as an angel of light" (2 Corinthians 11:14). He came as the most cunning beast of the field to the first Adam and came as a pompous ruler with lavish offerings to the last Adam (Jesus). He also comes to us with false promises of pleasure that lead only to eternal death. David's gift to Uriah was treacherous murder covered in chocolate kindness; like the evil king in Daniel 11:32, "With flattery he will corrupt." Paul admonished, "For such men are slaves, not of our Lord Christ but of their own appetites; and by their smooth words and flattering speech they deceive the hearts of the unsuspecting" (Romans 16:18).

People who smile while bitter envy consumes their heart are those who "kill with kindness." We even hear believers use that terminology: "Kill them with kindness!" We should not need to wonder what master they are serving nor what manner of spirit they are. Conspiring lust, bitter envy, and treacherous contempt destroy loyalty and honor. Kindness is a fruit of the Holy Spirit and He would never use what is holy to wound or kill. To kill with kindness is Satan-inspired, and treacherous hypocrisy. Be kind, but only to heal. Kindness used to hurt or retaliate is a fruit of the Devil cloaked as fruit of the Spirit. Madness!

For Study:

Job 32:22
Job 17:5
Proverbs 6:24, 7:21

Psalm 5:9, 12:2
Ecclesiastes 7:5
1 Thessalonians 2:5

Day 130

Who is My Neighbor? (Part 1)

Read (Luke 10:25-37).
"A man was going down from Jerusalem to Jericho and fell among robbers, and they stripped him and beat him, and went away leaving him half dead."

Jesus answers the question, "Who is my neighbor?" with a parable. This means that every person, place, thing, and event, were purposely chosen by Him to not only answer the question, but also to veil other heavenly truths. Each detail possesses a spiritual meaning in need of being mined because there are specific reasons why He chose them. Before we arrive at our ultimate answer we must first examine some other thoughts. For start, why was the man departing *Jerusalem* and going to *Jericho*?

The road from Jerusalem to Jericho was a major highway and was so straight that you could see very far down it. This would restrict robbers from attacking people in the daytime, so very likely the man was traveling all alone in the dark. Jerusalem means "foundation of peace." It symbolizes being in a place of wholeness and rest inside of God's covenant of peace. Jericho was the greatest stronghold of the enemy in Joshua 6. God said, "The city and everything in it are set apart for destruction," and "keep yourselves from" it or "you will be set apart for destruction" (vs. 17-18). God destroyed that city by His own mighty hand and then declared, "The man who undertakes the rebuilding of this city, Jericho, is cursed before the Lord."

Therefore, the man was abandoning the place of wholeness, rest, and peace in hopes to find something of value in a cursed place that God had already destroyed. He was basically leaving the refuge of God to go back to an old stronghold of sin, and the fact that he was traveling all alone in the darkness strengthens that point.

"Thorns and snares are in the way of the crooked; whoever guards his soul will keep far from them" (Proverbs 22:5). Never leave the dwelling place of God's blessing for a cursed illusion of pleasure. Never leave the lighted path of righteousness for the darkened path of sin. It is an affront to Jesus the Good Samaritan that saved you once before from this path. Have you entertained thoughts of revisiting an old sin? The robber of your soul, who only comes to kill, steal, and destroy, is lurking on that road. "A rebellious man seeks only evil, so a cruel messenger will be sent against him" (Proverbs 17:11). Never try to return to a stronghold that God has pulled down; you may not live through it.

For Thought:

Why did Jesus not have the Good Samaritan show up and rescue the man while he was being mugged?

Hint: It has to do with true repentance.

Day 131

Who is My Neighbor? (Part 2)

Read (Luke 10:25-37).
"A priest was going down on that road, and when he saw him, he passed by on the other side, likewise a Levite also, when he came to the place and saw him, passed by on the other side."

A priest was a servant in the temple. A Levite was a descendant of Levi and a superintendent of the temple. A priest's greatest concern was seeing that every detail of the sacrificial system was in order; priests were the mediators. The Levite's concern was over the inanimate objects, including the tabernacle/temple itself. Therefore, Jesus' usage of a priest and a Levite must be centered on their religious duties.

Traveling priests were likely leaving Jerusalem after their tenure of religious duties. If a priest were to touch a naked man, especially one thought to be dead, they would be disqualified from those duties for an entire day of ritual washings (Leviticus 15). He would also have to present very expensive offerings and go to a section of the temple reserved for unclean priests (it was a shameful thing). Levites took great pride in their ancestral status and their exclusive position of taking care of the temple. God said, "Any unauthorized person who comes near it must be put to death" (Numbers 1:51). He also said the "Levites belong to Me" (3:12). Moreover, God commanded that they were to "send away anyone who has a bodily discharge, or who is defiled because of a corpse" (Numbers 5:1, 2).

Their priestly and Levitical religious duties forbid them to touch this man who was surely bloody and very likely thought to be a dead corpse. The law demanded cleanliness but also demanded expensive restitution offerings for uncleanness. So to help this man was extremely risky and costly. Their religious pride was too precious to sacrifice for compassion. Religion will not save a soul. Religious people pass by what would risk their prestigious positions, pious images, and pocketbooks. These "heroes of religion" were surpassed by a Samaritan dreg. It was a radical rebuke from Jesus to those who were listening. Jesus is saying that loving the Lord by loving your neighbor will cost you everything. The question is, "Is He worth it?"

For Thought:

There may also be an allegorical truth in this parable: Since the old religious system would end at the beginning of Christ's Gospel Dispensation, the priestly and Levitical roles would also "pass." Just like in the parable, standing alone to save "dead men" would be the half Jew, half Gentile Samaritan. This speaks of both Jew and Gentile being saved from eternal death and united in One Man, Jesus (Romans 1:16; Galatians 3:28).

Day 132

Who is My Neighbor? (Part 3)

Read (Luke 10:25-37).
"He went over to him and bandaged his wounds, pouring on olive oil and wine. Then he put him on his own animal, brought him to an inn, and took care of him."

This act is all about the costliness of compassion. The eastern customs of that time determined that once he touched the man he took responsibility for him. If the man had died under his care he could have been liable for his death, and the avenger of blood could have come after him (the avenger of blood had the right to execute the one responsible for the death of his kinsman). The Samaritan was putting his own life on the line; today's western mindset misses this important truth.

This Samaritan was probably wealthy. People who rode donkeys were generally wealthy, and many were kings. It was another custom for wealthy travelers to wear expensive robes to mark their importance, especially if he were a king. When the Samaritan came to the man, the man was stripped naked; which meant the Samaritan would need to cover him. This implies the need for the Samaritan to use his own expensive robe. Costly compassion just got costlier, but it doesn't stop here. The Samaritan could not tell if the naked man was Jewish or not (they were usually distinguished by their clothing). This meant there was a chance that once the man recovered he might never repay the debt because Jews detested Samaritans. The Samaritan was willing to love without worldly repayment, and without the praises of men. Compassion got even pricier, but continues more.

The Samaritan then put the man on his own donkey, where two grown men could not fit. This meant that he would have to walk like a servant in front of his own donkey while the man wearing his own expensive robe sat in the high place of honor (see Philippians 2:5-8). The Samaritan was willing to take on the form of a lowly servant with the possibility of other people thinking the man on the donkey was the wealthy master or king.

What remarkable humility! What selfless sacrifice! Compassion costs our pride, our money, and possibly even our own life, all for love's sake. Love is dead to self and alive to God. That is why Jesus said in Matthew 5:46-47, "If you love those who love you, what reward will you get? Are not even the tax collectors doing that? And if you greet only your own people, what are you doing more than others? Do not even pagans do that?" Jesus was willing to suffer and die for a world that would mostly never love Him back. He calls you and I to do the same. Consider the cost of compassion!

For Thought:

Read 2 Corinthians 5:15. Does this describe your Christian walk?

Day 133

Who is My Neighbor? (Part 4)

"They stripped him and beat him, and went away leaving him half dead" (Luke 10:30).

Is not this the way our enemy leaves us after we have departed from God to pursue what the enemy offers to gratify our selfish desires? You were certain that divorce was the right path—at the cost of your children. You just knew that there was gratification downtown at the strip club—at the cost of your ministry. You just had to click on that website—at the cost of your marriage. You just had to tell your mother and all your close sisters about what your husband did—at the cost of both of your reputations. Winning that account for your lavish vacation this summer was so important—at the cost of your integrity. Winning that argument with your spouse felt good—at the cost of her honor and yours. Calling that old drug dealer just one more time seemed reasonable—at the cost of your life, and the lives of a widowed wife and fatherless kids.

Everything gets broken: Families, hearts, relationships, hope, bodies, minds, and ultimately eternities. The person is stripped, beaten, and left for dead by the enemy. He or she is now left to ponder "Where in the world was the good Samaritan when I needed Him?" That is a good question indeed.

In Jesus' parable, why did He not have the Samaritan heroically show up while the man was being attacked? Why did he wait until the near death and ultimate ruin of the man to save him? The answer is, he would never have appreciated his rescue. He only needed assistance before, but now he needed a Savior. You must come to the place of utter brokenness, stripped of every man-made covering, and dead to the old life. That is when Jesus, the Good Samaritan shows up. Never does He come to spare you from that, because He knows if He did you would only be glad He gave you more time to love your idols. He knows you would only continue down the same road to sin and destruction you were traveling. Jesus did not come to assist people in living godless lives; He came to rescue people from them. He always purposes to show up at the last hour of despondency and desolation. Jesus begins at your end. Paul had also come to the end of himself on a similar road to destruction (the destruction of innocent Christians). Therefore he was able to say, "I have been crucified with Christ; and it is no longer I who live, but Christ lives in me" (Galatians 2:20).

Every child of God, was beaten, stripped, and left for dead in his or her sin. "Who is my neighbor?" Jesus tells us our neighbor is the Samaritan that risked everything, even his own life to shower us with mercy and costly compassion. He then says the way to love Him is to "Go and do the same" (Luke 10:37), without repayment, without the praises of men, and as a lowly servant willing to lift up an equally undeserving lost world.

Day 134

When Instruments Conquered Instruction

"If anyone does not obey our instruction . . . do not associate with him . . . yet do not regard him as an enemy, but admonish him as a brother" (2 Thessalonians 3:14,15).

The word for admonish here is *noutheteō*. It means, "I admonish, warn, counsel through instruction; appealing to the mind by supplying doctrinal and spiritual substance. This exerts positive pressure on someone's reasoning, which urges them to repent and choose God's best."[18] This is the ministry known today as confrontational biblical counseling. This ministry was one of the largest parts of the early church and was fervently in continuous operation. Biblical counseling and the church were inseparable. Now they are rarely seen together.

The culture that we live in calls good evil and evil good. Television and media constantly bombard us with worldly lusts, and while they can provide useful sources of communication, much of what they convey is ungodly and selfish. For example, through advertising, there is constant pressure to buy what the advertisers claim will bring fulfillment and happiness, usually using sex and sensuality. God, holiness, and the church, are mocked in sitcoms and late-night entertainment shows. Over a period of time, the propaganda instilled by a sensually charged media has the effect of desensitizing believers to sin, exacerbating their already lukewarm spiritual slumber.

With that said; if there ever was a time where biblical counseling was needed most, it is now! And yet somehow it has been severed from the church as "non-evangelistic" and "nonessential." Find a church with a biblical counseling department and you have found gold; find a church with a paid worship leader and you have found nothing special.

Financially limited, the church leadership looks at a talented musician and then looks at a trained biblical counselor; guess who gets the spot? Good music, people like; good admonishment, people hate. Dictated by the church growth movement, growth in numbers outweighs spiritual growth. Good music never offended anyone; confronting sin, lust, and pride through bold admonishment of the Truth is highly offensive—especially to the majority who despise submitting to authority. Do we want ears tickled or lives changed? Do we want fuzzy emotions, or flaming hearts?

For Thought:

We are inundated with pleas from the church to pray for our nation. Who is going to petition God for a spiritual awakening in the lukewarm church? Saint, will you? What cost will you pay? Your prayer life will determine it.

Do we need true revival or more retreats? Do we need more fun programs or fervent prayer?

Day 135

Choose Your Table Wisely

"You cannot partake of the table of the Lord and the table of demons" (1 Corinthians 10:21).

In the book of Second Samuel, David had finally ascended to his rightful position as king of Israel. Saul and his son Jonathan had tragically died and even though Saul had tormented David for several years, David still wanted to "show kindness to Saul's family" (9:1) because of his unfailing love for Jonathan. He found a son of Jonathan's named Mephibosheth who was probably left alive because of his crippled affliction. He was found in Lo-debar, a dreg-ridden place so named because of its pasture-less condition. It was a place without green fields for grazing which implies its low economic status. It was quite common for outlaws to frequent, take refuge in, and even take residence in towns such as this one. No one of any prominence had any desire to come to such a poverty-stricken place, so fugitives, riff-raff, and dregs of society were many times the majority of the population.

Can you imagine the petrifying fear of Mephibosheth, knowing he was a grandson of Saul, David's most tormenting enemy? "He's here to kill me!" he must have thought. On the contrary, the king was there to pour out his loving-kindness upon this undeserving cripple to have the lifelong honor of eating at the king's table "just like one of the king's sons" (9:11).

All of us as saved saints were undeserving cripples maimed with sin, and by our old Adamic ancestry, we also were enemies of the King of kings (see Romans 5:10). But Jesus in His unmerited mercy came to our own dreg-infested Lo-debar to seat us with Him in the heavenly places (Ephesians 2:6), at the King's table for the eternal "marriage supper of the Lamb" (Revelation 19:9).

Numerous believers secretly dine at the enemy's table, drink from his poisonous cup of sin and lust, and then come back to Jesus so He can remove the poison. What's astounding is that Jesus does it nonetheless, because He is mercy. He knows their hard hearts will either soften and be won over, or they will grow harder, leaving them with no excuse when they stand before Him. From which cup are you drinking, the cup of communion or the cup of rebellion? From which table are you eating, the King's or the enemy's? You cannot keep partaking of both. Lord forbid we even entertain the treacherous thought!

For Thought:

In Revelation 3:16, the Lord said He would spit out the lukewarm. It is a known fact that tepid beverages are loathsome and trigger gag reflexes. Lukewarm Christians are that way because like Ephraim in Hosea 7, they mix with the cold, dead lifestyles of the world.

Read 1 Kings 18:21.

Day 136

They Abandoned their Idols

"Like a bursting flood, the LORD has burst out against my enemies before me . . . The Philistines abandoned their idols there" (2 Samuel 5:20-21, HCS).

King David had just witnessed God's mighty power "burst out like a flood" against His enemies, defeating them to the point they had to abandon their idols. This must have been quite some outburst of God! Keep in mind, pagan nations depended on their idol worship; they believed victory and conquest was contingent upon appeasing their false gods with ritual. For the Philistines to abandon their idols meant one of two things: 1) Either they were so utterly overpowered that they saw the worthlessness of their idols and forsook them as such, or 2) they were so overwhelmed with God's sudden flood of strength that they were forced to flee so fast that they left behind their idols. It is possible that both are true. Nonetheless, God's conquering flood at *Baal-perazim* was an awesome victory indeed, enough to be recorded in the annals of biblical history.

This may also remind us of Noah's flood that swallowed a world full of God-hating enemies. Think of all the idols that must have been scattered upon the ground after the floodwaters receded; they were certainly abandoned by their worshipers. What is unmistakable is that God is an enemy to those who make themselves enemies of His by their worship of idols. "You adulteresses, do you not know that friendship with the world is hostility toward God? Therefore whoever wishes to be a friend of the world makes himself an enemy of God" (James 4:4).

When The Lord finally bursts forth like a flood, all Christ-rejecting people will see the worthlessness of their idolatry and godless worship.

Every vain idol will be abandoned, and every idol-worshiper will be swept away. Isaiah writes, "The pride of man will be humbled, and the loftiness of men will be abased; the LORD alone will be exalted in that day, the idols will completely vanish" (2:17-18).

For Thought:

Many believers grossly err by thinking only of objects, vices, inordinate behaviors, and cultish religions as idolatry. The blunder is in overlooking the biggest idol of all, the worship and love of self. Hopefully they will see their error, repent, and abandon their idolatry before that great Day of the Lord bursts out like a flood upon them. Let us be sober, watch, and pray.

God hates great swimmers; they never drown, and therefore never need to be resuscitated and resurrected. They say, "Look how good we can swim!" God says, "Look how well you never died!"

Day 137

Don't Be a Stranger

> "The ark of the LORD remained in his house three months, and the LORD blessed Obed-edom and his whole family" (2 Samuel 6:11, HCS).

It is a foolish thing for God to be a stranger in your house. But it is a fearful thing to be a stranger in God's house. Just ask the man in Matthew 22:12-13 who tried to sneak into the king's wedding banquet without the authorized attire. Ask Nadab and Abihu who also came into the presence of God in an unauthorized manner. Truth is, the only reason people remain strangers to God is because He remains a stranger to them. The remedy to being a stranger in the house of God is not merely by allowing His dwelling, but rather by giving Him your house to be His permanent dwelling place.

Obed-edom had a spiritual insight even greater than David. He willingly took the ark into his house. This was "the ark of God, whose name is called by the name of the LORD of hosts that dwells between the cherubim" (2 Samuel 6:2). Surely he must have mulled over what happened to Uzzah when he took hold of the ark and God's anger struck him dead for his irreverence. Remember, David was so perturbed by this event that he wanted nothing to do with the Ark. It does not make sense that David was glad about God's prior outburst against the Philistines but was angry at God's outburst against Uzzah (2 Samuel 5:20 and 6:6-8). David could see the Philistines as a blatant enemy of God, but could not see the secret opposition of pride in Uzzah's heart that only God must have seen. Because of his ignorance, David missed out on three months of blessing, but at least it only took him that long to learn. What did Obed-edom know that David did not?

Obed-edom knew that God is only hostile to those who are hostile to Him, but the opposition that God is concerned about is that which is in the heart. God's presence will not reside forever in a heart where His enemies are welcomed and loved. Obed-edom also knew the reverse was true. He knew that God blesses those who bless Him from a worship filled heart. This implies that Obed-edom had a pure heart and he knew it. He knew that if God were to search his heart and see if there be any wicked way within him, He would find none unconfessed. God knew his heart and he knew God's heart, therefore there was peace and fellowship between them.

Clear your home of all that is opposed to the Lord; do the same with your heart. The wonderful result will be when God's presence fills the dwelling that you have given Him to possess. He doesn't just bless you; He blesses the whole family. Then you will not only have a heart for God; you will be the heart of God, and never again a stranger.

For Thought:

Is Jesus your Husband or a roommate?

Day 138

Strangers in God's House

"You brought in foreigners, uncircumcised in heart and uncircumcised in flesh, to be in My sanctuary to profane it" (Ezekiel 44:7).

The rebuke here is not toward those who are sin-sick and newcomers to the church. For what is the church's mission but to be a hospital for sick souls? The rebuke is to churchgoers, whose lives should be exhibiting the image of Christ Jesus and His holiness, but on the contrary continue to remain as worldly as the unsaved. Foreigners that come into that assembly have no contrast of standard by which to judge. They are new strangers of God coming into a gathering of old ones.

Foreigners wander in seeking a higher standard, real help, new hope, and an authentic representation of this holy and powerful God of transformation that the people and marquis champion. Instead they discover only religion and people demanding they change their dress but not their heart. They hear weird language and even more bizarre behavior, or they see their own breath from the coldness of the air. Either way they come into an atmosphere that should be a reproach to their old way of life, but instead is very conducive and similar to it.

Hence both the newcomer and the old comer are devoid of true worship of God, willfully ignorant to the teachings of the Spirit, and without desperate need for real intimacy and fellowship with Jesus. They rebel against self-denial, humility, and holiness, and are illiterate to the non-legalistic, joyful practices of such. They are blind to their own condition, convinced that they are "good people with good hearts and bad habits."

With seared consciences they are numb to the cutting of God's Word, and dumb to the deceitfulness of the sin they practice. Strangers to contrition of heart, true repentance, and joy-filled worship, they are also strangers to the unadulterated Gospel of Christ, His finished work, and His divine truths. Their hearts proceed untouched by God, un-pricked for sin, unhealed by Jesus, and untransformed. The pain, desperate groaning, and shameful tears at the revelation of sin and rebellion are never felt. So they are left in an unrepentant, natural, and unconverted state. The lusts of the eyes the lusts of the flesh, and the pride of life and are never exhorted to be denied and never admonished if they are not. All this has been brought into His Holy Sanctuary, thereby profaning it.

God's house must be cleansed not only of the idolatry and sin, but also of all the paraphernalia used for their worship; that means the removal of every instrument, place, ideal, and every person associated with them. Just as it was with Josiah's reformation, once it is purified, there will be an unprecedented celebration of the Lord for His returned presence (see 2 Kings 23:4-25).

For Thought:

Revival comes to the sheep only after the shepherd.

Day 139

Bark, For Heaven's Sake!

"His watchmen are blind: they are all ignorant, they are all dumb dogs, they cannot bark; sleeping, lying down, loving to slumber" (Isaiah 56:10, KJV).

There was a house we used to pass as kids when riding our bikes. It had a fenced in yard with a very large dog that had an even larger bark. The sidewalk was maybe a foot from the fence and we would never know if the dog was sleeping or awake until we were right next to the fence. If there was a detour to avoid it, we would have taken it, but there was none. Every so often we would ride past without a peep from the dog. But most times we would think it was sleeping and it would catch us by surprise with a bark so viciously loud that some of us would nearly wreck. Oh how we hated that dog!

One of the reasons people keep dogs is to be a watchdog whose bark not only sounds the alarm, but also frightens away undesirable intruders. Watchdogs that bark are only doing what they are supposed to, and what they were designed by God to do. Mute watchdogs that lie down and sleep all the time are useless to their masters' intentions. When warning is needed they fail to do what they were purchased, bred, and designed to do. They become a cumbersome burden to their masters who have to feed them for nothing in return. Even worse, they become gluttonous frauds that reside in a position of protection, yet offering none whatsoever. Once I learned this, I actually looked back with much appreciation for that dog I hated as a child. I also realized that even though the dog was asleep sometimes, we would still ride by very cautiously. So even when the dog was rightfully taking a snooze, it was still effective, because it did its job well when it was awake.

Immature compromise-loving believers hate barking dogs; mature Christians not only love them, they acknowledge their desperate need for them. Careless pastors and elders who refuse to assail sin, worldliness, and idolatry from the pulpit, or preach a watered-down message are mute watchmen. They do nothing but eat, grow fat off the people's offerings, and slumber. They are worthless to the Kingdom of God; they are gluttonous frauds like Eli. Just as Isaiah writes in the following verse, "These dogs have fierce appetites; they never have enough" (56:11).

This devotional is designed to do what most watchmen will not do—bark! To those who call themselves leaders of God's people, if you are mute for Him, He will be mute to you. Love and feed your sheep by sounding the alarm and waking up from your slumber. Be the barking watchmen that your Master purchased, bred, and designed you to be. If you are just an average lay believer in the church, you also have a charge not to be silent. There is world of lost people. "Go into all the world and preach the gospel to all creation" (Mark 16:15). Bark, for heaven's sake!

Day 140

The Bread that Ends All Bread

"The manna ceased" (Joshua 5:12).

Manna was heavenly food provided for earthly people. In Exodus 16:4, God said, "Behold, I will rain bread from heaven for you; and the people shall go out and gather a day's portion every day, that I may test them, whether or not they will walk in My instruction." The first part of the verse God gives an unconditional promise; the second part He gives a conditional premise. This was to teach them how to be dependent on God as the Provider of their "daily bread." When bellies grumble so to people. When provisions are scant so is faith. Oh how we need to be taught to walk by faith rather than by sight. Proverbs 3:5 says "Trust in the LORD with all your heart and lean not on your own understanding."

God was bringing them to the end of human ability and wisdom, and into the blessed state of poverty of spirit. Poverty of spirit is the state of utter powerlessness and the acknowledgment of self-nothingness. This is where the faith of many Christians collapses. If they cannot fix it, see it, or control it they panic and flee from the will of God. Jesus said this would happen; "The worries of the world, and the deceitfulness of riches, and the desires for other things enter in and choke the word, and it becomes unfruitful" (Mark 4:19).

The manna was a type of Christ, a shadow of things to come. Jesus said that He is the Bread of Life, the Living Bread that came down from heaven (John 6:35, 51). The manna would satisfy hunger temporarily; Jesus would satisfy hunger eternally. In Exodus 16, God said there would be no manna on the seventh (Sabbath) day, but on the sixth day He would give a double portion. The Sabbath symbolized the Great Day of the Lord. This implies God's rest from providing bread; they would have to draw from yesterday's doubled graces. No other bread can enter into the Presence of Jesus, the Living Bread of the Presence (see Exodus 25:30).

In Joshua 5, the manna ceased for good once they crossed over the Jordan into the Land of Promise. Crossing the Jordan into the Promised Land typifies entering into heaven. Entering into the Sabbath rest of heaven is hinged upon whether the former life partook of God's grace provided by the broken Bread of His Son at Calvary.

In heaven, manna is no longer needed. No provision is necessary in an eternity with *Jehovah-Jireh* (God our Provider). It was the season of harvest for the Israelites, and the miraculous provision of manna was replaced. Miracles will cease once the fullness of Christ is obtained in the heavenly harvest. Jesus, the greatest miracle will be forever enjoyed. We will be eternally filled with the broken Bread from Heaven, with our souls ever captivated in worship of Him. "The eyes of all look to You, and You give them their food in due time" (Psalm 145:15). Our spiritual eyes will be eternally fixed upon the slain Lamb of God who took away the sin of the world.

Day 141

Love is Always Crucified! *"To destroy the works of the Devil"* (1 John 3:8)

There is an immeasurable difference between seeing people added to your church and seeing souls being liberated from the power of the enemy. Jesus came to "seek and save the lost" (Luke 19:10). The church is His body and its mission must be identical to His. How often do we see the church building to impress the lost? How often do we the church delighting in the works of the Devil by neglecting to confront those devilish works in the lives of its members? A popular mega church pastor was confronted with the question "Why don't you preach the whole truth, against sin, or about the cross?" His answer was, "If I do that I will lose most of my members!" What rebellious neglect and selfish apathy for the souls of people!

Calvary is the full expression of God's passion for souls and hatred for sin. Our love for souls and hatred for sin cannot be formed in a different mold. If a man does not preach the cross and carry his own, he knows not the love of God nor does he exhibit it, no matter how much he smiles. Calvary is also the full revelation of Jesus Christ's intercession between God and man. If a preacher does not preach the cross, he has sealed up heaven for all his listeners and followers! Calvary obtained fellowship with God. If a man despises the cross he despises fellowship with God.

Jesus is the great Intercessor for souls and He has called His church to be the same to a lost world. The true intercessor enters into a direct spiritual warfare between God and the Devil for the sake of souls. Can a prayerless church do this? God has called His church to be His "holy" hands and feet (1 Peter 1:16). The word for church is *ekklesia*, which means "called out of the world and belonging to God."

He has liberated us from our bondage to sin and rebellion for us to fill up the wounds in His palms that our sin and rebellion caused. Paul said, "I rejoice in my sufferings for your sake, and in my flesh I do my share on behalf of His body, which is the church, in filling up what is lacking in Christ's afflictions" (Colossians 1:24). Those who despise this will have their own hands and feet forever bound in chains of darkness. In Christ's parable, the king said, "Bind his hands and feet and throw him into the outer darkness, where there will be weeping and gnashing of teeth" (Matthew 22:13).

For Thought:

God is love, and love extends itself to a lost and dying world at its own expense. Anyone who claims they have God's love without radically dealing with sin or suffering loss for the sake of others is a liar and a charlatan. This is true because he or she has made the love of God something other than what God exemplified through the crushing of His own Son at Calvary. Love is always crucified!

Day 142

Fearers of Mirrors see Clearer

"Satan stood up against Israel and moved David to number Israel" (1Chronicles 21:1).

David again is falling in lust for beauty. How easily the exalted are tempted to turn inward to find beauty. How swift they are to forget the One who has made them beautiful, clothed them with fine linen, and crowned them with His glory and splendor. However, this time for David it was not lust for a woman, but for the beauty of his kingdom. The vanity of a mirror has brought many kings and princes to utter ruin. By what other explanation can we speak of the fall of Lucifer to Satan? The biblical examples of fallen men that fell in love with themselves strongly point to this. Nevertheless, the enemy comes with the tantalizing whisper, "Look what glory you can have apart from God."

God said of His beloved Israel, "I put a beautiful crown on your head . . . so you were exceedingly beautiful and advanced to royalty . . . but you trusted in your beauty and played the harlot because of your fame" (Ezekiel 16:12-15). God bestowed the same lavish blessings upon David, but he lusted after his kingdom apart from God? He wanted to number his kingdom to satisfy his self-importance by relishing in its size. Nebuchadnezzar did the same thing with the building of a statue of himself. "Nebuchadnezzar the king made an image of gold, the height of which was sixty cubits (90 feet) and its width six cubits (9 feet). He set it up for all to worship at the strike of musical instruments.

What is the church that is fixated upon "numbers" doing but turning inward, taking a census, trusting in its own beauty, playing the harlot, and setting itself up as an image to be worshiped at the strike of the musical instruments? There are too many similarities here to dismiss a sober inquiry. David's arrogance and presumptuous pride cost the lives of seventy thousand people to die by the chastening plague of God. How many countless thousands have died in the plague of unrepentant idolatry because they worshiped a church rather than Jesus? Heaven help us!

Not literally, but spiritually, we should be fearers of mirrors unless they help us see clearer the ugliness of our pride and selfishness and the beauty of Jesus. Let us only gaze into the mirror that reflects the glory of the Lord and transforms us into His image (2 Corinthians 3:18).

For Thought:

Read 2 Corinthians 4:6. The word "face" means countenance or presence. True knowledge of God comes from much time spent in His presence.

If the tremendous light of Jesus were to expose what is hidden in your heart would people see Jesus or idols? Would they see the Word of God or the god of this world?

Day 143

See God, Not Rome!

"I must also see Rome"
(Acts 19:21).

There is no doubt that the conditions of our world, our nations, and their governments are precarious. As a result, churches, small groups, and pulpits are being flooded with conversations of world-watching Christians. The atmosphere is at best panic and at worst toxic—"The news, the President, health bills, and political parties!" If Christians were as radically concerned with the sin and worldliness that severs their relationship with Jesus, they would be less concerned with the world and more concerned about souls. Consider the following:

Rome, like Babylon, symbolized the world and secular society. Paul was very eager to get to Rome, but only to preach. Nero was emperor when Paul arrived. Nero was one of the most despotic and insane rulers ever. He poisoned his own stepbrother, killed two of his wives, and his only restraints from absolute tyranny were his two wise counselors Burrus and Seneca; the former died and the latter he murdered. Nero heavily taxed the people while he lavishly gambled with the fortunes he gained from them. He almost certainly burned down two-thirds of Rome, and accused the Christians of the arson. He became the first emperor of ten who would render unspeakable persecutions against Christ's elect saints. Rome in Paul's time was tyrannically misgoverned and being plowed into poverty.

Scandal, dictatorship, immorality, chaos, revolt, murder, heavy taxes, and oppression describe the conditions of biblical Rome. However, almost all of the above information comes from the records of secular historians, not Paul's writings. Paul lived shackled to a Roman guard as an innocent prisoner during all of this, and there is not a trace of him discussing the "bad news" of Rome. Paul wrote his joy-filled Epistle to the Philippians in the midst of these ill-favored circumstances. Philippians has been called the Epistle of "joy, excellent things, right-mindedness, and unity."[19] Paul's concerns were to preach the Gospel of Christ, strengthen the body, and encourage believers. He did not "see" Rome; his eyes were on Jesus and His Gospel.

People ask, "What kind of Christian doesn't get concerned about world news and politics?" The answer is, "An Apostle Paul kind of Christian." Those who are constantly worrying about world affairs are showing where their eyes and hearts are dwelling most. They likely have forgotten that every good and perfect gift comes down from the Father (see James 1:17). Trust and know that God can rain down bread from heaven, make water gush from a rock, and swallow up every enemy that oppresses you. See Him, not Rome!

For Thought:

Whatever you fix your interests upon will sway your heart, win your trust, and dictate your peace. If you watch a lot of news, you had better be watching twice that much Jesus.

Day 144

The Word Versus the World

"Whoever wishes to be a friend of the world makes himself an enemy of God" (James 4:4).

The world exalts the proud and humiliates the lowly; the Word of God exalts the lowly and humbles the proud. The world says be the best and look out for number one; the Word says be the last and consider others as more important. The world says the way up is to climb on people's backs; the Word says the way up is to fall at Jesus' feet. The world says high self-esteem is vital; the Word calls that pride, and pride is fatal. The world says you can only love others if you love yourself first; the Word says you cannot love others because you love yourself. The world says you are a good person; the Word of God says there is none that are good. The world says believe in God and go to heaven; the Word says even the demons believe, and demons have fallen from heaven. The world says hold a grudge and give them the cold shoulder; the Word says forgive or you will not be forgiven. The world says do your duty and go home; the Word says go the second mile with joy. For comfort, the world says eat and play; the Word says fast and pray.

The world calls chronic drug, pornography, and alcohol use a foolish addiction; the Word of God says it is flagrant idolatry. The world says preserve your life; the Word says lose your life for Jesus. The world says store up treasure for retirement; the Word says do not store up earthly treasures, but only treasures in heaven. The world says save up for a rainy day; the Word says He will rain down daily bread. The world says mourning is pitiful; the Word says blessed are those who mourn. The world says not returning evil for evil is a good thing; the Word says do good to those who do evil to you and this is just the standard.

The world says you have a mental disorder; the Word of God says your heart is desperately wicked. The world calls evil behavior a sickness; the Word calls it sin. The world calls rebellion "oppositional defiance disorder" and calls guilt "a neurosis." Self-pity is "low self-esteem;" depression, fear, and anxiety are "mood disorders." Pride and a haughty spirit is "narcissistic personality disorder," and sexual sin is an "addiction." Thievery is "kleptomania" and gluttony is an "eating disorder." Repentance is unnecessary if you believe the world.

Everything of the world's system is hostile to the Word of God. The world is obsessed with pleasure and self. Therefore, we need to separate ourselves from it if we are to enjoy a vibrant walk with Jesus. Love the people, not the things of the world. The person who lives mostly for this world is wise only for a moment, but is a fool for eternity! If you think you can continue a worldly lifestyle and walk in victory with Jesus at the same time, you are only fooling yourself. "Come out from among them and be separate, says the Lord, and I will welcome you" (2 Corinthians 6:17).

Day 145

If the World's Appealing, Heaven's Appalling

"Store up for yourselves treasures in heaven . . . where thieves do not break in or steal" (Matthew 6:20).

Imagine a neighborhood street with large fancy houses, but with one dilapidated shack. It is safe to bet the expert thief will not target the shack for burglary. Notice Jesus said in this passage that thieves "do not" break in to steal, rather than "cannot." Thieves see no value in heavenly treasures so they do not break in to steal them. A thief is selfish; he "works for his own self-interests, but his desires remain unsatisfied" (Ecclesiastes 6:7). Thieves covet only worldly things that cater to their earthly and sensual desires. Heavenly treasures mean absolutely nothing to the earthly-minded; these treasures are like the shack that promises no payoff. Heavenly treasures are safe and secure because they are holy and eternal. They are appealing to those who love Jesus, and appalling to those who love themselves and this world.

Souls saved because of faithful minsters of the Gospel are heavenly treasures. Some of the heavenly treasures mentioned in Revelation are: The right to sit with Jesus on His throne (3:21); being made a pillar in God's heavenly sanctuary (3:12); being dressed in eternally white garments with your name inerasably written in the book of life and acknowledged before God and His angels (3:5); receiving authority over the nations with Christ (2:26); eating the hidden manna, and being given a new name on a white stone (2:17); receiving the crown of life (2:10). Jesus also said when people insult you, persecute you, and falsely say every kind of evil against you because of Him to "be glad and rejoice because your reward is great in heaven" (Matthew 5:11).

Not only is heaven a safe place to hide your treasure, hide it also in your heart. David said God's Word was his most valuable treasure and he protected it as such in his heart (see Psalm 119:11). Jesus, "The Treasure" of heaven must be the litmus test that determines if the treasure in your heart is good. We must fervently rid ourselves of every stored treasure in our hearts that Jesus does not value. The more you have in your heart that thieves would love to steal, the more you have to close it and keep it locked. That is why heavenly-minded people have the most open hearts. The more that worldliness is appealing, the more heavenliness is appalling. If people envy your worldly prosperity rather than your spiritual posterity you stand on shaky ground, not holy ground. Where do you stand?

For Thought:

Read Isaiah 45:3. It can be said, "Whomever you live your life for declares your treasure and determines with whom you will spend an eternity."

Day 146

You are Treasure Too

"The kingdom of heaven is like treasure, buried in a field, that a man found and reburied. Then in his joy he goes and sells everything he has and buys that field" (Matthew 13:44, HCS).

If you have been a Christian long you have heard the parable of the treasure in the field. It is very likely that you have heard Jesus being referred to as "the Treasure." You have heard how much the fortunate finder willingly gives up for the sake of possessing such a prize. This is all true and sound in interpretation. But did you ever ponder this parable from the perspective of "you" being the treasure and Jesus being the "Man"?

As blood bought saints, we have been plucked out of the earth like treasure from the ground, and brought into the kingdom of heaven. Undoubtedly, we were all found in a "buried in the earth" spiritual condition.

Before the flood, the Lord searched the entire earth for the treasure of righteousness and found only one (Noah). Before God destroyed Sodom and Gomorrah, He searched and again found only one (Lot). Each one of us were also painstakingly searched for and found. We were living dead people headed for an eternal grave, buried in our trespasses and sin. We can all say, "I was the *one* lost sheep that the Shepherd was willing to leave the other ninety-nine to find." When He found us He dug us up from our grave and "reburied" us in Himself. "For you have died and your life is hidden with Christ in God" (Colossians 3:3). Before, we were buried in death. Now we are "buried with Him in baptism and raised up with Him through faith in the working of God, who raised Jesus from the dead" (Colossians 2:12).

Jesus left His heavenly throne to take up a Roman cross. He set aside His Royal Crown to put on a crown of thorns. He left the palaces of heaven and lived like a nomad in the world He created. He was born the target of assassination, served like a pauper, and suffered and died like a criminal. Jesus did not consider His divine equality with God as something to be held onto, but instead He "emptied Himself . . . and being found in appearance as a man, He humbled Himself by becoming obedient to the point of death, even death on a cross" (Philippians 2:6-8). In Hebrews, it says, "For the joy set before Him, He endured the cross" (12:2). Emptied, humbled, and sacrificed: This is the "Man" that joyfully left all He had to find you, sold all He had to purchase you, labored with all He had to raise you up from the dead, and spent all He had to rebury you with Him in eternal life. Apparently, He sees you as that very precious treasure. Can you see Him the same way?

For Thought:

We often find ourselves under so much teaching to treasure Jesus that we forget that He infinitely treasures us. Overflowing with love, He created us as receptacles of His love, and then died to prove it!

Day 147

What's in Your Temple?

"My house shall be a house of prayer" (Luke 19:46).

Greedy men were using the Temple to favorably line their pockets with profit. Jews would come from near and far with eagerness to have their sins atoned for yet another year. Some would travel from so far they were unwilling to bring their own animals for fear of their dying or getting sick along the way. Empty-handed Jews were then forced to pay for animals with grievous interest. Money in large coin was brought due to the need to minimize traveling weight (Carry ten thousand pennies or a single hundred-dollar bill?). These circumstances would be any swindler's dream. "You're going to have to spend the entire hundred dollars, because we don't have change for that." Roman coin was also forbidden in the Temple treasury because of the idolatrous image of Caesar (some Jews were paid in this coin for their work). With no set standard for exchange, this provided a perfect opportunity for deceitful profit. All of this not only shows they had defiled the Temple of God with greed and deceit, but also they had secularized what was built for spiritual purposes, namely prayer.

All Jesus found in the Temple were ritual sacrifices, secular marketing, and the deceitfulness of riches, but no prayer. If a pastor wants to find who might be the true saints in the church, call a prayer meeting on Sunday night. If he really wants to distinguish the true flock, he will call a prayer meeting every night. True Christians are praying saints; they love to pray because they love intimate fellowship with Jesus. They love to pray because it is their spiritual worship to Him. They love to meet for prayer because prayer is a small fire, and small fires when put together become a raging fire of God. Praying for souls, one another, the poor, the church, the lost, repentance, and true revival, all these are the spiritual activity missing in churches today. The flesh hates prayer; it will sacrifice long hours at the church, give large offerings, and even go on mission trips—anything but pray! Fatally, believers who are absent in prayer are fleshly governed, not spiritually. "The mind governed by the flesh is death, but the mind governed by the Spirit is life and peace" (Romans 8:6, NIV).

Jesus came to His Temple and found only fleshly sacrifices, but no fervent spiritual prayer. He had once before said, "Go and learn what this means: 'I desire mercy, not sacrifice'" (Matthew 9:13). Prayer is a spiritual act of mercy. Have you learned? What will He find in your temple?

For Thought:

"Prayer is the highest activity of the human soul, and the ultimate test of a man's true spiritual condition. Everything we do in the Christian life is easier than prayer."—Dr. Martin Lloyd Jones

Day 148

Much in Prayer

"Pray without ceasing" (1 Thessalonians 5:17).

Prayer is the mightiest exercise of faith; it grasps hold of the Hope that has entered the Holiest Place behind the curtain (Hebrews 6:19), knowing this Hope never disappoints (Romans 5:5). Prayer tells God we want what He wants, we know who He is, and we know He will accomplish His will as He sees fit. Prayer says, "Father, You said, and Your Word always comes to pass." Prayer is omnipotent; it can do everything that God can do. And when it does, faith not only grows, it gets harder like cement. Jesus was much in prayer, and He is the Living God. Those who are much in prayer will have the Living God coursing through their lives like electricity. This will do more to prosper the Kingdom of God than all the efforts of man, media, and mega-churches put together. Below are some of the finest quotes from some of the finest saints of God who learned that the secret to the true Christian life—passionate, unceasing prayer. Meditate on these, *prayerfully*:

"Prayer is the soil that faith grows in."—Andrew Murray

"Pray hardest when it is hardest to pray."—Charles H. Brent

"Beware of prayer-less tears and beware of tearless prayers."—Anonymous

"Happy are they who suspend their desires until they know their Father's will through much prayer."—A.B. Simpson

"We must trust God and pray, not only *when* we do not understand, but *because* we do not understand."—Unknown

"A praying man stops sinning; a sinning man stops praying"—Leonard Ravenhill

"*In His Name* signifies that our prayers are to be grounded upon the finished work of Christ and our redemption rights through His death and atonement."—A.B. Simpson,

"A single word, coming fresh from lips that have been kindled into heavenly warmth, by near fellowship with God, will avail more than a thousand others."—Horatius Bonar

"Praying people know they're weak."—Jeff Colon

"All decays begin in the closet; no heart thrives without much secret converse with God, and nothing will make amends for the want of it."—Berridge

For Thought:

The Lord's desire is to reproduce Himself in His people. We cannot sail by another standard. Leonard Ravenhill wrote, "There's nothing more transfiguring than prayer. People often ask, 'Why do you insist on prayer so much?' The answer is very simple: 'Because Jesus did!'" [20]

Day 149

No "If" About It

"When you pray, go into your inner room, close your door and pray to your Father who is in secret" (Matthew 6:6).

Jesus said, "When you pray," not "If." And He said when you do, "go into your closet." How many times have you heard the phrase, "prayer closet?" What in the world is this place? "The inner room, closet, secret chamber, private place"—all of these are English translations of the Greek word *tameion* (tuh-ME-on) that Jesus used. However, this word actually derives from a root word that meant "storeroom" or "dispensary chamber." It was the room where medicines were safely stored to keep from corruption. The fact that Jesus is purposely using this word is of great spiritual importance. He is trying to teach us that when we pray we indeed enter into this medicinal storehouse; in fact it is the Most Holy place behind the curtain that we are entering. In this room the holy presence of God dwells, and He infinitely possesses every ointment that the heart, soul, mind, and body will ever need. Furthermore, He alone is the only One that knows how to properly apply it.

This is why Jesus says to close the door. This means intentionally shutting out every other medicinal alternative, every other care, and all other affections. By doing this we are declaring that only He possesses what we truly need, acknowledging we are coming into the presence of the infinite Dispenser of mercies. It is a Most Holy place because no foreign or unholy thing can enter. It is a secret place because it is a transaction solely between the child and the Father. Every distraction, attraction, and infraction is shut out to make the holy transaction. The child is completely alone with the wonderful Savior. This is the way Jesus prayed with His Father and this is how He teaches us to pray. The secret to effective prayer is praying in secret. Come into the medicine closet with Jesus. Let Him apply the blood bought bandages to heal your wounded heart, the Oil of the Holy Spirit for your fire, and the wine of salvation for your joy (wine is the spiritual symbol of "joy"). Note: It is very interesting that the medicinal supplies that the Good Samaritan had to apply to the man beaten, stripped, and left for dead (see Luke 9:34) were "bandages, oil, and wine."

Bandages heal: Our ultimate healing was at Calvary where sin was lifted away by the Living Word. Oil anoints: The gift of the Holy Spirit is the Anointing Oil of God. Wine brings joy: David pleaded, "Restore to me the joy of Your salvation" (Psalm 51:12), and Jesus has accomplished that very thing. His blood is the poured-out wine that continuously restores the joy of salvation. Healing, anointing, and joy await you in your prayer closet. Close the door on doubt. There is no "if" about it.

For Thought:

"Closing the door," declares that we shun every affection and all alternatives that compete for our hearts, and agree that Jesus Himself is our all in all.

"Closing the door," also means shutting out all fear, doubt, and unbelief.

Day 150

150 Days Behind the Wooden Door

"The water prevailed upon the earth one hundred and fifty days" (Genesis 7:24).

At this point, all living things, except for those that dwelled in the sea and those in the Ark, had long been dead. For five (Jewish) months Noah was submerged into God's life-preserving refuge in complete dependence. God's wrath had been poured out and it was all consuming. One hundred and fifty days worth of it certainly declares not only His thoroughness to eradicate sin and rebellion, but also the measure of His hatred for it. Surely Noah must have nervously wondered if he had followed all of God's instructions or if he had missed anything. One minutely overlooked detail and they were sunk. If God's people would only live with such meticulous obedience today, they would not be sinking and drowning like faithless unbelievers.

Faithless humans were swept away, and much too late came the realization of their ignorance. Death and horror broke upon them like an unexpected tsunami. They had scoffed at every warning, and given themselves over to the careless pleasures of this world. Their ears were closed because such were their hearts, and the Ark doors closed upon them. The Ark symbolized Christ, so those outside of Christ will be swept away forever.

Noah lived in the ambiance of devotion because he knew that it was the very breath of God (Genesis 2:7) that sustained him. Five months in the Ark demanded no real change in his spiritual life; he was used to being shut in with God and walking with Him in righteousness (Genesis 6:9). The only difference was that now every distraction and opposition to his devotional life had been erased from the planet. The world was closed off and washed clean; independence and self-will were inoperative and irrelevant. Noah would experience one hundred and fifty days of resting in God, dwelling in His holy place. However, it was not a curtain, but a wooden door that separated all the righteous of the earth from the condemned, as well as life from death. By faith Noah built the Ark; through obedience to God's command he entered it (7:1). One hundred and fifty days later he was still depending on the Ark, resting in the depths of God's saving mercy. Are you? Notice what Day you're on.

For Thought:

Sin (*hamartía*) means, "to miss the mark." Its antonym is the word for "intercede" (*entugchánō*). *Entugchánō* comes from the prefix *en* ("the innermost depth") plus *tugchánō* ("hitting the mark"). Put them together and it means, "Being deep inside what always hits the mark." Noah got in the Ark, which took him to God's proper destination. Are you abiding in Jesus in that way? He always hits the bull's-eye. Sin comes from neglecting to abide in Him.

Day 151

When Peter Demanded Hell

"Peter took Him aside and began to rebuke Him, saying, 'God forbid it, Lord! This shall never happen to You'" (Matthew 16:22).

Can you ponder a set of circumstances where you begged God not to do something, but He did it anyway? Can you look back on any of them now and enthusiastically praise Him for not listening to you? Jesus had just told His disciples that He was going to Jerusalem, but this time He would suffer many terrible things, and that was not all. After these horrible sufferings, He would then be killed ("and resurrect three days later" but they missed that part). If God had listened to Peter and "forbid it," any existing life on the planet would be in a miserably hellish state headed for an infinitely worse eternal hell. It is certainly safe to say that we can all lift our praises with great zeal to heaven and thank God for not listening to Peter! If God had conceded to Peter's plea, there would be absolutely no hope for mankind through Calvary.

Jesus said, "Get behind Me Satan!" Peter could not understand such a seemingly harsh rebuke; but we sure can. However, the plot thickens with a deeper look. Rabbis had prospective disciples. To become an actual disciple, the aspiring prospects not only had to go everywhere the Rabbi went, they also had to do what he did. Jesus was greater than any Rabbi, so to honor Him meant they must follow Him in every way down to the tiniest detail. Therefore, when Jesus told His disciples where He was going and what would happen to Him, Peter understood this from the Rabbi-disciple perspective. This meant all that would happen to Jesus would likely happen to him as well. Jesus was basically saying, "I'm going to the cross, are you following?"

At first glance, it looks like Peter loves Jesus so much that he was tenaciously against anything that would separate them. From the Jewish custom of "Rabbi does, disciple follows," we see Peter with an outward concern for Jesus, but also an inward preservation of self ("If Jesus suffers death so will I"). Peter thought the only way he could spare himself from suffering yet keep his righteous reputation would be to convince Jesus to abort His "suicidal" mission. Peter could not see what he was really demanding—If Jesus didn't suffer death, all would suffer eternal death in hell. This teaches us to prayerfully seek the heart of God and carefully examine His will before we impetuously start hurling petitions at Him. God forbid He answer one of those self-willed appeals; there is no telling what anguish that would bring. It also exposes the selfish heart that refuses to follow Jesus and covers it up with false affection for Him.

For Thought:

Read 2 Corinthians 4:17. Peter had an excuse; he did not have the resurrection of Jesus yet. We do!

Fear not and follow your "resurrected" Shepherd.

Day 152

Let's Go to Judea Again

"Rabbi, the Jews were just now seeking to stone You, and are You going there again" (John 11:8)?

As kids, whenever we would experience a fun ride we would say, "Let's do that again!" But when is the last time we faced death-threatening danger and then said, "Hey, let's do that again"? Here we have the disciples again expressing their deep concern for the life of Jesus. Twice the Jews in Judea had tried to stone Him, and the last time it seemed as if they would have actually succeeded. Now Jesus was saying, "Let's go to Judea again," and with confusion they asked Him why. He had previously told them the Father had granted Him authority to lay down His life and take it up again; that no man had the ability to take it from Him (see John 10:17-18). He reiterated this truth with his reply, "Aren't there 12 hours in a day?" In other words, just as the lifespan of the sun is divinely appointed and unalterable by man; so was the lifespan of the Son of God divinely appointed and unalterable by man. This was His way of calming their turbulent hearts and declaring His sovereignty.

Jesus had just learned that His dear friend Lazarus was on his deathbed in Bethany. Jesus, knowing He had the divine authority to heal, lingered where He was. Jesus is no waster of time and He would use His delay as an opportunity to teach. The disciples could not see that Jesus was teaching them with His stillness and seeming neglect. Rigor mortis sets in on the fourth day, and Jesus was purposely waiting that long to demonstrate upon Lazarus His power over bodily corruption as well as the soul's. This teaches us not to say, "Lord, Why are You refusing to move?" When Jesus did finally move He set course for Judea that not only seemed as if He intended to skip over Bethany, but also seemed to promise certain death by stoning for all of them.

This may remind us of when the disciples were facing the fierce storm in Mark 4:38. "Jesus was in the stern, sleeping on a cushion. The disciples woke him and said, 'Teacher, don't you care if we drown?'" The word "we" included Jesus too. Here we have Jesus teaching them again by being still and carefree. Who other than Jesus can teach the greatest fundamentals of faith without moving or speaking? He rebuked the storm, which taught them an ultimate truth after His death, resurrection, and ascension. They would personally face the fiercest storm—preaching the Gospel to a Christ-murdering world. They would each "go to Judea again" compelled by love and devoid of fear. You must go through the storms of life to personally experience Jesus. It is by faith in His resurrection power and its resulting glory that you endure them. Confident resurrection yields steadfast endurance. Your lifespan is also divinely appointed. Spend it wisely for Jesus; He spent His for you.

Day 153

It Must Be Broken

"He took the five loaves and the two fish, and looking up toward heaven, He blessed the food and broke the loaves" (Mark 6:41).

This is Mark's account of Jesus feeding of the five thousand. Matthew tells us that there were five thousand "besides women and children" (14:21). It was customary in the Jewish culture not to count women and children in censuses. Therefore it is safe to assume that there could have been somewhere between ten and fifteen thousand people present. This great multitude was so eager to see Jesus that they traveled on foot what would be over twenty miles. They anticipated where He was going when He got into the boat to retreat and they arrived at that place before He did. These people were desperate to see Jesus!

John tells us in his account that the five loaves and two fish came from a young boy. Could you imagine being that boy? In a crowd of ten to fifteen thousand people you would have been no one special. Then Jesus asks the disciples to "go and see" if they could find food, and you (the boy) are the only one in the entire multitude that has any.

Some might say that the others were so eager to get to Jesus they forgot about food; but you could say that you were the only one smart enough to bring food for such a taxing journey on foot. Nevertheless, in a single moment you go from being a "zero," blending into the crowd, to a "hero," standing out among them. This would be similar to being at a concert arena to see your favorite group, and being pulled up on stage with them. Out of thousands you have something that no one else has, and the Star of the event calls for you to come and bring it to Him. Your heart is racing and you are nervous. Everyone is looking at you. "Who is this young lad? What is so special about him?" they ask among themselves. But there is something special about you; you have bread and Jesus is going to take what you have to feed thousands. You have something of tremendous value to bring to the Master and you cannot wait to give it to Him and see Him honor you for having it. You get to Jesus, hand Him your bread, and what does He do with it? He breaks it!

Whatever you have that you see of value for the Master's use, it is of no value until He breaks it. It must be broken if it is going to be used for the Kingdom. Just as the stallion must be broken before its master can get right use out of it, so must all your possessions, ambitions, talents, even your very life be broken. Bring it all to the feet of Jesus; let Him bless it, break it, multiply it, and distribute it for the sake of feeding other hungry people.

For Thought:

The Lord loves the broken. He detests the unbroken because they reject their need for Him and demand to keep that they have for themselves.

Day 154

The Basket that Never Empties

"He blessed the food and broke the loaves and He kept giving them to the disciples to set before them" (Mark 6:41).

The bread has been blessed and broken, but how on earth is Jesus going to feed ten to fifteen thousand people with five loaves and two fish? Would He in His divine power make a massive smorgasbord of bread and fish to appear? This is not even close to what we read. It says "He kept on giving" out bread and fish to the disciples.

One mammoth sized miracle would have been sufficient, simple to perform, and awesome to see. However, this is not how the Lord fed them. Jesus knows that people love to glorify big things, and how inclined they are to set their desires and hopes upon them. Skyscrapers, mega churches, cathedrals, towers, superdomes, and "big" miracles, how easily they captivate the wonder of the heart. These things speak kindly to our pride and expose the tower building trends that lie dormant inside of us. On the contrary, Jesus fed this vast multitude of people one loaf and one fish at a time. This shows His humility to serve and His labor to meet every single need personally. In other words, Jesus turned His back on the vainglory that would love to see one "big" demonstration of miraculous power. Instead He meekly performed about ten to fifteen thousand small but "personal" miracles.

That is not all. It was also a rebuke to our self-sufficiency. It is true that if there had been five million people there, He would have performed that many miracles. But the principle commonly missed is this: Every time Jesus reached His hand into the basket there was another fish. There was no running out! This is a rebuke to our humanistic reasoning that cannot see beyond what is natural, thereby remaining blind to the supernatural. Our bent towards trusting in our own abilities paralyzes our faith to trust in God. Christians are afraid they will "run out" if they give too much. When provisions are low and bank ledgers are turning red, they stop giving. They have never experienced the spiritual law of "Blessed are the merciful, for they will receive mercy" (Matthew 5:7). If you live to give, He will continually fill your basket with mercy.

It takes faith to reach into a basket that should otherwise be empty. If there are only two fish, and two people just claimed them both, reach your hand into the basket anyway; you will be humbled by what you find. Jesus is the broken Bread of life. Your faith may be low but His basket is always full.

For Thought:

Read 2 Kings 4:1-7.

The miraculous outpouring continued to flow as long as there were empty containers. It is only our faith that runs out, never His provision.

Smith Wigglesworth, a Pentecostal evangelist of the early 20th Century told a boy with no feet to go buy shoes. It was documented that the boy did, and as he put on the shoes his feet grew. [21]

Day 155

The Habit of Listening and Responding

"I spoke to you, but you would not listen. Instead you rebelled against the command of the LORD, and acted presumptuously... The Amorites who lived in that hill country came out against you and chased you as bees do, and crushed you" (Deuteronomy 1:43-44).

We who hear the voice of the Holy Spirit speak words of warning but do not take heed to them, do not understand the preciousness of the gift we are rejecting; nor do we understand the greatness of the sin we are committing. It is a miracle of mercy that we can even hear the still small voice of the Spirit. The problem is not merely the act of forsaking of His voice; the problem is *why* we do it. Remember the last time you got annoyed with someone and ignored them while they were talking? The issue is not that you ignored them; the issue is your annoyance toward them caused you to deem their words worthless.

A preacher or pastor will say, "Do not squelch the voice of the Spirit because it is bad." But the reality is that "bad" is not the word for it. Heresy is the espousing of opinions that are contrary to biblical truth. The Holy Spirit speaks God's Word. If I am ignoring His voice, I am basically saying God's Word is annoying, contrary to my current opinion, and thereby not worthy enough to follow. Squelching the voice of the Holy Spirit is just a step or two away from heresy, and if not repented of can eventually become just that. One of His main ministries is to "guide you into all truth" (John 16:13), and if He is consistently ignored, you will certainly fall into error and heresy. God's Word will be found worthless in light of your opinion, and your opinion will be what you follow and teach.

Keep this obstinate habit, and you will rashly venture into the enemy's territory without God's protective blessing, the enemy will swarm you like bees, and his sting is one of crushing death. We declare our thankfulness for the gift of hearing and receiving the Gospel of Jesus Christ by listening and obediently responding to His Words. This is the way we worship Him in Spirit and in Truth. Get into the habit of listening and responding and you will discover a joy and a freedom you never knew.

For Thought:

For anyone who hears the Spirit's prohibitions but suppresses the truth by squelching His voice, then wanders into the enemy's territory with vain contempt and the gall of pride expecting not to be defeated and consumed—there is no greater folly!

The more you listen and respond, the more you will see the divinely Orchestrated appointments with which He loves to amaze us, increase our faith, and bless others.

Day 156

Are You a Burning Bush? (Part 1)

> ... *And he looked, and behold, the bush was burning with fire, yet the bush was not consumed. So Moses said, 'I must turn aside now and see this marvelous sight, why the bush is not burned up'"* (Exodus 3:2-3).

What was the marvelous sight that compelled Moses toward God's holy presence? It was not a speaking bush, as the voice of God had not yet resounded. It was not merely a "burning" bush. The thing that drew Moses with such a compelling "I must," was the fact that the bush was consumed with a blazing fire *but not destroyed*. The sign, miracle, and wonder of an object naturally flammable being engulfed with fire yet without one single ash would, I propose, compel any person toward awestruck investigation.

"Our God is a consuming fire" (Hebrews 12:29). In the Old Testament, the fire of God was a celestial fire, which consumed the entire sacrifice. But today, God commands us to be *living sacrifices*. If we truly love Jesus by keeping His commands, we would surely not neglect His imperative to present ourselves as "living sacrifices, holy and pleasing to God" (Romans 12:1). Therefore, since Jesus Christ is unchanging, if we were continuously putting our entire life on the altar as *living sacrifices*, we would also be consumed by the fire of God but not burned up. What a marvelous sight the glorious Bride of Christ is when she is a blazing fire speaking as oracles the Word of God in thunderous Holy Ghost power and authority!

It was a lowly thorn bush, most likely a wild acacia, with which we know the region to be quite populated. This conveys 1) the humility necessary for the divine glory of God to be made manifest, and 2) the way God chooses that which is humble and abased to display His glory. Consequently, we would do well to learn the abhorrent nature of pride and how it works in hostility to God's glory. Lord, forbid that we should boast in anything except the cross (Galatians 6:14).

For Thought:

Name some things that you boast about more than Jesus?

The fiery presence of God drew Moses to the bush; today most are only drawn by what caters to their lusts and selfish pleasures.

Read Psalm 46 and describe what it means to have God in your midst.

Day 157

Are You a Burning Bush? (Part 2)

". . . And he looked, and behold, the bush was burning with fire, yet the bush was not consumed. So Moses said, 'I must turn aside now and see this marvelous sight, why the bush is not burned up'" (Exodus 3:2-3).

One symbolism of the burning bush was the fiery trial of Israel's current afflictions in Egypt and their deliverance. They were consumed but not burned up. Another symbolism was one more distant, namely those persecutions of the early Church of Christ (not omitting the individual saint sold out for Christ Jesus). Peter encourages us, "Beloved, do not be surprised at the fiery ordeal among you, which comes upon you for your testing, as though some strange thing were happening to you" (1 Peter 4:12). Paul also gives us hope through his own fiery trials as he steadfastly proclaimed, "Persecuted, but not forsaken; struck down, but not destroyed" (2 Corinthians 4:9). The Israelites, along with these two Apostles of Christ were consumed with fiery trials but not destroyed because, like the lowly thorn bush, "God was in their midst!"

We should remember in the book of Daniel when this same miraculous wonder was manifested to three uncompromising men of God. Dumbfounded, Nebuchadnezzar said, "Was it not three men we cast bound into the midst of the fire?" . . . I see four men loose, walking in the midst of the fire, and they have no hurt; and the form of the fourth is like the Son of God" (Daniel 3:23, 25). These men came out of a super-heated fire and, like the lowly thorn bush, were without one single ash upon their clothing, and even the scent of smoke avoided them. They too were consumed by fire but not burned up, because God was in their midst.

Much is to be learned from the outcome of this marvelous scene (read Daniel 3:28). Because these men said, "We will not serve your gods . . . our God whom we serve is able to deliver us from the furnace of blazing fire," God proved these words to be trustworthy to all who watched, and a God-denying king turned to praising the Name of God.

The burning bush—whether blazing with the consuming fire of God or engulfed with the fiery trials of affliction—prospers when it possesses God in its midst. And when it speaks the uncompromising Word of God, the ground through which its roots burrow becomes holy ground. As a result, other people will also turn aside to see the marvelous sight and be transformed into God-worshiping servants. Are you a burning bush?

For Thought:

Would you face a fiery furnace for your faith? Do you abandon ship when life or temptations get hot, or go down with it?

In your fiery trials, do you take refuge in knowing that God is in your midst? How do you know He is?

Day 158

What is My Strength?

"The joy of the LORD is your strength" (Nehemiah 8:10).

What was the joy of our Lord Jesus? His joy was perfect devotion to the Father's will, and being in complete oneness with Him. Before the cross, Jesus had never known separation from His Father. Though He certainly had contemplated it, being the Lamb slain from the foundation of the world, it was something He could only experience to truly know. It is safe to assume that separation from God was something virtually impossible for Jesus to grasp before the cross. As Jesus prayed in the garden, *"Father, let this cup pass from Me. Nevertheless, not My will, but Yours"* (Matthew 26:36-46), it was not the suffering of the cross that Jesus was pleading to miss. It was something infinitely worse; it was being separated from His Father.

Jesus perfect obedience caused His being separated from God for just six hours, and to Him that was eternity. Just a single glimpse of it in the garden nearly killed Him. "My soul is swallowed up in sorrow—to the point of death" (26:38). It is indeed our self-will and disobedience that causes our separation from God our Father. Can you ever imagine your obedience causing separation from God? Impossible!

Jesus again did the impossible. He suffered separation from His Father through His pure obedience to bridge the abyss of separation that our disobedience caused. Now we have the Way of devotion to God the Father opened through Jesus. This is our joy and ultimately our strength. Lasting strength comes from lasting joy. Lasting joy is always fresh and new because it gathers its life from today's abiding in Christ. David said, "In Your presence is the fullness of joy" (Psalm 16:11). When our circumstances fill us with depression and fear, these reactions are indicators that we are not dwelling in His presence. The Apostle Paul also learned the secret to contentment and joy in all circumstances, and he disclosed his secret as being surrendered to God's will.

So many of our sorrows are born out of our own disappointments because we were putting our hopes in things and visions that were not necessarily the Lord's. At first glance it seems absurd that God's will was for His Son to be "crushed for our iniquities" (Isaiah 53:5). It also seems absurd that there is joy in losing our lives for Jesus. But this is the center of His will, and that is where true joy is found. Jesus' joy was to give His life on the cross to ransom us (Hebrews 12:2), and He said to *go* and *do* that same mercy for others (see Matthew 9:13; Matthew 28:19). Those that need mercy the most are usually those we deem the most undeserving. But the Lord's joy was in selfless intercession not selfish adulation. When our joy is the same as His, therein is the mightiest of strength for us as saints.

For Thought:

Jesus' greatest display of strength was His willingness to remain on the cross to redeem you.

Day 159

When Jesus Stood Up

"Behold, I see the heavens opened up and the Son of Man standing at the right hand of God" (Acts 7:56).

Ask the question "Who was one of the boldest, wisest, most Spirit-filled saints in the New Testament?" Most would answer Paul or John, Peter, or perhaps Priscilla and Aquila. What about Stephen? He was "full of grace and power, performing great wonders and signs" (6:8). His wisdom was so great and the unction of the Holy Spirit was so powerful when he spoke, that his enemies were unable to stand up against him (6:10). His face was illumined with such a holy radiance that the people said he had the face of an angel (6:15). He was able to recount the entire history of God's people from the Old Testament to the present, all by memory. His Holy emboldened sermon was so fiery that it cut to the quick of every evil heart that listened, exposing them as betrayers and murderers of God's promised Messiah, and as hypocritical frauds. So they decided to stone him.

Immediately before the stones began to rain down upon him it says Stephen, "filled by the Spirit, gazed intently into heaven, and saw the glory of God" (7:55). He saw Jesus, but Jesus was doing something peculiar. Luke, the author of Acts had before written, "From now on, the Son of Man will be seated at the right hand of the Power of God" (Luke 22:69). Everywhere else in Scripture that speaks of Jesus being at the right hand of the Father also reveals Him as being in a "seated" position. But recording the events of Stephen, Luke says that Stephen saw Jesus "standing" at God's right hand.

Oh how beautiful this is! Jesus cannot just sit there and watch this extraordinary event. This was the first Christian to struggle against sin to the point of bloodshed (see Hebrews 12:4). This was the first believer who would lay down his life for the Gospel. This is the first man who stood up for Jesus at the price of death. Just as fanatic sports spectators stand up when things get exciting, Jesus is doing the same thing. This speaks a glorious truth: "If you stand up for Jesus, He stands up for you." Stephen was not worried about what other people thought about him; he just made a stand for Jesus and joyfully paid for it with his life.

For Thought:

Jesus, filled with the Spirit, prayed for His Father to forgive those who were crucifying Him. Stephen, standing up for Jesus rather than himself, also prayed the same Spirit-filled prayer: "Lord, do not charge them with this sin" (Acts 7:60).

Who do you often stand up for? Do you stand up to fight for your rights to yourself, or do you stand up for Jesus to fight against sin? Have you ever become so excited about Jesus that you spontaneously stood up to worship Him in a meeting? If you kneel before Him first you can stand up for Him forever.

Day 160

The Good Soldier

"Suffer hardship with me, as a good soldier of Christ Jesus" (2 Timothy 2:3).

Just a couple of weeks before VE Day, a young soldier approached his captain and reported that he had been there since D-Day-one. His captain began to commend him for his survival, but the soldier interrupted, "And I haven't fired my weapon once!" At first his captain was stunned, but the young soldier continued. He explained with great anguish that every time the rounds begin to burst his muscles freeze to the point of immobility (Fear paralysis was not yet a popular diagnosis). With his confession the soldier requested a court-martial, seeing this as the only fitting action for his "cowardly actions." His captain responded with a strange smirk, "Son, you don't need a court-martial; you need to stop thinking you're still alive! Not until you accept the fact that you are already dead will you begin to fight. Your life ended when you signed on the dotted line, raised your right hand, and swore-in."

That young soldier was immediately set free from his paralyzing fear. He went on to become one of the most decorated war heroes of the entire battalion. He becamse so fearless his fellow soldiers said he was crazy. One day just a few days before he was supposed to return home, his platoon was caught in vicious sniper fire. One-by-one his buddies were being picked off, so fast that no one could pinpont where the rounds were coming from. He came out from behind his covering, told his brothers to watch carefully, aimed his rifle down range, and darted for an old building where he supposed the sniper was perched. "Stop!" His captain yelled to no avail. Haphazardly he continued to run as he screamed, "I see where you are!" The sniper fired and down the fearless soldier fell, instantly dead. However, his brothers followed his orders to watch and were able to spot the fire-flash of the sniper's rifle and they took him out, thereby sparing many more lives. The young soldier had ceased struggling to save his life, and began doing what he signed up to do—fight for the lives of his brothers and the freedom of his country. He was a "good soldier."

A "good soldier" is someone who, at one point in life, wrote and endorsed a blank check made payable to his country, for the amount of "*up to and including his life.*" A "good soldier of Christ" is someone who did the same thing for Jesus and His Kingdom. When you were baptized into Christ, your life ended, along with your claim to it. Have you accepted it? Whose life are you fighting for? Oh what freedom awaits you once you realize the prison doors have been open all along!

For Thought:

Did you know that the more rights you fight for, the more you must labor to maintain them? The man who has died to many of his rights suffers few wrongs.

Day 161

The Value of Living for Jesus

"I count my life of no value to myself, so that I may finish my course and the ministry I received from the Lord Jesus, to testify to the gospel of God's grace" (Acts 20:24).

Self-denial is not despising self. Paul's life was of supreme value, not to himself, but to Jesus and His Gospel. He did not despise his life; he valued it only to the extent the Lord did. The value of Paul's life was in how efficiently it had become fashioned to its God-given design and purpose. His life's value was in how it could be spent for the Kingdom of Christ and the edifying of His church.

Railroad tracks have value only in how well they support and carry the train engine from point A to B. Train engines have value only in how well they remain on the tracks. Both the tracks and the engine were designed for one another. Railroad tracks no longer carrying trains are a nuisance. Decommissioned train engines are useless, but derailed ones are destructive. What would happen if an engine decided to derail itself from the tracks and venture off into the surrounding countryside? Hundreds of tons of iron would destroy the entire landscape creating a disastrous mess.

Destruction, disaster, and train wrecks are inevitable when believers derail from their God designed tracks. Lives, families, and marriages are in shambles because they hold their lives dear and valuable only to themselves. The will of God and His Word are the tracks; we, His redeemed people, are the engines. Our course mission is to testify of the free grace given to forgive sin and restore man's fellowship with God through faith in the finished work of Jesus Christ. The old course of being lovers of self and living only for worldly desires was a course set straight for eternal death. Instead, because of the Lord Jesus, we have been given a new course.

Paul's old course led many early Christians to an early death, and would have led him straight to a Christ-less eternity in hell. However, Paul adhered to a new course, one specifically given to Him by Jesus Christ, and he knew that His life only had value as long as it remained on the tracks of this course. He also knew if he valued his life by any standard other than its Kingdom value, he would derail and create a train wreck for many. His life's value had been redeemed and redirected from self to Jesus and others. Paul's life was rich because it was one with Jesus, the Pearl of great price.

For Thought:

Is your life valuable to only you, or does it have value only in being used for the King? How much of your life is being spent for Jesus? Your prayer life, devotional life, and passion for lost souls will tell the answer. Your knowledge of His great mercy and love for you will be the constant fuel.

Day 162

The Grasping Hands of Faith

"God himself will provide the lamb for the burnt offering, my son. And the two of them walked on together" (Genesis 22:8).

God had first instructed that the burnt offering must be only "clean animals," but then commanded Abraham to offer his son, Isaac. Therefore, the abnormalities of God requesting a "human" sacrifice were not few. But the one that appears most odd is God's apparent contradiction. Why would God contradict Himself by asking for a "human" (unclean with sin) sacrifice after mandating that the sacrifice must be both clean and animal? He wouldn't! In other words, this was no ordinary sacrifice, and we can be sure that Abraham was also aware of this. An ordinary animal sacrifice would have contained no faith-building ability. But this unusual sacrifice would bring Abraham to the end of himself. Sifted of all his religious knowledge and preconceived notions, he was left with nothing but faith grasping hold of God's promise.

God commanded Abraham to climb up Mt. Moriah and sacrifice the one He had promised to be his covenant heir (Genesis 17:19). However, before the command, God had given him a promise. At the bottom of the hill, Isaac asked, "Where is the lamb?" Abraham answered, "God Himself will provide the lamb." This shows that he knew his faith was being tested (he knew a dead son could not produce descendants and fulfill God's promise).

We talk much of Abraham's faith, but what about Isaac's faith? His only dialogue was the inquiry to his father about "the lamb." Surely Isaac grew a little nervous climbing a hill for a burnt sacrifice, carrying the firewood on his back, yet without a sacrifice. This implies that from Isaac's perspective, either he or his dad was going to be sacrificed. Both options being highly unfavorable, he inquired about the sacrificial lamb and his dad said God would provide. Isaac never responded back, and it says they "walked on together." This implies he was at peace with his daddy's answer, believed it with child-like faith, and recklessly abandoned himself to his father's will.

Both Abraham and Isaac were teetering on the notion that if God doesn't provide, "My family and I will suffer!" With confidence that God's provision was ahead they walked on together. Oh if believers would trust the Father that way! When the cupboard is used up, bank accounts are drying up, and the bills are stacking up, our Father says, "I will provide, just keep walking with Me." Do you have Isaac's child-like faith and Abraham's promise-grasping faith? At the bottom of our mountain we cannot see the provision and ask God where it is. It is only at the top where we will see it, so we keep climbing because He promised it is up there.

Abraham told his servants, "*We* will come back" (22:5), which proves he had such faith in God's promise that if Isaac were killed, God would resurrect him (see Hebrews 11:19). It isn't that God needed assurance of Abraham's faith; it was Abraham himself who needed to experience it. God knows our inability to keep His commands without first receiving His promises.

God's commands for us carry with them the notion of being wholly given over to Him—all of which are absurdly impossible without first receiving the comforts of His Gospel promises. A strong man can work first and receive the wages of a meal later; a weak and starving man needs food first before he can work. We all come to Jesus weak and famished, and we need the nourishing benefits of God's promises in Jesus before we can keep the duties of His commands.

Christ's call to us is one of death before it is one of life. With that call comes the stripping of all human ability to *walk on together* with Him apart from the nourishment of His promises. "Without faith it is impossible to please God" (Hebrews 11:6). It is not just believing-faith that God is pleased with; it is faith in motion to His call. This obedient motion requires faith grasping His everlasting promises. Obedience proves faith. You can only be a *living sacrifice* once you first receive the faith-filled assurance of His promises. Never put the commandment before the promise; you'll never finish the climb! Cling to what you have in Jesus and you will have continuous strength to climb.

For Thought:

Want increased faith? Use what you already have!

Day 163

All Alone and No One To Hide

"So all the people took off their earrings and brought them to Aaron. He took what they handed him and made it into an idol cast in the shape of a calf" (Exodus 32:3-4).

A month and a half had passed since Moses left again for Mt. Sinai, and the people were growing more anxious and weary by the day. Moses went up the mount to be in the presence of the Lord. Moses' reckless devotion to God had cost him everything. He had turned his back on the easy life of shepherding sheep in Midian, and taken up his cross to suffer the costly life of shepherding people. Twice the people had tried to get rid of Moses because of their fear and unbelief. The one friend it seemed he had was his brother Aaron, his co-leader.

Aaron had watched in amazement the mighty miracles God had produced through Moses. He had seen the holy boldness by which Moses spoke to Pharaoh. Aaron had witnessed Moses remain unmoved by the faithless grumblings, complaints, and agitations of the people. Many times, they had pressured him to do what they wanted, but Moses' fear of God could not be swayed by fear of man; he lived to please God not people. Aaron so wanted to be like Moses, but when his fiery trials came he did not have Moses' walk, and he fell. Aaron wanted *what* Moses had, but not *Who* he had.

Aaron was left in charge and here his true spiritual condition was stirred to the surface. Aaron had come into this position at no cost, and where there is no cost there is little value in what is obtained. Out from behind the coverings of Moses, the real Aaron was exposed. He was more impressed by man rather than by God. Because of this, it was easy for people to persuade him to make them an idol. Since they assumed Moses had forever departed, they reasoned God had also left. Aaron, therefore, was left to his own devices. This is always a state to be pitied and feared. Whoever people are living for—God, or man—is determined by who they are most driven to please.

Who are you living for? Who do you strive to please the most? What are you doing when you are alone? This is where "the real you" is revealed. Do not be astonished at what you see; rather know that God saw the desperate necessity for you to see what He sees, and dispel your deception once and for all. God puts His children in desperate situations where only He can deliver them. He must put you in "I'll never make it" places where your weakness and failure are exposed and He is revealed. But once He comes in all His glory and might and pulls you through, you will never again trust in the arm of flesh, be driven by the fear of man, or attempt to do a single thing apart from Him.

For Thought:

Read John 15:1-8.

Day 164

Do You Have the Passion?

"Save others by snatching them from the fire" (Jude 23).

"What can we do to cultivate a greater passion for the lost?" The answer is, "Dwell near the heart of Jesus!" A greater passion for lost souls comes from a greater revelation of one's own salvation, and this demands much time spent near Jesus. Paul radically asserted in Romans, "For I could wish that I myself were accursed, separated from Christ for the sake of my brethren" (9:3). Paul lived so close to the Lord that he had developed the Lord's heart for the lost. Those who see what foul sin and fiery death they have been snatched from cultivate this passion. Those who have been forgiven much love much.

Those who have truly seen their hopeless and wretched condition in light of the cross, and humbly received the unmerited comforts Christ purchased for them there, they will have an insatiable desire to live near Him. They come to depend on His presence. They realize without it they would be left in an eternal state of deception and darkness. The more God disillusions them to their true spiritual condition, the more they will see the vileness from which they have been saved. This helps them to more wonderfully see the Savior. The more they see their Savior, the more they desire to be like Him. The more they desire His likeness, the more they desire fellowship with Him. Love of fellowship with Him produces hatred of sin that separates. People love to be told they have been saved from hell; but many of them hate to be shown that it is really themselves from which they need to be saved. A truth that few ever acknowledge is that hell is just an eternal collection of souls who were never delivered from their selfish pride.

Believers that get a sight of themselves and the cross and truly repent, get set free from the maddening circles of self-passion (see John 8:32). It is like being gyrated off a rapidly spinning merry-go-round because you let go of it. They never forget the insanity and bondage from which they have been delivered. These are typically the saints who obtain a blazing passion for lost souls. However, it is a super costly passion because once you obtain it you take on the desire to lay down your life to intercede for a world full of sin-sick souls. The right to govern your life is crucified and you become nothing but clay in the hands of the Potter. This becomes your new passion, and you will joyfully cultivate it with no need of being coerced by people. What must you do to cultivate this passion? Dwell near the heart of Jesus in deep devotion and with unbroken fellowship.

For Thought:

You were snatched from one fire to be consumed by another—the fiery passion for souls. Love is the manifest power of the presence of God overflowing out of a life emptied of selfish lust and pride. It is the only true fire!

Day 165

Raised to Make a Difference

"For this reason, since the day we heard about you, we have not stopped praying for you" (Colossians 1:9).

What do Joseph, Moses, Esther, Daniel, the allied forces of WWII, the Apostle Paul, and Jesus all have in common? All were raised by God to make a difference. Joseph was raised from an outcast prisoner to second in command of Egypt and saved his father and brothers—the core of the entire nation of Israel—from starvation (Genesis 41-42). From a Hebrew baby nearly murdered, Moses was raised twice; first as shepherd to deliver the Jewish people from cruel oppression (Exodus 3:6-8), and second as an intercessor to deliver them from God's wrath (Exodus 32:31-32). Esther was raised from a Jewess nobody to the highest position any woman could have, the Queen of a world superpower. Her intercession thwarted Haman's plan to have the Jews exterminated.

Daniel was raised from a Jewish prisoner to a position over all the presidents and princes, even the entire kingdom of Babylon (Daniel 6:3). He was in the position to intercede for his nation's return from captivity. His faithfulness to God spared him from the lion's mouth, which granted him even more favor among the kings. This favor eventually trickled down to King Cyrus, which softened his heart enough that the Lord could move him to let the Jews return home. Otherwise, they would have been assimilated, thereby losing sight of their God and their privilege of being a set apart people to reveal God and His plan of redemption to the world.

The allied forces of WWII were raised to victory, which ended the tyranny of Hitler and his Satan-inspired desire to exterminate the Jews.

Paul was raised from self-righteousness to an Apostle, where unceasing prayer and preaching the cross became his difference-making lifestyle.

Jesus was raised, suspended between heaven and earth on a cursed tree, to deliver all who would follow Him from eternal death and destruction. "Therefore God exalted Him to the highest place and gave Him the Name that is above every name" (Philippians 2:9).

In order to save His people from starvation, cruel oppression, His own wrath, extermination, and worldly assimilation, God raised up faithful intercessors to special positions who would risk their own lives to make a difference for many. You have also been raised to make a difference. Intercessory prayer puts you right at the feet of the King of kings. And as a princely coheir with Him, you are in the position of highest authority to make a world of difference to an otherwise indifferent world. Are you making a difference?

For Thought:

Read James 5:16-17. What kind of man and what kind of prayer can make a difference? Why?

Day 166

The Peril of Backsliding

"Israel is stubborn like a stubborn heifer" (Hosea 4:16).

It was a heavy rebuke for God to refer to Israel as a heifer. A heifer is a young female cow that has no offspring. God often refers to His people in the feminine gender (e.g. "the Bride of Christ"); and to not bear children was considered a shameful and disgraceful thing. For women such as Hannah, Sarah, and Rachel, whose wombs were barren, their anguish was a very heavy burden to carry. People considered them afflicted outcasts cursed by God. Therefore, God was rebuking Israel for being spiritually barren and not producing holy offspring.

Some translations use the word "backsliding" instead of "stubborn." But *stubborn* and *backsliding* are synonymous. Backsliding has long carried the implied meaning of falling back into old sinful behavior patterns, or more plainly, "not being the Christian that we should be or once were." This weak usage enables the one who is backsliding to minimize the perilous danger of what they are really doing. The backslider thinks that he or she is just "sliding backward," but this is not the case. Here is an illustration: A shepherd leads an animal up to a gate of entry but the animal sits on its hind end refusing to enter. This renders it immovable, but it also causes the back to slope, hence the "backslide." In this position a horse or donkey cannot be ridden and nothing can be carried on its back, and an ox or cow cannot be yoked to do its work. The animal is virtually useless.

Backsliding is obstinate rebellion rendering Jesus your Master unable to guide you. Backsliding says, "I will not surrender the right to myself to You!" The Lord wants to take you where He wants, but just like the stallion, the Master can only use the one whose stubborn self-will has been broken. Moreover, stubborn rebellion is basically the same as saying "I will not enter the gate!" Since Jesus is the Gate to the heavenly sheepfold (John 10:7), what do you think unrepentant stubborn rebellion could ultimately keep you from? The heifer can believe she is in the right place all she wants, but as long as she continues to "backslide" she will remain outside until she submits. Again, Jesus cannot save anyone He cannot command. Therefore, a "stubborn heifer" is one who sits on its hind end, refuses to be led, produces nothing for the Kingdom of God, and never enters into it.

For Thought:

Read Matthew 3:8, Luke 3:8, and Acts 26:19-20. Are you producing fruit?

Have you entered into the pasture of being joyfully ruled and reigned by Jesus?

"God will give His power to every heart that will let Him hold the reins." [22]—A. B. Simpson

Day 167

Hindered Prayer is Hazardous

"That your prayers may not be hindered" (1 Peter 3:7).

Prayer is our number one weapon against the spiritual forces of evil in the heavenly realm (Ephesians 6:12). We cannot wage war against spiritual powers by physical means. We must be engaged in Spirit-empowered prayer if we are to be effective in our battle. However, it is absolute folly to battle against our adversaries with blunted blades and shattered swords. In other terms, since effectual prayer is our greatest weapon, then hindered prayer is our weapon's greatest foe. It blunts our blade.

In 1 Peter 3:5, Peter preached on the relationship of Christ-exalting marriage. He commands the husband to treat his wife as a "fragile instrument of great value" (*asthenās skúŏs*). This command is given great incentive by Peter's admonishment that failure to do so results in hindered prayer. Husbands, if you are not treating your wives like "fine china," your prayers go about as high as the ceiling, and you have a broken blade to fight the sworn enemy of both your and her soul.

Un-confessed and unrepentant sin mutes prayer. David said in his Psalm, "If I regard wickedness in my heart, the Lord will not hear" (66:18). Ezekiel also writes that those who delight in idolatrous images cannot inquire of God (14:3). James assures us those who covet selfish and sensuous pleasures are wasting their breath in prayer. "You ask and do not receive, because you ask with wrong motives, so that you may spend it on your pleasures" (4:3). Mark confirms that un-forgiveness, resentment, and bitterness incapacitate prayer. "Whenever you stand praying, forgive, if you have anything against anyone" (11:35).

James also reveals the prayer hindrance of doubt. He says of one who prays while doubting God, "That person should not expect to receive anything from the Lord" (1:7). The writer of Hebrews reveals the hindrances of unbelief and disobedience, because of which we are unable to enter (3:18-19). Since prayer is entering into the most Holy Place with God, disobedience, doubt, and unbelief certainly hinder our prayers.

We love to talk about prayer, but we utterly fail if we neglect to teach and warn about prayer's hindrances. These hindrances are mortal enemies; they must be removed at all costs. Deal with them because they are obstructions between you and the Lord. Without Him you have no effective weapon against the Devil and all his demonic cohorts.

For Thought:

Are there hindrances in your prayer life? Besides salvation, this is probably one of the most serious questions you could be asked; so search your heart. If family and lost souls are precious to you, prove it by dealing with these hindrances.

Day 168

The Removal of Achan

"I coveted them and took them; and behold, they are concealed in the earth inside my tent" (Joshua 7:21).

God's temple will be called a house of prayer and you are the temple of God (1 Corinthians 6:19). God's first dwelling place was a "tent" (*ohel*); hence it was called "the tent of meeting." In Exodus 33:7 it says, "Moses took a tent." This implies that it was his own tent, and he consecrated it to the Lord for His dwelling and use. Any unclean or unholy thing would be an accursed obstruction to the holiness of God's dwelling place, therefore, any hindrance to prayer could be considered equal to an accursed thing concealed in your tent, greatly needing to be removed.

All the things that we bring into our "tents" that obstruct our fellowship with God are only there because of our sinful and covetous desires. In fact that is why we, like Achan, purpose to "conceal" them; we know they are forbidden and sinful. God had commanded all of Israel, "Keep yourselves from the things set apart, or you will be set apart for destruction. If you take any of those things, you will set apart the camp of Israel for destruction and bring disaster on it" (Joshua 6:18 HCS). Achan apparently did not believe that God spoke as authoritatively through Joshua as He did Moses. Or perhaps he was thinking about setting up his family's financial security and future prosperity. Nevertheless, he decided to help himself to the glimmering plunders that God had forbidden. His secret sin and rebellion cost the lives of thirty-six good men, produced that many widows, and cursed rather than blessed his entire family. God cannot abide with the hindrance of secret sin in His camp, and Achan was the hindrance. Therefore he, his family, his possessions, and all he had secretly stored in his tent were brought to the Valley of Achor to be stoned, incinerated, and buried. There God's righteous anger was appeased, and His presence and favor returned to Israel.

God's abiding presence produces hope (see Psalm 16:11). The Valley of Achor meant, "Valley of Trouble." However, Hosea called it "a gate of hope" (Hosea 2:15), because the hindrance to God's presence was abolished there. Every Achan must be removed; none can remain! Each must be brought to another place of death called Calvary (Colossians 2:14), where the debt is cancelled and the eternal "Gate" of hope is opened. *Hearts* are what God desires to be brought there, not things. Bring your heart to Him and He will open up for you a new radiant life of hope and holy purpose. Consecrate your tent to the Lord and His abiding presence will shine brighter and brighter unto that glorious day (see Proverbs 4:18).

For Thought:

The cross of Christ turns our *Valley of Trouble* into a *Gate of hope*. Expound, or meditate upon this.

Day 169

The Eternity of Abiding

"He who abides in Me and I in him" (John 15:5).

How would you feel and what would you think if your spouse, parent, or immediate family member spent the last four days avoiding you or not speaking to you? Maybe you would think, "What did I do wrong?" Perhaps you would feel they were angry with you, or just plain despised you. You might think they see you as undesirable, unneeded, or unworthy. Regardless, their behavior declares your fellowship has been currently deemed repugnant to them.

There is no universe large enough to contain the greatness of the glory of Jesus' Incarnation. There is no poet with the words to describe the beauty of Jesus' humility to suffer death for a world that by majority would declare with their lifestyles they wish He had never come. How greatly this Gospel message is muted when it is only mentioned as God's way to pardon our sins. If the overarching purpose of God's desire to fellowship intimately with us continues to be the lesser motive, that is exactly what it will remain to be from our perspective. There will continue to be little value in abiding in the presence of Jesus. Prayer will be drudgery; His intimacy will remain undesirable; His revelation and leading will remain unneeded; hearts will remain unchanged. These attitudes describe hell not heaven! Heaven is the eternal dwelling of intimate and unveiled fellowship with the Lord of lords. Everlasting joy, worship, and basking in His presence is heaven's atmosphere, and its hymn is "Holy, Holy, Holy are you Lord God Almighty" (Isaiah 6:3; Revelation 4:8).

If God were not completely unlike us, He too might feel we were angry with Him or despised Him when we avoid spending time with Him. However, it is not about whether He "feels" that way; it is about whether our actions are declaring it. The fact is, if you spend days without seeking His face in prayer and meditating upon His Word, your actions are declaring you do not need Him or desire Him. If people despise fellowship and intimacy with Jesus now, why would they want heaven? Heaven is the eternity of abiding, and those who would have it all about streets of gold and mansions truly show where their hearts are. Achan coveted gold and silver and riches and despised the presence of God. Everyone wants to miss hell; but few desire the reality of heaven, which is the eternity of abiding in Jesus.

For Thought:

Read Genesis 3:8-10. "Where are you?" Could God say those words to you right now? Sin caused Adam and Eve to avoid God; is something causing you to avoid Him?

Read 1 John 2:16. Heaven is popularly described with endless buffets, golden streets, and mansions. It's striking that all three are respectively congruent to the lust of the flesh, the lust of the eyes, and the pride of life.

Day 170

The Loyalty of Abiding

"How beautiful are your tents . . . like gardens beside the river, like aloes planted by the LORD, like cedars beside the waters" (Numbers 24:6).

There was a very large lilac tree we wanted to transplant from one place to another. We split it up into four separate plants because we envisioned four large and beautiful ones. Any landscaper knows that transplanting is risky because it majorly stresses the plant, often to the point that it dies. Nevertheless we followed through with our original plan. Several years later, only one survived. In retrospect we realized the three that died were the ones that were hauled by amateurs who did not know how to properly handle them. They were roughly battered in the trip and insufficiently covered (the roots must be covered or they begin to die). A professional transported the other, thoroughly covered it with a blanket, and handled it with great care. This one survived and prospered.

In the book of Numbers, Israel was right where they were supposed to be, the place where God had divinely chosen to plant them for the time being. They moved only when and where the Lord did, and remained planted when He commanded them to stay put. Only He knows the hidden earthly springs of water that can sufficiently nourish His people where they drop anchor. And for when they are mobile, He is also their covering that keeps the roots from dying. This abiding loyalty was elegantly displayed in Ruth, "For where you go, I will go, and where you lodge, I will lodge" (Ruth 1:16).

Many believers fall into spiritual burnout. They substitute the spiritual loyalty of abiding with the physical counterfeit of work, human ability, good management, and religious duties. They are busy *Martha's* who neglect the one good thing of sitting at the feet of Jesus. God wants to plant them in a certain place, but in self-reliance they move and become stressed and withered. Then when God says, "I'm moving," they stay planted and their soil becomes parched without the Living Water. They are not "planted by the LORD" but rather by self. They are not "cedars beside the waters" but dried up Junipers in the wilderness (Jeremiah 17:6), because they trust in their own strength. The more they continue to operate independent of the Holy Spirit, the more they become like the three lilacs that died.

Slow down and do not be so eager to always be on the move. Get alone often with Jesus. Allow yourself to be deep-rooted and firmly established by abiding in Him with loyalty. Be sure He has filled your heart before you run off to labor, or else you'll be sacrificing on a broken altar.

For Study:

Paul was frequently imprisoned, severely flogged, repeatedly exposed to death, scourged five times, pelted with stones, shipwrecked three times, and constantly in danger. He never suffered "burnout." Why?

Day 171

God's Number One Hit Song

"The sin of Judah is written down with an iron stylus; with a diamond point it is engraved upon the tablet of their heart" (Jeremiah 17:1).

The stylus was an engraving instrument used by scribes to record sacred writings. It had a diamond fastened to the point because of its unique ability to cut. If you have ever owned an old gramophone, you know that originally its stylus (the needle) also had a diamond tip. Whenever you listen to one of those old gramophone records you will hear annoying sound disturbances. These are made as the stylus runs over particles of dust and dirt that have nested into the groove. This causes the stylus to make unintended movements not related to the originally engraved music.

There was an interesting method in the production of the early gramophone records. The recordings were made as the stylus engraved one continuous groove that spirals toward the center of the disc. Additionally, the musical groove could only be erased by a special machine that would shave off the entire surface of the recording disc, providing a new clean surface for carving a new one. This could normally be done only once.

Judah was persisting in unrepentant sin. The waywardness and hardness of their hearts was like the diamond stylus carving one continuous groove of rebellion. But their groove spiraled "away" from the center. They began in the center of God's will but were spiraling further and further away. Their groove had accumulated countless dirt particles of sin, and if placed upon a record player would have surely been unbearable for God to listen. Judah was writing a song in their heart that God was not. Babylonian captivity would be His special abrasive to erase the old sin-carved groove and prepare a smooth new surface. This would provide the Lord a clean record for engraving His new song.

Persisting in a lifestyle of willful sin, little to no devotion to God, or idolatrous habits, will make you just like Judah. Your sin-carved groove will continue to spiral outward from the center of God's will. The playback of your record will become more annoying and unpleasant to the ears of the Lord, and He may be compelled to use a very abrasive method to erase it and make a new song. Written and recorded by God Himself, there is a new song in heaven and it must be ours as well: "And they sang a new song before the throne and before the four living creatures and the elders. No one could learn the song except . . . who had been redeemed from the earth" (Revelation 14:3). God wrote a number one hit song that will remain on the top of the charts for an eternity. Is it on your record?

For Thought:

You cannot add His new song to your old record.

Day 172

Getting Alone with God

"Samuel said to Saul, 'Tell the attendant to go on ahead of us, but you stay for a while, and I'll reveal the word of God to you'" (1 Samuel 9:27).

Whenever God is about to give his child a new identity, one that is transformed from the natural to the spiritual, He must first get the person all alone. Saul was about to be anointed the first king of Israel. He would go from a natural member of the lowest tribe of Israel to her first royal leader. But Saul first had to get alone with God's messenger, Samuel, through whom the word of God would be revealed to him.

Before Jacob could become Israel, God had to get him alone. Jacob sent all his servants, his possessions, and his entire family across the Jabbok River to be left all alone with God's messenger. Here we have the natural man wrestling with the spiritual man right before the transformation.

Before Saul the persecutor became Paul the Apostle, he also would get alone with God. On the road to Damascus, he had a revelation encounter with the fully glorified Jesus. This vision brought three days of blindness. It is only imaginable what wrestling he must have gone through knowing that he had been persecuting the Son of God and what was most precious to Him, His Bride. Three days worth of darkness and solitude preceded the transformation, as Saul of Tarsus went from being filled with the leaven of the Pharisees to being filled with the Holy Spirit. From Saul to Paul, he transformed the Gentile world with the Gospel.

Elijah was alone in the desert ready to die. Wrestling with his own self-pity, the Lord came and led him to Mount Horeb to get him all alone.

It was there that God appeared to Elijah in a way He had only done with Moses, and transformed Elijah from a naturally defeated preacher to a spiritually designated prophet.

We can grope about through the naturally overwhelming trials we are facing, and we can speak of how difficult the Christian life is. But what is certain is that we have no grounds for complaint if all the troubles remain because we refuse to get alone with God. Do not cling to the comfort of possessions, the companionship of family, or the busy schedules of your lucrative career. You must send them all away for a time. If you are looking for spiritual transformation, then you must allow God to get you alone where you and He can wrestle it out. Only He can choose where this takes place.

For Thought:

Jesus alone with the Father in the garden of Gethsemane is the most intense display of the natural wrestling with the spiritual. The agonizing struggle was that the will of God would require Him to be separated from His Father.

Day 173

Henotheism in God's House

"They took Dagon and put him back in his place" (1 Samuel 5:3c)

Read 1 Samuel 5:1-12

Henotheism is the worship of one god, while accepting the existence of other gods also considered worthy of worship. Today henotheism thrives where the buzzword, "tolerance" is most present, and where Spirit-inspired worship of the one true God is most absent.

God allowed the Ark to be captured by the Philistines and taken to Ashdod where it was placed right next to their favorite god, Dagon. They were henotheists believing that the God of Israel could be added to their collection and "add some value to their success." An interesting fundamental of henotheism is that deities are considered to have regional sovereignty; meaning that a particular god is most powerful where it is worshiped the most. This is important to know because the true God of Israel was about to prove that wrong by His absolute supremacy. He alone is the boundless God, incapable of being regionalized or placed in the presence of another god and it remain standing.

Notice the Philistines set the Ark next to Dagon. However, they woke the next morning to the sight of their pathetically lifeless god prostrate on its face before the Ark. They set him back up, which shows that they thought it was a fluke. The following morning, Dagon was again on his face, this time with head and hands dismembered. This confronted their skepticism and declared the supremacy and authority of God Almighty.

As a Christian believer you may be thinking how indigestible henotheism seems; "We worship only Jesus at our church and in our family!" But have you thought that you could just add Jesus to your collection of other idols? A grave mistake of believers today is thinking as long as we are monotheists (believing in only one God) we are safe. However, many have done exactly what the Philistines did by attempting to bring the holy presence of God into their dwelling place and set Him right next to other gods. Then every time God pulls them down, they just set it back up again.

The heart is His tabernacle and He will not reside in the presence of other gods, especially ourselves. He is not to be added to our life like an ornament for selfish prosperity. Our wise choice is to fearfully fall on our face and worship Him, rather than lose our heads and hands. Our heads possess our mind, affections, and will, and our hands possess our strength and ability; all of which must be consecrated to the single worship of God. Whatever is not used for His worship will be cut off on that Great Day of the Lord. "The Lord alone will be exalted on that day. The idols will completely vanish" (Isaiah 2:17-18).

For Thought:

Read John 18:1-6. They all "fell to the ground."

Day 174

Self-Sufficiency Strikes Jesus Twice

"Must we bring water out of this rock for you?" (Numbers 20:11).

God had commanded Moses quite specifically to take the staff and assemble the people, and then "speak to the rock" at Meribah to yield water for them to drink (see 20:8). Moses instead struck the rock two times with the staff and God punished him by revoking his entry to the Promised Land. Many believers reason it was because he struck it twice thereby showing his lack of faith. The truth is God never told Moses to strike the rock at all.

The staff was for assembly purposes; God said "speak" to the rock (20:8), not strike it. This event really goes all the way back to the first Promise God made in Genesis. Referring to the serpent, God said He would put hostility between his (Satan's) seed and Eve's seed (Jesus). God said, "He will strike your head and you will strike His heel" (3:15). The rock at Meribah was a typology of Jesus the Rock that yields streams of Living Water (see 1 Corinthians 10:4). Now we can understand that Moses striking the rock was equivalent to him striking Jesus, twice. Moses had usurped God's divine will, which singled out Satan as the only one authorized by God to strike Messiah.

Furthermore, God specifically commanded Moses to speak to the rock, and His purpose was for the spoken Word of God to produce the miracle of quenching the people's thirst. Striking the rock was a display of fleshly human effort and ability, which is what much of the church is doing today ("We, with all our awesome abilities, will quench your thirst"). By Moses saying, "Must *we*," the holiness and glory of God was obscured and robbed. Whenever the glorious presence of the Holy Spirit is absent, the pride of human effort is present. Moses was saying, "Look what *we* can do" rather than what

God can do. Self-sufficiency strikes Jesus twice. The second strike proves that the first was not an accidental slip.

Moses and Aaron took much of the glory of God's work and the wondrous demonstration of His manifest power unto themselves. Their actions were done as if through some ability or worthiness of their own. God's punitive measures upon Moses (Aaron died soon after) were well deserved. The punishment was a charge against the high spiritual crimes of 1) usurping God's authority, 2) stealing His glory 3) selfish independence, and 4) disobedience. What pandemic spiritual crime is this today? How absurd it is that anyone who calls himself God's messenger would take credit for a message and miracle he did not create. It says, "Look at *me*, not Him!" What do you boast in besides the Lord? How much are you doing apart from Him? Whatever the answers, they are obstructions to His splendor, power, and holiness, and strike Him like the spear in His side . . . twice!

Day 175

Are You Hungry?

"Everything is ready; come to the wedding feast; but they paid no attention and went their way" (Matthew 22:4-5).

There is something about hunger and a buffet that go together like peas in a pod. One might propose that it is the plethora of food; another may submit that it is the great selection. Nevertheless, a large buffet-style banquet is very appealing when the appetite is fierce. However, people normally do not opt for a buffet when they are already full.

Although it may seem odd, there are people who go to buffets and somehow get the same thing every time. Why would they do that? The answer is there is something quite pleasurable about being in the presence of so much variety; knowing that you are not constrained to just one option brings comfort. With the widespread increase of consumerism, people are demanding more variety, and the Gospel of Jesus Christ is just one of the many choices to get to heaven. Anything that is narrowed to just one option is dubbed unpalatable, even dogmatic. "We want variety!" the world protests, and so churches submit and give them what they want. And therefore, the one option people truly need is condescended to "just another choice on the menu!"

For instance, "Losing your life for Jesus" is just a side dish that goes with loving this world and "believing in" God. Jesus' words, "Anyone who does not give up all he has cannot be My disciple" (Luke 14:33), is twisted to mean, "That is just for people who go into ministry and become preachers and missionaries."

In Matthew 22:1-10, the King in this parable symbolizes Jesus who labored to prepare such a lavish feast. Everything was ready except His people. However, this feast is not a buffet offering endless variety; it is a holy and eternal feast with one option: The broken Bread of life. What it comes down to is this: The reason no one came is the same reason people do not come today—They are not hungry! The reason they are not hungry is because they are already full. They are full from eating at the endless buffets of sin, self, lust, and the world (see 2 Timothy 3:1-5). People want variety, and they go from church to church to find it because they do not want just Jesus! They want pleasure, comfort, and eternal security, but not joyfully suffering loss for the sake of Jesus. They love programs but despise prayer. Thus they remain blissfully ignorant to the fact of thousands per hour entering into a Christ-less eternity. The question is, "Are you too full to long for, ache for, and hunger for Jesus and His passion for souls? "Everything is ready." Are you?

For Thought:

Roughly 8,635 unsaved people die per hour; that's 144 people per minute entering an eternal state of despair, darkness, and unrestrained evil!

Day 176

Revelation without Gethsemane Corrupts

"And He took with Him Peter and the two sons of Zebedee, and began to be sorrowful and distressed" (Matthew 26:36-37).

Untested faith, revelation, and knowledge are the same as unused muscles; they will atrophy without resistance, and corrupt without a test. Salvation is free because Jesus paid its cost in death on the cross. Faith is also a gift but becomes costly when called to action. Many are enamored with faith, revelation, and knowledge but are emasculated when their right use is required. Visions are exciting; revelations are riveting; faith is phenomenal; prophecies are prolific; all of which continue to be cheapened and sold at a "steal" these days. We no longer need to climb Everest; we have helicopters to lift us. Testing is avoided or eliminated so the gifts remain cheap. The summit is coveted but the trial of the climb is removed; so without the climb, the summit is trite. It would be just another neat excursion—one more sightseeing event to add to the family vacation album.

Peter, James, and John were the only disciples who went up the mount with Jesus and witnessed His transfiguration. They saw Him glorified in a way no other has or ever would, and were commanded to speak nothing of it to anyone. Oh what unique faith they must have thought they had when they saw the momentary resurrections of two of their heroes of the faith, Moses and Elijah. Oh what exclusive vision as they witnessed Jesus being transfigured before them; Oh what revelation as they heard the audible voice of God speak, "This is My beloved Son . . . listen to Him" (Matthew 17:5).

Fast-forward to Gethsemane. Jesus chose the same three to come with Him deeper into the garden of suffering and prayer where He cried, "My soul is swallowed up in sorrow to the point of death" (vs. 38).

Jesus was foreshadowing the immense cost of the climb to Mount Calvary. Gethsemane tests if we are willing to suffer the cost of living out what we have received. Only those who have had a sight of Christ's glory are enabled to enter the fellowship of His sufferings. Faith, revelation, and knowledge that never enter the Garden of suffering with Jesus will not only corrupt; they will corrode you from the inside out like a cancer (pride). Gethsemane is the valley of testing for the glory received on your mountain. If you dodge and finagle your way around all that would lead you into your Gethsemane; if you are addicted to the rush of divine graces, then you have reduced them to a black-market sale. If there was little cost, you got them from a peddler not Jesus—they were a steal that reduced the price of Calvary to just another momentary "wow" experience. A revelation without a Gethsemane has no depth, no cost, and no place in the Christian walk. Let Jesus take you deeper into your Gethsemane. The cost may be great but the depth of your relationship with Him will be greater. Is the prize worth it?

Day 177

Washing Your Hands in Pilate's Sink

"After tying Him up, they led Him away and handed Him over to Pilate, the governor" (Matthew 27:2, HCS).

Deceived by a disciple, probed by a prefect, ridiculed by royalty, flouted for a felon, scorned by soldiers, and crucified with criminals; Jesus suffered Himself to be handed over like yesterday's garbage. His own people freed a killer in sin to kill the Freedom from sin. Those He painfully came to redeem used a secular crucifixion of death to eliminate the sacred Creator of life. A complete stranger was forced to help Him carry His cross while one of His dearest disciples—who promised he would have gone "to death with" Him—was nowhere to be found. Jesus had been handed over for removal by death. Have you handed over Jesus?

In all four Gospels, Pilate's resistance to crucify Jesus is seen. In Matthew he "washes his hands" of his responsibility. In Mark, he is very reluctant. In Luke, he finds no treachery in Jesus. And in John, Pilate finds no guilt in Him. Therefore, Pilate "reluctantly" handed Jesus over to His death. Does reluctance excuse responsibility? Pilate's role as prefect was collecting taxes, having limited officiating ability and only a small auxiliary army at hand. An uprising would be highly uncontrollable and unfavorable, so Pilate assumed a position of neutrality. Does neutrality neutralize responsibility?

Not standing up for Jesus is equal to standing against Him, is it not? We as Christians did not physically drive the nails into His hands, though we speak of our responsibility. Pilate may not have sanctioned Jesus' crucifixion, but his permission to hand Him back over to those who did makes him responsible. Maybe he was too comfortable to deal with a Jewish uprising. Maybe he was too afraid of his superior Roman legate or being deemed incompetent. Whatever the case, he chose his comfort, ease, and pleasure over fighting for Jesus. And to cleanse his conscience of his bloodguilt, he washed his hands in the waters of his own reluctance (Matthew 27:24).

"Surely He must understand how heavy that temptation was, and how hard it was to hand Him over to His crucifying enemies to scratch that lustful itch." "I didn't *mean* to deny Jesus to accommodate my friends," believers contemplate. This is just what Pilate did; he washed his hands in his own self-made waters to cleanse his conscience. Whenever you minimize and justify sin, you are not only bypassing repentance, you are washing your hands in Pilate's sink as you send Jesus away.

For Thought:

Going to Pilate's sink deems Christ's blood unworthy and insufficient, and leaves our hands and hearts desperately unclean.

Day 178

Seeking God's Wisdom

"You have made Your servant king in place of my father David, yet I am just a youth with no experience in leadership" (1 Kings 3:9, HCS).

It is well known that those of youthful immaturity and inexperience make incompetent leaders. The question is, "How was it possible for such an inexperienced young man such as Solomon to become one of the wisest kings ever, as soon as he became king?" Talent and skill cannot account for it, because these come from refining practice, which Solomon was not afforded. We cannot say it came from being mentored by David. Aaron had long watched and learned from Moses, and when Aaron was forced to stand on his own legs of leadership, he failed miserably. It was not progressive because we see its immediacy in Solomon's resolving the tricky situation between the two prostitutes (3:16-28). Israel heard about this wise judgment to the point "they stood in awe" and "saw that *God's wisdom* was in him" (vs.28), and that answers our question. However, this leads to a deeper inquiry: What did God see in Solomon that prompted the outpouring of such an unrivaled portion of His wisdom?

The first quality Solomon portrayed was confession. He agreed with God's perspective rather than his own; that although he was king in the eyes of men, in God's eyes he was just a young servant. The next was poverty of spirit where Solomon recognized his absolute insufficiency. Humble dependence and intimacy with the Lord followed next. Jesus teaches that the way we abide in Him is through yielding obedience and fervent prayer (John 15-17). This is exactly what we see in Solomon's request for understanding. The Hebrew word for *understanding* comes from *shamä*, which means, "to listen obediently."

People are devoid of God's wisdom because they are too full of their own. Samuel's rebuke to king Saul (1 Samuel 15:17), "When you were little in your eyes," says it all. God cannot—indeed will not—pour His wisdom into a container that insists on keeping the foolish wisdom of this world (see 1 Corinthians 1:20). We must renounce our own understanding and acknowledge Him in all our ways (Proverbs 3:5-6); we must listen obediently, and judge only by the infallible standard of God's Word; we must have a servant's heart and a single view toward how God's wisdom can bless others and edify His Kingdom. Many say, "Lord, here's my cup, fill it up," yet are deaf to His reply, "I cannot; there is too much foreign material in it!" To be full of God's wisdom you must be broken, emptied, and willing to stay empty of every ounce of selfish ambition and pride. The two cannot mix.

For Thought:

God's wisdom is poured out *behind the curtain* through devotion and prayer; it must be sought, bought, and wrought before it can be taught.

Read (2 Kings 4:38-41).

Day 179

Is There Death in the Pot?

"There's death in the pot, man of God" (vs.40).

We have heard the phrase, "Don't eat the berries!" Not knowing what you're eating or what you're serving is risky business. The earth contains myriads of edible looking produce that could drop a healthy human dead in a matter of heartbeats. In Genesis, we read the ill-fated words, "The woman saw that the tree was good for food and delightful to look at" (3:6). Eve at least had been told that there was death in the fruit; nevertheless, she delighted in it, shared it with the entire population of the earth, and it resulted in death for all.

For Elisha, just because there was famine in the land didn't mean there must also be spiritual famine. He was engaged in breaking spiritual bread for the hungry souls of these young prophets who were gathered before him. This teaches us that though earthly bread may be scant, there is always an endless supply of the broken Bread of life prepared for the devoted saint. When provisions run low, do not let your devotion follow suit. Concerning the stew, Elisha had entrusted someone else to go gather food for the stew and the servant gathered unknown gourds from a wild vine. The pot was poisonous and could have killed them all if God had not intervened.

Who are parents entrusting to teach their children, and what are they being taught without their parents' knowledge? We live in the age of a great paradigm shift where secularized public school, television, media, have become the teachers and mentors; where all that is death and poison to holiness and eternity is laid out as a cheap smorgasbord. Husbands and fathers, who are to be spiritual leaders, are allowing sexual sin, idolatry, and anger into their heart and feeding their families from this death-pot. From what fields are church pastors gathering produce? A watered-down gospel (which is no Gospel), half-truths (lies), puppet shows, comedic videos, worldly compromise, and crude jokes; all are bitter wormwood and death in the pot for the soul. They gather bitter gourds from a wild vine and feed it to countless victims.

Elisha's response to discovering the ill effects of the poisonous pot was one of urgent haste. The meal/flour that he threw into the pot contained no known natural abilities to remedy the poison, but rather speaks of a miraculous attendance of divine healing. What is in your pot? Are there foreign contaminates that could kill you, poison your family, or make your church bitter? You had better seek the Master for the miracle meal to cure the poison. If the poison is false teaching, go to God's Word. If it is false living go to His cross.

For Thought:

Read Acts 17:11. A "Berean" always checks the pot for any wild or poisonous ingredients. Be one.

Day 180

Jesus, The Purpose of Life

"In the beginning God created" (Genesis 1:1).

*T*ruth has both a determined beginning and end; the beginning and end never have to be conjured, and therefore the contents in between flow without need of distortion or embellishment. Lies have to conjure a beginning to secure their desired end. Just watch someone caught in a lie strain to present the origin and contents of their story. Truth can be spoken in very few words because truth is elegant. Lies are generally spoken with long, drawn-out explanations, and then supported with a ruse of intellectualism. Just watch a child explain why he or she did what got him or her in trouble. Truth is mature; lies are childish.

The Word of God gives an answer for the contents of life having a determined beginning and end. Evolution has to reject all determined beginnings, because to accept a purposed origin demands an answer to what originated it. Evolution also rejects all determined ends to life for the same reason. This is why the evolutionist must look to earthly or cosmic calamities for origin, purpose, and end. Furthermore, to have a purposed origin and end to life means there must also be purpose in its content. This blows evolution's whole preposterous theory that claims there is no purpose to life. This theory says, "Since we evolved from and are heading toward a purposeless nothing, we are an accident of chance." To say we are an accident and have purpose are self-refuting statements.

Truth lends itself to be simple; lies tend to be complicated. With five simple words, "In the beginning God created," we have a commanded origin. With evolution and its countless words incomprehensible to the unscholarly mind, we have a conjured origin. With another five simple words, Jesus declares Himself "the beginning and the end." He is the purposed end of what He purposed to begin. Again, the Word of God is the only source that gives a confident purpose to life's contents. "For I am confident of this very thing, that He who began a good work in you will perfect it until the day of Christ Jesus" (Philippians 1:6).

Only the Author of life can give life purpose. He created man in His image but man fell from this grace. He came to earth to recreate man into His image and will bring the repentant back to the fullness of this grace. The Bible ends with "the grace of the Lord Jesus" (Revelation 22:21). Jesus is the purpose of life. Those who are not living for Him are wandering in a temporal state of insatiable desire, and heading toward an eternal state of insatiable desire. They have chosen to live like a nomad in the desert. They thirst but refuse to come to Jesus to drink the living water that satisfies. "If anyone is thirsty, let him come to Me and drink," (John 7:37). Jesus suffered death so we could have intimate fellowship with Him. Honor His graceful purpose through daily devotion *behind the curtain*.

Bibliography

1. Meldrum, Glenn, *Rend the Heavens, What Revival Is: Revival is a Sovereign Act of God*, chapter 2. (Covert, MI, Wisdom's Gate Publishing, 2005. See Glenn and Jessica Meldrum at ihpministry.com. (DAY 8)

2. Gurnall, William. *[The Christian in Complete Armour . . . The Sixth Edition.]*. Vol. I. London: n.p., 1820. Print. (DAY 11)

3. Andrews, Rex, *What the Bible Teaches About Mercy*, Zion Faith Homes, Zion, Illinois, 1985, Chapter 1 (DAY 14)

4. *Oh, How I Love Jesus*, lyrics by: Frederick Whitfield and Thoro Harris; (DAY 27)

5. Barnes, Albert, H. C. Leupold, and Robert Frew. *Barnes' Notes on the Old and New Testaments: A Practical and Explanatory Commentary*. Grand Rapids, MI: Baker Book House, 1949. Print. (DAY 36)

6. *I Surrender All*, Lyrics by: Judson W. de Venter; Music by: Winfield Scott Weeden. (DAY 41)

7. Luke Gilkerson, http://www.covenanteyes.com/2011/03/23/john owen on accountability part 2 of 4; inspired from *Of the Mortification of Sin in Believers*, chapter 8. (DAY 43)

8. Owen, John. *Of the Mortification of Sin in Believers: The Necessity, Nature and Means of it with a Resolution of Sundry Cases of Conscience, Thereunto Belonging. By John Owen, D.D*. London: Printed for Joseph Marshall, 1721. Print. (DAY 60)

9. Owen, John. *Of the Mortification of Sin in Believers: The Necessity, Nature and Means of it with a Resolution of Sundry Cases of Conscience, Thereunto Belonging. By John Owen, D.D.*, Chapter 8. London: Printed for Joseph Marshall, 1721. Print. (DAY 71)

10. Simpson, A. B. *The Life of Prayer*, Chapter 1: "Hindrances to Prayer". Harrisburg, PA: Christian Publications, 1925. Print. (DAY 77)

11. Simpson, A. B. *The Life of Prayer*, Chapter 5. Harrisburg, PA: Christian Publications, 1925. Print. (DAY 78)

12. Howells, Rees, and Doris M. Ruscoe. *The Intercession of Rees Howells*, pg. 58. Guildford, Surrey: Lutterworth, 1983. Print. (DAY 78)

13. Meldrum, Glenn, *Radical Jesus*, "Radical Faith", chapter 10. In His Presence Ministries, Phoenix, Arizona, 2013. See Glenn and Jessica Meldrum at ihpministry.com (DAY 90)

14. Howells, Rees, and Doris M. Ruscoe. *The Intercession of Rees Howells*, pg. 58. Guildford, Surrey: Lutterworth, 1983. Print. (DAY 90)

15. Murray, Andrew, *Sanctification Or The Highway Of Holiness: An Abridgment Of The Gospel Mystery Of Sanctification*. (DAY 100)

16. *Love Lifted Me*, lyrics by: James Rowe; music by: Howard E. Smith (1912) (DAY 100)

17. Murray, Andrew, *Abide in Christ*. Westwood, NJ: Barbour, 1985. Print. (DAY 110)

18. Courtesy of biblos.com: http://biblesuite.com/greek/3560.htm. (DAY 134)

19. Fields, Wilbur, *Philippians-Colossians-Philemon*. Joplin, MO: College Press, 1969. Print. (DAY 143)

20. Ravenhill, Leonard, *The Gospel of Prayer*. Copyright (C) 1994 by Leonard Ravenhill, Lindale, Texas—http://www.ravenhill.org. (DAY 148)

21. Hibbert, Albert, *Smith Wigglesworth: The Secret of His Power* (Tulsa, OK, Harrison House, 1982. (DAY 154)

22. Simpson, A. B. *The Life of Prayer*, Chapter 5. Harrisburg, PA: Christian Publications, 1925. Print. (DAY 166)

About The Authors

David Frazier was born and raised in the Louisville, KY area and now resides in Bedford, IN. David is a former Marine and has great kinship for all veterans who serve. David was radically saved out of a lifestyle of darkness, drugs, and the intoxicating worship of fame in the music business. David is a graduate and alumni of *Master's International School of Divinity* and holds an MA in Biblical Studies with an emphasis in Biblical Counseling, and is currently finishing his Doctorate in Theology (Th.D.). David has been serving four years as a biblical counselor for *Pure Life Ministries*. Presently, David itinerates as an evangelist, Bible teacher, and Revivalist. He and his wife Kim travel with a fervent heart cry for passionate prayer, longing for intimacy with Jesus, biblical literacy, and spiritual awakening to return to the church. They invite all to join with them in unceasing prayer for genuine revival and spiritual awakening in this desperate hour.

Glenn Meldrum and his wife, Jessica, comprise the husband and wife team of *In His Presence Ministries*. Glenn is ordained with the Assemblies of God and holds an MA in theology and church history from Ashland Theological Seminary. He has ministered as an evangelist since 1997. His 15 years of pastoral experience has included an urban multicultural church, a rural church and a Romanian congregation. Glenn, who was saved out of a life of drugs and alcohol, also ministers in prisons and rehab programs such as Teen Challenge and Victory Outreach.

The other half of *In His Presence Ministries* is Jessica Meldrum who teaches women's groups and is a speaker for Christian Women's Clubs, a ministry aimed at presenting the reality of Christ to the un-churched.

Made in the USA
Lexington, KY
24 December 2014